Strategic Planning and Management Control

Strategic Planning and Management Control

Systems for Survival and Success

John C. Camillus
Graduate School of Business
University of Pittsburgh

Lexington Books
D.C. Heath and Company/Lexington, Massachusetts/Toronto

Library of Congress Cataloging-in-Publication Data

Camillus, John C.
  Strategic planning and management control.

  Includes index.
  1. Strategic planning. 2. Budget in business.
I. Title.
HD30.28.C353   1986   658.4'012   85–40001
ISBN 0– 669–10315–2 (alk. paper)

Published simultaneously in Canada
Printed in the United States of America
International Standard Book Number: 0– 669–10315–2
Library of Congress Catalog Card Number: 85–40001

The paper used in this publication meets the minimum requirements of
American National Standard for Information Sciences–Permanence of
Paper for Printed Library Materials, ANSI Z39.48–1984. ∞™

86 87 88 89 90 8 7 6 5 4 3 2 1

To my mother, with love and gratitude

Contents

Figures

Tables

Part I
A Framework for Planning and Control in Organizations

1
Planning and Control in Organizations: The Need for New Perspectives

Planning and control have long been accepted as fundamental to the practice of management. Early treatises on management, such as that of Fayol (1949), viewed planning and control as the beginning and end of the management process. Later, experts began to recognize the complex and diverse nature of planning and control in organizations. Anthony (1965), for instance, offered a seminal analysis of the vastly different purposes, processes, time horizons, and levels of managers involved in various planning and control activities in organizations. But his excellent framework does not recognize the different kinds of organizations that may be involved, nor does it readily lend itself to translation into systems that managers can use.

There have been constant developments in the theory and practice of planning and control over the last three decades. In the 1950s, budgeting systems were considered the answer to managerial planning and control needs. The 1960s saw the emergence of long-range planning systems. And the environmental volatility and management aggressiveness of the 1970s led to the development of strategic planning systems.

Despite the enormous progress that has been made, managers are still driven by the need to develop better systems of planning and control. The corporate corpses that litter the economic landscape of the 1980s are perhaps a symptom of the pressing nature of the need for better planning and control systems. Another symptom is that many organizations that pride themselves on their managerial prowess and view themselves at the forefront of management technology have recently been overhauling their planning and control systems. General Electric, Texas Instruments, and Westinghouse are typical of such organizations.

The popular press (*Business Week*), managerial magazines (*Planning Review*), and judicious journals (*Sloan Management Review*) have been forums for voicing widespread disenchantment with planning and control systems. The increasingly complex, demanding, and even hostile climate facing organizations in the private and public sectors accentuates the need for better planning and control systems.

The planning and control systems developed and discussed in this book are designed to respond to the shortcomings of present practice. The techniques and processes described here represent carefully developed, tested, and significant departures from the current conventional wisdom regarding the design of planning and control systems.

There are three important differences between traditional approaches to the design of planning and control systems and the novel approach proposed here. First, the proposed approach is highly integrated along some important dimensions. For instance, certain kinds of planning and control activities are so intertwined that it is difficult to label them as one or the other. My approach to design sidesteps the highly subjective and somewhat unnecessary task of categorizing activities such as defining the organization's mission or raison d'être as either planning or control. It is a planning activity in that it charts the future directions of the organization. It is also a control activity in that it limits the range of businesses or programs that the organization can consider. Instead of trying to define such activities as planning or as control, I will discuss how to orient these activities toward promoting greater flexibility or greater stability, toward anticipating the future or understanding and learning from the past, toward greater effectiveness or greater efficiency.

In addition to integrating the planning and control activities that are intrinsically inseparable, my approach focuses a great deal of attention on how to integrate or link planning and control activities that occur at different levels and locations in the organization. Planning and control activities that are carried out by top management need to be linked with the planning and control activities carried out by lower-level managers. A variety of mechanisms for bringing about these linkages will be identified and their appropriate use described.

The fact that I will be examining these linkage mechanisms is indicative of another distinctive aspect of this book. Unlike the usual practice of focusing solely on strategic planning or on management control, I will consider both. Thus I will not only look at how organizations should determine their aspirations, but also how these aspirations are translated into managerial actions and decisions and then modified in the light of improved understanding of the environmental context and organizational capabilities.

A further integrative characteristic of the approach is that planning and control activities are viewed as part of a broader administrative system that executives must manage in order to affect organizational performance. The relationship of planning and control systems to organizational structure, competitive strategy, and management style is explored at the conceptual and pragmatic levels.

The second important difference between my approach to planning and control and conventional perspectives is that the type of organization is explicitly considered. Organizations with a single product line are both different from and similar in some ways to organizations that operate in multiple unrelated businesses. Understanding how these differences affect planning and control is crucial for effective system design. At the same time, recognizing the similarities between these different organizational types greatly simplifies the task of the system designer. My approach highlights the key differences between types of organizations but also identifies the planning and control activities that are identical across organizational types.

The third important difference is that the systems I will develop are much simpler and more efficient than the traditional ones. At the same time, the new system designs will accomplish even more effectively the entire range of purposes that conventional systems claim to serve.

The greater efficiency and effectiveness of my approach stem from several factors. Conventional systems have evolved over the years to meet new challenges or accomplish new purposes. Not surprisingly, they are a patchwork of subsystems, additions to the original edifice that are much less efficient and effective than a system built from the ground up to meet today's challenges and needs. By not recognizing the key differences and similarities among various types of organizations, conventional systems built in both ineffectiveness and unnecessary complexity. Finally, a combination of happenstance, necessity, and creative thinking has in recent years resulted in the development of nontraditional, near-heretical techniques and processes that have proved to be effective in practice and that offer alternative paradigms, new ways of thinking about the theoretical underpinnings of planning and control.

These new perspectives offer the prospect of responding to or avoiding troubling questions that have plagued designers who look at systems from traditional perspectives. The arbitrary, often ambiguous, and sometimes misleading distinction between formulation and implementation of plans is no longer an impediment. The apparent conflict between "rational" imperatives and "behavioral" dictates is squarely confronted, and a symbiotic resolution is offered. The debate between those who espouse a formal, comprehensive approach to planning and control and those who favor informal, incremental approaches is addressed by incorporating the best that both schools of thought offer. These new, simple, proven processes and techniques will constitute the backbone of the systems that we design. The underlying theory that justifies their use and explains their effectiveness will be discussed, but my emphasis will be more on the rules of thumb, or operational guidelines, that will help translate this theory into effective practice.

I will begin by identifying the different kinds of planning and control activities that organizations need to carry out. The perspective I develop here modifies existing theories in the light of practical insights developed in recent years.

The second step will be to define a framework for classifying organizations that will identify the similarities and differences among various types of organizations that need to be considered when designing planning and control systems. Also, the subunits within the simple organizations down to the lowest level of managerial responsibility will be identified and classified in a manner that facilitates the design and implementation of planning and control activities at these levels. The classification scheme for subunits within simple organizations will be presented later, in the context of the design of management control systems.

The next step will address the design of strategic planning and control systems in simple organizations that operate in a single business, applying the framework developed in chapter 2. These systems focus on the identification of the organization's mission, on articulating the aspirations of its managers, and on developing broad guidelines for allocating the resources available to the organization.

Following this step, we will be in a position to explore the design of management planning and control systems in these simple organizations. These systems focus on the processes by which the organization translates its strategic aspirations into reality through the medium of plans of action and by monitoring the success of these plans.

On completing the design of strategic planning and management control systems in simple organizations, we will be in a position to examine the added features required for systems in more complex organizations. The first level of added complexity will involve divisionalized organizations that function in multiple but related businesses. The linkages between planning and control at the corporate headquarters of these organizations and the management level responsible for individual businesses or divisions will require particular attention.

The next level of complexity in the design of planning and control systems arises in the context of conglomerate organizations that operate in multiple unrelated businesses. The concepts and techniques appropriate for these organizations are quite different at the corporate level from those considered in the context of less complex organizations.

Next we will examine the two major devices by which we can link strategic planning systems and management control systems. First, there is the capital budgeting system that defines and manages major projects that give the organization new capabilities and new directives. Second, there is the issue management system that identifies and responds to unanticipated major developments, internal and external, that affect the organization.

We will then look at how planning and control systems fit into the context of the larger administrative system that is employed to manage organizations. Such administrative systems include the organizational structure, management style, and competitive strategy adopted by the organization's managers.

Having considered the design of planning and control systems in various types of organizations, we will proceed to describe the most appropriate approaches to implementing those systems. At this stage, the criteria for assessing the effectiveness of these systems will also be discussed.

We conclude by recapitulating some of the major problems commonly encountered with regard to effective planning and control in organizations and review the most significant responses to these key problems. This book is designed to provide both a pragmatic understanding of how to design effective strategic planning and management control systems and a clear conception of why the approaches recommended are likely to be effective. I hope that readers will not only be able to design and implement the systems described in the book but also be in a position to develop novel insights and new approaches that will increase the effectiveness of planning and control systems and add to the viability and success of an organization.

To summarize, this book responds to the need for fresh perspectives on the key managerial functions of planning and control. The planning and control systems developed in this book are significantly different from current conventional wisdom in that:

1. They are highly integrated.
   - Planning and control are treated as inseparable and simultaneous in situations where such is the case;
   - Planning and control occurring at different levels in the organization are carefully linked;
   - Both strategic planning and management control, formulation and implementation are considered;
   - Planning and control are linked with the larger administrative systems in organizations.

2. They are tailored to the type of organization.
   - The complexities stemming from the differences between types of organizations are recognized;
   - The simplicity permitted by similarities between organizational types is exploited.

3. They are much simpler and also more effective.
   - Redundancies that have resulted from the historical evolution of planning and control systems are identified and eliminated;
   - New processes and techniques that do as much as traditional processes but with much less effort are described;
   - Arbitrary, theoretical distinctions between "formulation" and "implementation" are laid aside when appropriate;

- "Rational" approaches are integrated with the best that "behavioral" insights have to offer;
- The conflict between "incremental" and "comprehensive" approaches is substantially resolved;
- Complex theories are translated into pragmatic rules of thumb.

References

Anthony, Robert N. *Planning and Control Systems: A Framework for Analysis.* Boston: Division of Research, Harvard Business School, 1965.

"Eight Half-Truths of Strategic Planning: A Fresh Look." *Planning Review* (January 1985): 22–27.

Fayol, H. *General and Industrial Management.* London: Pitman, 1949.

"The New Breed of Strategic Planner." *Business Week* (September 17, 1984):62–68.

"Strategic Planning under Fire," *Sloan Management Review* (Summer 1984): 57–61.

2
A Framework of Planning and Control

The development of a framework of planning and control requires us to adopt a common understanding of planning and of control. It is surprising, considering the unquestioned importance of planning and control as elements in the process of management, that no commonly accepted definitions of the terms exist. On various occasions when practicing managers and students of management were asked to define the term *planning*, the answers tended to range over a spectrum of ideas. Some of the definitions proposed were: "Planning is thinking ahead"; "Planning is deciding what you can and should achieve"; and "Planning is deciding what to do." Although all of these definitions possess merit, they clearly represent different and fragmented views of planning.

A similar problem exists with regard to control. The concept of control ranges from specific, limited notions to broad, amorphous ideas. Control in a limited, remedial perspective can be seen as correcting something that has gone wrong. Control from a broad, future-oriented point of view can be perceived as the exercise of influence over the actions and decisions of others.

We need definitions of planning and control that are relevant in the context of the management of organizations, that are comprehensive in scope yet parsimonious enough to permit focused managerial effort and that offer guidance to the designers of planning and control systems.

Definitions

Planning

An early, comprehensive, managerially relevant definition of planning was offered by Brian Scott (1963, 8): "Planning is an analytical process which involves an assessment of the future, the determination of desired objectives in the context of that future, the development of alternative courses of action to achieve such objectives and the selection of a course (or courses) of action from among those alternatives." This definition integrates the three notions of planning already presented and possesses additional positive attributes, though it is not without shortcomings.

Scott's definition appears to be broad enough to be applied to planning for any activity from running a household through managing a large corporation or directing military operations to governing a country, but it was developed specifically in the context of the management of organizations. It is a comprehensive definition that embraces both the development of goals and the specification of means to achieve these goals. Yet it identifies in a parsimonious fashion the range of activities that must necessarily comprise the planning function: analysis of the future, formulation of goals, generation of alternatives, and evaluation of these alternatives. Moreover, it also characterizes the nature of the activity as implicitly rational, given the description of the process as "analytical." Surely it provides useful guidance in terms of needed activities to the designers of planning processes in organizations.

Despite its appealing characteristics, this definition has shortcomings. First, it is simplistic in that it suggests a linear sequence of activities from analysis to action. This is far from the painful reality. The real process is inevitably iterative and heuristic in character. Objectives might need to be modified if there are no acceptable ways to reach them, for example, and further analysis might be required as innovative alternatives reveal new possibilities.

Second, it biases the manager toward analysis of external developments. The definition implicitly stresses identification of environmental opportunities and threats. The key considerations of resource availability and organizational competences are not readily brought to mind.

Third, it does not recognize the reality that planning takes on different characteristics in different contexts. Planning that takes place at the corporate level of a multibillion dollar, multibusiness, multinational conglomerate such as ITT is vastly different from planning in the purchasing department of the owner-managed, single-location supplier of work gloves to industry that exists in a small steel town in southwestern Pennsylvania.

Fourth, its easy and appealing characterization of the planning process as analytic in character does not recognize the exercise of power and the reflection of managerial values that this process often represents.

Despite these significant shortcomings, Scott's definition is powerful and relevant enough to serve as the foundation for the framework I will develop in this book, providing we bear in mind the four caveats. A stylized representation of the planning process can be derived from this definition of planning (figure 2–1): the expected future, matched with the organization's competences, influenced by managerial preferences and values, and responsive to the priorities and power of others with a stake in the outcome of the process, gives rise to the plan, which includes an articulation of objectives, a specification of how (strategies or actions) to achieve these objectives, and an understanding of the needed resource commitments.

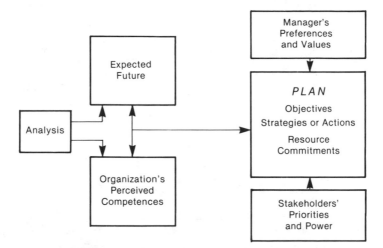

Figure 2–1. Generic Planning Process

This generic process must be tailored to particular contexts. The organization or subunit of the business and its characteristics must be explicitly recognized, the relevant future delineated, the stakeholders and their priorities identified, and the concerned managers' preferences articulated.

Control

No definition of *control* that is suited to our purposes is available in the literature. In its broadest terms, control is a process intended to increase the probability of achieving the organization's planned objectives. Again applying the criteria employed in selecting a definition of planning, it is possible to suggest a definition of *control* that is comprehensive yet parsimonious and a basis for designing effective systems:

> Control is a behavioral process that involves measurement and evaluation of the performance of organizational units, the identification of deviations from planned performance, the initiation of appropriate responses to these deviations, and the monitoring of remedial actions, all done with the intent of ensuring that managers' decisions and actions are consistent with planned organizational objectives.

Some significant aspects of this definition merit elaboration. First, the process is viewed as behavioral in character. This highlights the basic purpose of control: to motivate and assist managers to achieve results consistent with the organization's planned objectives. Second, planning is a necessary prerequisite for control to take place. Without planning objectives, control

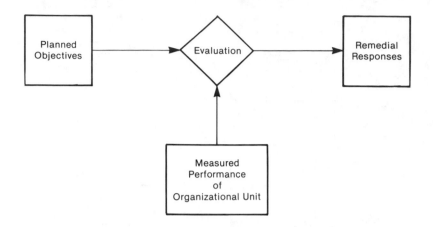

Figure 2–2. Generic Control Process

cannot exist. Third, the activities identified in the definition of control are not intrinsically valuable or necessary; they assume value and importance only insofar as they accomplish the basic purpose of control as described.

It is somewhat more difficult to derive a useful generic process or model of control than it was to develop a meaningful generic planning process. A simple generic process as diagrammed in figure 2–2 provides little added understanding, particularly when it is not explicitly linked to an organizational context. But overlaying the generic process on a model of the organization such as the classic input-process-output model developed by Miller and Rice (1967), it is possible to identify some key considerations of relevance to the designer of control systems.

In its simplest form, the input-process-output model views the organization and its subunits as a mechanism or process that converts inputs, such as money, human effort, and raw materials, into desired outputs, such as profits. The model envisages a manager of the organization or subunit who exercises authority over the inputs and process and holds responsibility for obtaining the desired output (figure 2–3).

The managerial model of control that is obtained by integrating the generic control process with this organizational model is diagrammed in figure 2–4. The four blocks from figure 2–2 relating to control circumscribe the four blocks from figure 2–3 relating to the organization.

The managerial model is fairly straightforward. Objectives derived from planning guide the selection of parameters of performance. These parameters describe the input, process, and output of the organization and are measured and fed to the evaluation activity. Measured performance is compared to planned objectives, and remedial responses are determined and communi-

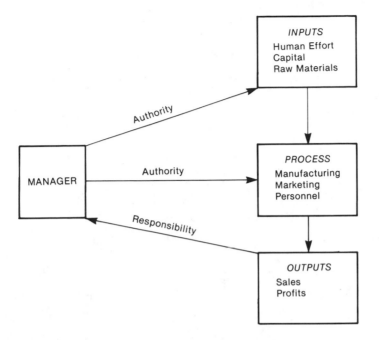

Figure 2–3. Input-Output Model

cated to the manager of the organizational unit. Remedial responses also include the possibility of modifying the planned objectives.

The strongest behavioral influences on the unit manager are from the objectives and evaluation aspects of the control process. These links are the two most significant of the behavioral aspects of the control process.

This model has two shortcomings. First, the possibility of preventive control—ensuring that deviations do not occur (as opposed to remedying deviations after they occur)—is not explicitly considered. Second, the model does not fully distinguish between control as a hierarchical concept where superior controls subordinate, and control as an individual activity where self-control is exercised; however, hierarchical control and self-control exist simultaneously in organizations, and the model implicitly accepts this reality.

Relationship between Planning and Control

The classic perspective on planning and control views them as two distinct activities under the umbrella of the process of management. Often planning is listed as the initial management activity and control as the last, possibly even post facto activity. We will adopt a different perspective on planning and

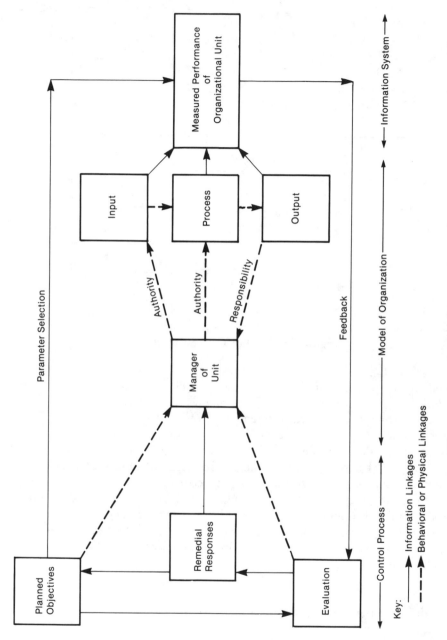

Figure 2–4. A Managerial Model of Control

control. To the extent that they are distinct and separate, we will search for ways to bring about a symbiotic relationship and to minimize possible negative influences one may have on the other. But as we will demonstrate, planning and control are often so closely intertwined as to be indistinguishable.

The most obvious relationship between planning and control is that it is not possible to control without having planned. The need to plan prior to the exercise of control stems from the fact that planning is the means by which objectives and courses of action are decided upon in the organization. Without these guidelines, it is not possible to determine whether an organization or an executive is deviating from what is expected. Control is not possible without the benchmarks and guideposts that can be provided only by planning. Neither is it reasonable to conceive of planning that is independent of control. Control ensures that the plan is reasonable. Also, planning without ensuring that implementation is effective and efficient is nothing more than an expensive exercise in futility.

The relationship between planning and control is not entirely or necessarily mutually beneficial. For example, the quality of planning can affect the exercise of control. Planned objectives that turn out to be excessively difficult or easy to achieve detract from the credibility of the control process. Given the behavioral character of control, this loss of credibility can be damaging.

Control can also negatively influence planning, though the nature of this influence is not as obvious. It is possible that the control activity can detract from the effectiveness of planning by inhibiting the creative elements of the planning process.

In order to be effective, all planning activity demands creativity, though the extent of creativity required varies from situation to situation. This need is particularly evident at the stage of identifying alternative courses of action. Moreover, the process of planning, in addition to requiring creativity (as an input to planning) for effective execution, also can be designed as a means for stimulating creativity. In fact, this stimulation of creativity in managers (as an output of planning) is often formally recognized as one of the primary reasons why planning is undertaken in organizations. Creativity essentially means originality, or developing alternatives and ideas that have not been tried before. Originality implies greater risk and thus carries with it a greater likelihood of failure. By definition, the higher the risk is, the greater is the chance of failure.

The control system constantly measures the degree of success or failure. Success is usually rewarded, and failure is either penalized or ignored. Managers are pressured or motivated by the control system to succeed. One way of ensuring success is to minimize risk, which means reducing originality and, in turn, inhibiting creativity. Consequently control might take away from the effectiveness of planning by reducing the critically important input of creativity and minimizing the expected output of stimulating managerial creativity.

These possibilities of a harmful relationship between planning and control make the design of planning and control systems complex and delicate. Effective planning both requires and is a prerequisite to effective control, but overly rigorous control can damage the quality of planning, and careless planning can destroy control.

Another complexity is that it is often hard to distinguish between planning and control. Given the definition of control that identifies its purpose as ensuring congruence between organizational objectives and executive decisions and actions, planning that involves lower-level managers in formulating objectives can reasonably be argued to be consistent with this definition of control. Planning in this sense is future-oriented control.

At the same time, the analysis that is defined as an integral part of planning is often carried out to a significant extent under the aegis of control. Also our model of control envisages the possibility of modifying planned objectives. Control in these contexts is hardly different from planning.

The traditional way of designing a separate planning system and a separate control system must be approached with caution, if not trepidation. Planning and control are highly dependent on each other for effectiveness. At the same time, the possibility exists that they can greatly damage each other. In addition, at times it is difficult to classify an activity as being either planning or control. Clearly a simplifying and novel perspective on planning and control is needed if the design of planning and control systems is to be carried out confidently and with reasonable assurance of effectiveness.

Anthony's Perspective

Until 1965, and not uncommonly even today, conventional wisdom held that planning and control in organizations should be separated. Each was viewed as being sufficiently disparate in nature, distinct in purpose, and different in activities that they should constitute two separate, homogeneous systems.

The concept of a single, possibly homogeneous, planning system gives rise to several problems. Take, for instance, the chief executive officer (CEO) of a national consumer goods organization and the manager in charge of the sales of a product line, say toiletries, in a territory comprising East Coast states. In terms of the definition of planning, both can be said to be involved in the planning activity of assessing the future, determining objectives, identifying alternatives, and selecting courses of action.

But these two managers have quite different objectives. The CEO is concerned with the company image and the continuing viability and growth of the organization over a period of five or even ten years in the future. The sales manager is concerned with sales volume, inventories, and customer relations over the period of a month, a quarter, or a year. The differences between the alternatives generated by the CEO and by the sales manager are so great as to almost defy comparison. In other words, the planning activities carried out by the CEO and by the sales manager are distinctly and drastically different along several dimensions:

1. Degree of complexity: Extremely high for the CEO and relatively low for the sales manager.

2. Time span: Several years for the CEO and months or a year for the sales manager.

3. Academic knowledge: Economics, labor relations, political science, accounting, statistics, forecasting techniques, and social psychology for the CEO and arithmetic, two-person interpersonal relationships and simple forecasting for the sales manager.

4. Number and hierarchical level of persons involved: Several senior staff and line managers for the CEO and relatively lower-level and many fewer personnel for the sales manager.

5. Degree of structure in the process: Highly unstructured for the CEO and quite amenable to structuring for the sales manager.

6. Ease of evaluation of the effectiveness of the planning process: Highly complicated, subjective, and, some would say, practically impossible for the CEO and relatively simple for the sales manager.

Thus although both the CEO and the sales manager are engaged in planning, the differences along several dimensions are so great as to make meaningless any attempt to use the same criteria for designing or evaluating a planning system for the CEO and the sales manager. An identical argument can be advanced in the case of control, again strongly suggesting that a single type of control system cannot work for both the CEO and the sales manager. The key dimensions along which planning and control differ depending on managerial level are highlighted in figure 2–5. These five dimensions—horizon or frequency, structure, focus, complexity, and ease of evaluation—have major implications in terms of designing planning and control processes and systems.

A major breakthrough occurred in 1965, when Robert Anthony of the Harvard Business School put forward a novel framework for the analysis of planning and control systems. Anthony's basic thesis is that thinking of planning and control as requiring two separate, presumably homogeneous systems in organizations is not only meaningless but probably dysfunctional. Instead of two categories of planning and control (a practice still supported by certain authorities), Anthony suggests that organizational planning and control be segmented into three categories: (1) strategic planning, (2) management control, and (3) operational control (Anthony 1965).

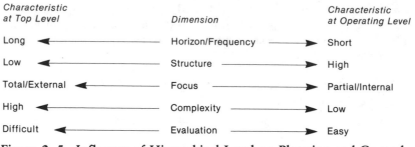

Characteristic at Top Level	Dimension	Characteristic at Operating Level
Long	Horizon/Frequency	Short
Low	Structure	High
Total/External	Focus	Partial/Internal
High	Complexity	Low
Difficult	Evaluation	Easy

Figure 2–5. Influence of Hierarchical Level on Planning and Control

Anthony believes that planning and control are so closely interlinked in organizations as to make their separation meaningless and undesirable. Instead, he suggests, it makes much more conceptual and practical sense to link together similar and intertwined planning and control activities into systems of homogeneous characteristics. For instance, to take the example of the CEO and the sales manager in the consumer goods company, Anthony would say that the planning and control activities carried out by the sales manager should be aggregated under the aegis of a separate system. Anthony's departure from the traditional view is diagrammed in figure 2–6.

It is important to note that Anthony's terminology, though widely accepted and in fact employed in the title of this book, is somewhat misleading. When Anthony says "strategic planning" he means "strategic planning and control." Similarly "management control" embraces both planning and control activities.

Strategic Planning and Control

Strategic planning and control is the responsibility of the apex of the organization. In large, complex organizations, it also occurs in subunits that function as independent businesses. According to Anthony, strategic planning and control involves the following:

1. Setting and modifying the organization's objectives.
2. Determining the resources that will be committed to accomplishing these objectives.
3. Defining the organization's policies regarding obtaining and using these resources.

Anthony's somewhat amorphous definition is acceptable. But his subsequent contention—that strategic planning is essentially an unstructured activity that cannot be formalized except for certain elements, such as the process of deciding on and sanctioning major capital expenditures—is not acceptable. I

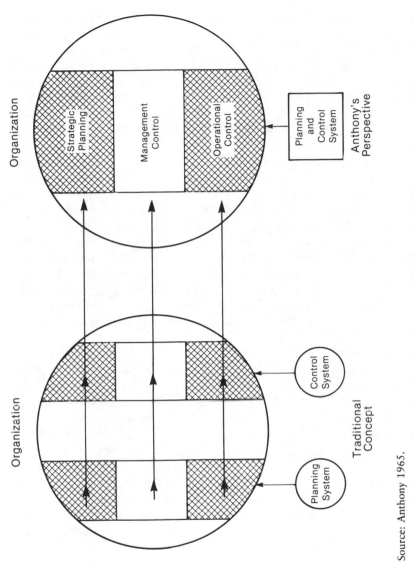

Source: Anthony 1965.

Figure 2–6. Traditional and Proposed Perspectives on Organizational Planning and Control Systems

propose that not only is strategic planning amenable to formal approaches but also that formalization is desirable if handled carefully. There is abundant evidence of the existence of formal systems for strategic planning.

In later chapters I detail the approach to formalizing strategic planning in different types of organizations. Very broadly, though, applying the definition of planning to top management's responsibilities for the organization, I suggest that top management can evaluate the relevant facets of the external environment—economic, social, political, technological, regulatory, and demographic—as well as competition in order to arrive at an understanding of the opportunities and threats facing the organization. At the same time, the organization itself can be assessed to arrive at a structured understanding of its strengths and weaknesses with regard to such facets as products and services, manufacturing and other operations, marketing, managerial capabilities, organizational structure, and planning and control systems.

By meshing the perceived external opportunities and threats with the identified internal strengths and weaknesses, top management, giving due importance to its own values and the priorities of those having a stake in the organization, would then be in a position to formulate the objectives of the organization and the strategies to be implemented, the resources to be committed, and the policies to be adopted in the quest to achieve the stated objectives.

Strategic control occurs in three ways. First, strategic planning is itself a form of control. Managerial discretion at lower levels in the hierarchy is circumscribed by the strategic plan. In other words, the boundaries of the feasible space for managerial decision making are defined and limited by the strategic plan. Also, the behavior of lower-level managers is affected by the nature and extent of their involvement in the strategic planning exercise.

Second, strategic plans are converted into reality not only by their influence on the management control activity but also by the key decisions regarding the allocation of resources. The capital budgeting exercise, as the formal resource allocation process is often called, is therefore a major form of strategic control. Capital budgeting or resource allocation systems illustrate the character of certain types of planning and control activities. These systems are simultaneously engaged in planning and control.

Third, while capital budgeting systems (CBS) can respond to requests for resources that are consistent with the accepted strategic plan, the period between formal, comprehensive strategic planning exercises can give rise to unanticipated changes in the environment or unexpected internal crises. The CBS cannot normally respond appropriately with the necessary modifications to existing resource allocation priorities because the strategic plan needed to guide these decisions may have been rendered obsolete and irrelevant. Moreover, an insensitivity to early indications of unanticipated developments is typical of strategic planning systems. It is imperative, therefore, that a flexible system providing quick responses to early signals of unexpected and important developments be developed. We shall call such systems strategic issue management systems (SIMS). These systems constitute a crucially important component of strategic control.

Management Planning and Control

Anthony views management planning and control as the processes by which (1) organizational objectives are achieved and (2) the use of resources is made effective and efficient.

Charles Rossotti (n.d.) offers an excellent description of what he calls "action planning," which involves activities that are typical in intent and nature of management planning and control. According to Rossotti, in action planning, the "prime focus is improved internal coordination, communication and motivation toward overall organizational goals. The most frequent form of this activity is the five year plan, which is compiled in a cycle similar to the more traditional budgeting."

In designing management control systems (MCS), certain other characteristics of action planning offer useful guidance. For example, it has been learned that the exercise of developing an action plan is less than optimally effective if time-bound tasks are not specified and the executives responsible for carrying out these tasks are not identified. Effective action planning, and by implication effective MCS, requires not only a statement of expected goals but also a detailed understanding of the specific actions to be carried out by identified executives in order to achieve these goals within a prescribed deadline.

Another traditional activity typical of management planning and control is the financial budget. Stedry (1960, 3) states, "First, a budget may serve as a plan. Second, a budget may serve as a control." Experience has shown that the mixture of planning and control in the budgeting activity is highly combustible. The dysfunctional relationships between planning and control are not uncommonly encountered here. Not surprisingly, therefore, much useful work has been done on the behavioral implications of budgeting practices. Our proposed MCS design will respond to these significant behavioral considerations.

Research (Bhattacharyya and Camillus 1977) has strongly indicated that an important element in effective management planning and control is the review and follow-up activity that is referred to as evaluation in our generic process of control. The design of this activity has been found to have a profound influence on the perceived effectiveness of the MCS.

Operational Planning and Control

Anthony views this third category of organizational planning and control as (1) focusing on specific, discrete tasks and (2) the process of ensuring that those tasks are done effectively and efficiently. This kind of planning and control is perhaps best illustrated by means of examples. The activities performed by the stores controller, who keeps track of inventory levels, initiates purchase orders addressed to prescreened, specified vendors when stocks fall below the reorder point, and ensures that the purchase quantity is in accordance with an appropriate economic order quantity formula, are essentially operational planning and control. Scheduling of manufacturing operations, most distribution activities, and the management of accounts receivable are other examples of activities that fall into the classification of operational planning and control. Generally any planning and control activity that is susceptible to the application of decision rules that ensure effective and efficient execution can be termed operational planning and control.

Strategic Planning and Management Control

This book will not address operational planning and control. The intrinsic qualities of these activities make them easy to perform well. On the other hand, strategic planning and control and management planning and control are complex, demanding activities that require insight, judgment, and experience to do well. Organizational survival and success can be greatly affected by the manner in which these activities are carried out. We will carefully examine the effective design and implementation of systems of strategic and management planning and control.

In order to conform to Anthony's choice of terminology and in the interest of brevity, I will refer to strategic planning and control as strategic planning and management planning and control as management control. Both terms, however, embrace planning and control.

Limiting the focus to strategic planning and management control in organizations, we can now identify four systems that must be examined in detail:

1. The strategic planning system (SPS), which defines the raison d'être of the organization, formalizes the organization's enduring objectives, identifies strategies for accomplishing these objectives, and defines the related broad resource commitments.

2. The management control system (MCS), which translates the organization's objectives and strategies into time-bound, measurable goals and related plans of action. It also ensures that available organizational resources are employed efficiently in accomplishing its goals.

3. The capital budgeting system (CBS), which links the SPS and MCS by converting on a routine, ongoing basis the broad resource commitments made by the SPS to specific allocations to particular projects and activities managed by the MCS.

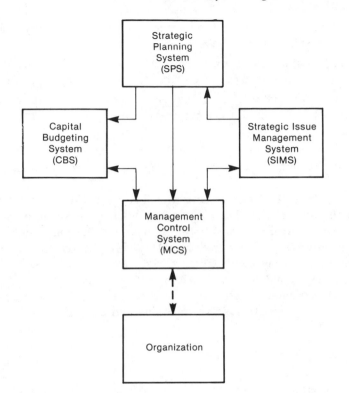

Figure 2–7. Four Key Systems of Planning and Control

4. The strategic issue management system (SIMS), which responds in a sensitive but powerful fashion to the imperatives of the inevitable, unanticipated, and significant changes in the environment and in the organization that the MCS cannot cope with and that the SPS is unlikely to recognize.

The interactions among these four systems of planning and control are illustrated in figure 2–7.

Organizational Context

These four systems of planning and control are dependent on and influence the organizational context in which they function. Five aspects of the organizational context are fundamental to the design of these systems:

1. Type of organization: Simple and small or complex and large.

2. Organizational structure: How responsibility and authority is shared by managers within the organization.

3. Management informations systems: The formal mechanisms for providing the information that is the lifeblood of planning and control.

4. Reward and compensation systems: The monetary and social mechanisms designed to influence managerial attitudes and the focus of attention.

5. Top management attitudes: The understanding of, commitment to, and use of planning and control by the organization's senior managers.

These five aspects of the organizational context will be common threads running throughout the discussion in this book of strategic planning and management control, offering opportunities and causing constraints that affect the design of planning and control systems. All five aspects are amenable to formal management, creating a kaleidoscope of possible contexts within which system designers can pattern planning and control to fit. All five aspects of the organization will be addressed with a view to ensuring more effective and appropriate design of planning and control.

References

Anthony, Robert N. *Planning and Control Systems: A Framework for Analysis.* Boston: Division of Research, Harvard Business School, 1965.

Bhattacharyya, S.K., and Camillus, John C. *Management Control Systems: A Framework for Resolution of Problems of Implementation.* New Delhi: Institute of Chartered Accountants of India, 1977.

Miller, Eric J., and Rice, A.K. *Systems of Organization.* London: Tavistock, 1967.

Rossotti, Charles O. *Two Concepts of Long Range Planning.* Boston: Management Consulting Group, Boston Safe Deposit and Trust Company, n.d.

Scott, Brian W. "Some Aspects of Long-Range Planning in American Corporations with Special Attention to Strategic Planning." Ph.D. dissertation, Harvard University, 1963.

Stedry, Andrew C. *Budget Control and Cost Behavior.* Englewood Cliffs, N.J.: Prentice-Hall, 1960.

3
Types of Organizations: Implications for Planning and Control

T hat organizations vary a great deal in a large number of characteristics is obvious. What is not as obvious is how these variations affect the planning and control requirements of each organization. In this chapter we will adopt a classification scheme that will enable us to understand the impact of organizational characteristics on planning and control. The scheme must be comprehensive so that the large majority of business organizations are covered by it, yet it must not include too many different categories in order to avoid unnecessarily fine or confusing distinctions.

Alternative Classification Schemes

A wide variety of approaches to classifying business organizations exists. Two of the most popular sets of approaches are schemes that emphasize the territorial coverage of organizations and those that emphasize the structural form of organizations. These two approaches are not entirely independent of each other. For instance, an organization that is multinational in territorial coverage will necessarily have to take on certain structural forms.

The task of selecting a scheme is greatly simplified and given direction by the fact that all we are interested in is the relationship between the type of organization and planning and control. Thus, while expanding territorial coverage or widening product lines may be the reason for certain organizational characteristics that have an influence on planning and control systems, we do not have to engage in a debate as to what the reasons are that an organization possesses certain characteristics. As will be abundantly clear in later chapters, planning and control systems are most closely linked with organization structure. In the case of management control, the key consideration driving MCS design is the internal structure of the organization. In the case of strategic planning, the structure of the organization both reflects and drives its strategy, thus implicitly defining the SPS design.

Classification schemes based on the structural form of the organization are what are relevant to the designer of planning and control systems. Of such schemes, one of the most popular, comprehensive, realistic, and surely the most elegant was developed by Larry Greiner (1972).

Greiner's Model

Greiner's model describes the stages through which organizations pass as they grow and mature. Considerable empirical evidence (Galbraith and Nathanson 1979) shows that this model accurately depicts reality. The model possesses an additional advantage in that there is a clear-cut distinction between each stage of growth and the next. The classification scheme is therefore intrinsic to the model and does not require us to slice a continuum arbitrarily at various points.

Greiner's model can be described by following a hypothetical organization from its origins in a shack in Waltham, Massachusetts, to its current situation, with international headquarters located in Boston, Massachusetts.

Entrepreneurial First Stage

American Chemical Enterprises, Inc., now more popularly known as ACE, started in November 1948 in Waltham, Massachusetts. Its founder, Mr. Berger, a 1941 graduate in chemical engineering from Rensselaer Polytechnic Institute, had worked with two large chemical companies before joining the U.S. Navy. On leaving the navy after saving some capital, Berger attempted unsuccessfully to put through a deal with another large chemical company to develop for it a maleic resin with applications in the manufacture of ink. His discouraging experiences with large corporations led him to decide to strike out on his own. With the few thousand dollars remaining of his savings, Berger acquired a small 700 gallon reactor at a bargain price. After spending three weeks cleaning the interior with a chisel, Berger made his first product, an alkyd resin, for a nearby firm.

ACE's facilities in Waltham were makeshift in nature. The operations were carried out in a building that was little more than a shack. Necessities like ovens for experimental purposes were fashioned by hand from bricks and hot plates. In the early years, it was not uncommon for Mrs. Berger to stir an experimental compound with their first child on her knee while her husband cooked up another batch of resin.

Greiner refers to this first stage in an organization's growth as the creative phase. I prefer to call it an entrepreneurial stage because qualities much beyond creativity are required to function in and survive this initial stage. This stage usually requires a monomaniac with a vision and a great deal of luck. What is not required at this stage is a formal planning and control system. Organizations at this stage will, therefore, not be considered further.

Functional Second Stage

For the first year or two, Berger continued to produce and sell alkyd resins but was constantly on the alert for possible new facilities. In particular, he had in mind a plant owned by a chemical company in Lowell, Massachusetts, that made products Berger knew were becoming obsolete. When this plant became available in 1951, Berger purchased it, borrowing heavily from a local bank. ACE moved from Waltham to Lowell in the same year. The new 1 acre plant included two reactors, each of 2,000 gallon capacity, which had to be modified considerably before they could be used.

Once the new reactors became operational, more products became feasible. For instance, at that time, ACE anticipated and responded early to the trend toward acrylics. Adhesives, plasticizers, coatings, and finishes were added to the product line in quick succession. The expanding product line was accompanied by expanding sales. ACE's sales of $50,000 in 1952 leaped to over $4 million by 1961.

The period 1951 through 1961 saw a great deal of change in how Berger operated. In 1951 he hired a former classmate from Rensselaer to supervise the production operations. In 1952 a sales manager was added to the managerial ranks. Berger continued to look after research and development (R&D) and the financing of the business but found it necessary to add an accountant, a shipping manager, and a personnel manager to his staff.

With only two reactors (ACE's original 700 gallon reactor was used solely for research after the move to Lowell) and many products, scheduling of production required the careful attention of the new production manager. Downtime of the reactors for cleaning and preparation became a significant issue. The large volumes in each batch made quality control and yields even more important than before.

The sales manager found himself stretched to find customers for all the products that Berger now found the time to formulate. With large volumes of production becoming available, competition with some of the other major firms in the industry emerged as a factor.

With new and larger customers, working capital management became one of Berger's constant concerns. He soon found it necessary to develop relationships with large banks because his original local banker soon began to feel overextended to ACE.

ACE's multishift operation made the hiring and training of workers a significant problem for the personnel manager. Alcoholism and absenteeism among workers caused constant friction between the personnel manager and the production manager.

Greiner refers to this second stage in an organization's growth as the directive stage. I will call it the functional stage. The organization at this stage has survived the rigors of the entrepreneurial stage. Its increased size makes expertise in the functional areas of management—manufacturing, marketing, human resources, finance, and so forth—vital. Formal systems become necessary to coordinate the activities of the various managers and to promote communication between the levels of management.

While the concept of business of the organization is apparently stable and well understood, it becomes increasingly necessary to select among options. Demand for resources often exceeds their availability, and the needs of the various functional areas have to be balanced.

A stylized, generic representation of the structure of a functional organization is illustrated in figure 3–1. (Figure 3–1 also contains representations of divisional and conglomerate organizations, discussed later. These structures are juxtaposed in one figure in order to permit an easier appreciation of their similarities and differences.)

Divisional Third Stage

In 1962 ACE embarked on a diversification path that was to continue successfully over the next decade. Diversification was triggered by Berger's brother, Joe. Joe had also graduated in chemical engineering from Rensselaer, had worked with DuPont for a few years, and then had completed his MBA at the Graduate School of Business at the University of Pittsburgh. While at Pittsburgh, Joe had gotten to know a research engineer working with a large oil company, and the two of them had convinced Berger of the untapped potential in petrochemicals. They persuaded him to invest in a plant near Oil City, Pennsylvania, which was a quick success and soon outstripped ACE's original product line in terms of sales volume.

In 1965 Berger became chairman and CEO of ACE. Joe left the Oil City operation in the hands of his engineer friend and moved to the company's new headquarters in Boston as president and chief operating officer (COO). The Lowell operations were taken over by the marketing manager, who was promoted and awarded the title of general manager.

Joe's dynamism and business acumen sparked a series of acquisitions of small companies in related chemical businesses. In order to help finance these acquisitions, ACE went public in 1967. By 1970 ACE's sales crossed the $100 million mark. Each new company acquired was left to function fairly independently under the charge of a general manager. All capital expenditures above $10,000 had to be approved by the COO or CEO. A corporate-level personnel manager with added responsibilities in the area of managerial training and development and a familiarity with incentive systems had been hired in 1968. Most managerial appointments throughout ACE were made with the cognizance, if not the approval, of the personnel manager. Salary scales were standardized throughout ACE by 1970, thus facilitating cross-divisional transfer of personnel.

By 1971 the COO began to rely heavily on his executive assistant, a

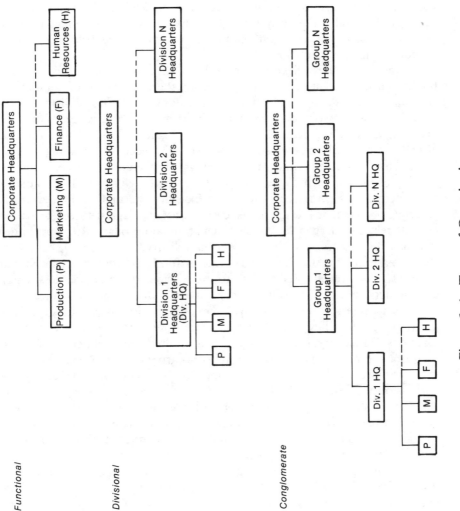

Figure 3–1. Types of Organizations

young Harvard Business School graduate who had taken elective courses in the area of formal planning systems. The CEO, however, continued to place his confidence in the corporate controller whom he had first hired as an accountant for the Lowell plant.

Berger particularly liked the controller's summary profit statements for the Lowell and Oil City plants and for each of the newly acquired companies. Although he broadly understood the businesses in which these divisions operated, he knew he was not as familiar with the markets and products of these divisions as were the general managers. He made it a point, therefore, to attend the quarterly meetings that Joe held with each of the general managers. He prepared for these meetings by asking the corporate controller to identify aspects of each division's operations that were not entirely satisfactory. Berger was somewhat uncomfortable with the new annual strategic planning process that Joe and his executive assistant had instituted. The exercise, he felt, encouraged too much speculation about business opportunities that had nothing to do with the chemical industry, which he felt he understood and in which ACE had been so successful. Even now, he believed that capital funds were allocated to the various divisions on somewhat less than a total understanding of the relative attractiveness of the various projects.

Greiner refers to this third stage in an organization's growth as the delegative stage. We will refer to the organizations of this type as divisional organizations. These organizations operate in multiple but related businesses. Corporate-level top management usually has grown up with one or more of the businesses and is more than superficially knowledgeable about the various businesses.

Corporate control is usually exercised over finance and personnel decisions. The choice between what should be kept under direct corporate control and what should be delegated to divisions is often a difficult question requiring the exercise of judgment.

Capital expenditures of any significance tend to be approved at the corporate level. Given their familiarity with the various businesses, corporate executives base these decisions on detailed reviews of the project proposals.

A generic representation of the structure of divisionalized organizations is provided in figure 3–1.

Conglomerate Fourth Stage

In 1973 Berger retired from ACE because of ill health. Joe was elected chairman and CEO. The executive vice-president of one of ACE's largest competitors was hired as the new president and COO.

In 1973 ACE acquired a large bottler of soft drinks and then several other unrelated businesses. By 1980 ACE's original divisions in the chemical industry constituted just one of three groups of divisions. Each of the two other groups of divisions was in entirely unrelated industries. One of these groups consisted of divisions operating in food and restaurant businesses, which had been built around the 1973 bottling acquisition. The other consisted of a somewhat heterogeneous set of divisions operating in what could loosely be termed the leisure industry. They included a manufacturer of board games, a manufacturer of skis and tennis rackets, and a producer of motion pictures and shows for television.

These acquisitions were masterminded by Joe's former executive assistant, who in 1974 had been appointed vice-president of corporate development. Joe continued to participate in major capital expenditure decisions but was guided primarily by advice from the vice-president of corporate development regarding the need for supporting the two new high-growth groups. The chemicals group continued to be profitable, but the excitement and electricity of the early years seemed to have vanished.

Each of the three groups was headed by an executive, titled group vice-president and general manager. All three group vice-presidents reported to the president and COO.

With sales of over a billion dollars in several industries and in several countries, in 1985 ACE moved its headquarters into a gleaming new glass tower in Boston. Berger, vacationing in the Bahamas, did not feel it necessary to attend the ceremonies that accompanied the move, despite a personal invitation from the charming new vice-president of public relations.

Greiner refers to this fourth stage in an organization as the coordinating stage. We will refer to it as the conglomerate stage because these organizations typically function in extremely diverse businesses that are often tied together only by financial considerations. Corporate management is far removed from product-market considerations and takes on responsibilities not unlike the investment managers of large pension or mutual funds.

Identifying businesses that are desirable investments and divesting divisions or groups of divisions that offer limited potential is the focus of corporate strategic planning. Control is exercised primarily in financial terms by the allocation of capital funds to the groups and by an emphasis on an attractive return on investment to be generated by each group. Formal planning and control systems become extremely important vehicles of communication in the organization.

A typical conglomerate organization is diagrammed in figure 3–1.

Special Types of Organizations

A type of organization that possesses a structural form different from the four discussed is the matrix organization. In fact, Greiner views the matrix organization as the next step in evolution past the conglomerate organization. This assertion is rather difficult to accept. In my view, matrix organizations are special cases rather than a natural step in the evolution of all organizations.

Typical matrix organizations are project engineering and consulting organizations. In these organizations a matrix structure emerges naturally. Engineering or professional disciplines form the first dimension along which the organization is structured. The second dimension of structure results from the specific projects to which engineers or professionals are assigned. Thus a matrix of relationships emerge, where each professional belongs to a group of individuals with similar expertise and also to a group that is responsible for particular projects.

A very special case of a matrix organization is the one adopted by Texas Instruments (TI) in the 1970s. In TI, the matrix consisted of operating and strategic responsibilities. Strategic projects were designed to cut across product, divisional, and group boundaries, thus creating a matrix structure in which individual managers had dual responsibilities. In the first place they were responsible for ongoing operations in a particular division or group and in the second place they were responsible for a strategic project that could involve managers from other divisions or groups.

A more common instance of matrix responsibilities is encountered within organizations that sell multiple product lines in multiple territories. This type of matrix is quite different from the Texas Instruments and project-oriented matrices. In the latter, each manager has dual responsibilities or loyalties. In the product-region matrix, two executives share some common responsibilities.

Matrix organizations are best dealt with as special cases. Techniques and approaches particularly relevant to these organizations will be identified in our discussions, but these organizations do not readily lend themselves to the kind of generalizations that are possible in the context of functional, divisional, and conglomerate organizations.

Implications for Planning and Control

That different planning and control systems are mandated by the different characteristics of functional, divisional, and conglomerate organizations is evident from the description of each of these types of organizations. Greiner provides further guidance by identifying the developments or crises that move an organization from one type to another. Entrepreneurial organizations take on a functional form as a result of a need for direction and specialized expertise. Functional organizations take on a divisional form because growth and product or territorial diversification create a need for autonomy. Divisional organizations that evolve into conglomerates experience a need for greater coordination and control.

The strategic differences among these three types of organizations are great, thus reinforcing the need for different planning and control systems. Corporate-level strategy in a conglomerate organization addresses questions pertaining to the set of businesses to engage in, portfolio balance between the businesses and related risk, and resource allocation between businesses. In functional organizations, strategy deals mainly with the determination of the scope of the business, deciding objectives within that scope, and identifying the means of competing within the scope of the business and the interdependencies of the various functional areas. In divisional organizations, strategy addresses issues relevant to both conglomerate and functional strategies. In the divisional organization, the scope of the set of businesses to be in is more limited than in conglomerate organizations, the means of competing are broader than in the case of functional organizations, and the critical, underlying focus is synergy between the divisions.

It follows that the strategic planning activities in conglomerate organizations are quite different from those of functional organizations and divisional organizations. The nature of strategic choice, the transactions between various units and subunits, and the focus of innovation are different; consequently the SPSs designed will also be different depending on the level and type of organization.

It is important to note that conglomerate organizations have nested within them divisional forms of organization, and divisional organizations, in turn, have functional forms nested within them. Thus, by starting with the design of planning and control systems in functional organizations, it is possible to address planning and control in divisional and conglomerate organizations by focusing just on the corporate level of these two more complex forms of organization and on the links between planning and control at the corporate level and the level immediately below.

A better appreciation of the planning and control imperatives of different organizational types can be obtained by examining the strategic planning needs of these three types of organizations in the context of two different stimuli. Strategic planning in organizations can be triggered by profit objectives' not being met. This gap between desired and actual performance can arise for a variety of reasons, two of which are inadequate resources to exploit fully the profit potential (a resource gap) and inadequate profit potential in the industry (a potential gap).

Juxtaposing the type of gap and the type of organization creates a framework from which desirable characteristics of SPSs can be derived (Camillus and Sadhu 1986). A functional organization facing a resource gap will have to address issues relating to finance (generation of additional resources) and process technology (better use of existing resources). The focus of the SPS will be primarily internal, with an emphasis on efficiency. The SPS would, in essence, be oriented toward domain navigation, or helping the organization do better in its existing business.

A potential gap faced by a functional organization should trigger an external orientation in its SPS. New uses for existing products, new markets, and new product-market combinations might have to be explored. Thus the SPS would aid in domain redefinition because it enables the organization to diversify out of its existing unsatisfactory business.

At the other extreme, a conglomerate organization encountering a resource gap would be faced with efficiency, divestment, and resource allocation decisions quite different from those dealt with by functional organizations. The SPS would have to assist in decisions relating to domain emphasis, or which businesses to stress and which to harvest or divest.

A potential gap would require the SPS to aid in making the resulting acquisition and divestment decisions. These decisions can perhaps be appropriately described as relating to questions of domain change.

The divisional organization's responses to resource and potential gaps are not quite the same as those of the functional or conglomerate organizations. In the context of a resource gap, the SPS would have to find opportunities for divisions to help each other. The synergies resulting from the relatedness of the divisions can perhaps be described as domain interdependence. In the context of a potential gap, the resulting efforts to change the organization's cluster of businesses, preferably by identifying and exploiting new

Type of Organization \ Type of Gap	Resource Gap	Potential Gap
Functional Organizations	Domain navigation (e.g., Commodore Computers, with price competition based on process technologies)	Domain redefinition (e.g., Apple Computers with recent attention to business markets)
Divisional Organizations	Domain interdependence (e.g., Sears, with development of integrated financial services)	Domain modification (e.g., Kodak, with thrusts into electronic imaging and applications in diverse markets)
Conglomerate Organizations	Domain emphasis (e.g., ITT, with recent efforts to consolidate and streamline holdings)	Domain change (e.g., U.S. Steel, with moves into chemicals and oil)

Figure 3–2. Impact of Organizational Type on SPS Design

synergies, are different from the domain redefinition activities of a functional organization in that several different competences can be considered and utilized in divisional organizations. To distinguish this activity from domain redefinition in functional organizations and domain change in conglomerates, we can recognize its wider-reaching and more limited character, respectively, by defining it as domain modification.

The framework and the focus of SPS in each cell are illustrated in figure 3–2. In order to aid understanding of the distinctions being made, well-known organizations that typify the focus of each cell are identified in the figure.

References

Camillus, John C., and Sadhu, Kunal S., "Contingency Perspectives on Gap Analysis." *Proceedings of the Midwest Decision Sciences Institute* (1986).

Galbraith, Jay R., and Nathanson, Daniel A., "The Role of Organizational Structure and Process in Strategy Implementation." In Dan E. Schendel and Charles W. Hofer, eds., *Strategic Management.* Boston: Little, Brown, 1979.

Greiner, Larry E., "Evolution and Revolution as Organizations Grow." *Harvard Business Review* (July–August 1972): 37–46.

Part II
Strategic Planning in Functional Organizations

4
The Scope of the
Strategic Planning System

U nderstanding the scope of the SPS requires an appreciation of what the system can and should accomplish, as well as a broad familiarity with the various components of the system. We shall, in this chapter, identify some of the more important and commonly accepted purposes that a SPS can serve. We will then explore what constitutes a strategic planning system in terms of five components that are amenable to manipulation by the system designer.

Purposes of Strategic Planning

Although a wide variety of purposes can be served by an SPS, five are commonly recognized and have stood the test of time. First, an SPS is most widely, visibly, and explicitly employed as a means of determining the enduring, long-term objectives of organizations and as a means of devising strategies for accomplishing these objectives. In order to arrive at a meaningful statement of objectives and strategies, the SPS has to help develop a concept of business or mission for the organization. These constitute some of the most important documentary outputs of the SPS.

Second, the SPS defines the framework within which management control takes place. The action planning and budgeting activities that are the heart of the MCS are nested within and guided by the concept of business, objectives, and strategies developed by the SPS. The framework required for the MCS to function well would also include an understanding of what constitutes acceptable performance, together with broad guidelines for the inevitable trade-offs between long-term and short-term financial performance.

Third, the SPS serves as a vehicle for communication between levels of management in the organizational hierarchy and between subunits in the organization.

Fourth, the SPS is an important means of developing needed managerial skills and perspectives in organizations. Time, Inc., and Sandoz use the strategic planning process to expose managers to new techniques, sensitize them to emerging issues, and instill in them an awareness of organizational needs and environmental imperatives that might not otherwise be apparent to them in their day-to-day functioning.

Fifth, the SPS can be designed to increase the level of creativity employed in managing the organization. Effective strategic planning demands the exercise of creativity by those engaged in the process of planning. Generating original, but feasible alternatives is one of the hallmarks of effective strategic planning, and obviously this demands creativity. Not so evident but nevertheless of great importance is the possibility of designing the SPS to encourage and facilitate the exercise of creativity and to increase generally the level of creativity employed in managing an organization. In one sense, the SPS can be viewed as a training device to help managers recognize and exploit their creative potential.

These five purposes of planning are not exhaustive, but for most organizations, they should constitute an adequate list of ends that strategic planning can serve. These purposes are not mutually exclusive. Any purpose or combination of purposes can be selected as appropriate to a particular organization at a particular time. The relative emphasis given to the various purposes, however, can and should affect the design of the SPS.

Other less laudable but at times more pressing reasons sometimes exist for instituting an SPS. Some organizations view SPSs as a means of demonstrating the avant-garde and sophisticated nature of management. Such systems rarely bear fruit of any value, though they often produce tomes used to impress visitors but that have little or no impact on managerial actions and decisions that affect organizational performance.

Another reason why organizations may attempt to produce a strategic plan is that external agencies sometimes require or mandate it. Financing agencies often require formal assessments, including pro forma financial statements, of the organization's future. Divisions or subsidiaries of business organizations sometimes engage in planning because the corporate headquarters or parent company demands it. Reasons such as these for engaging in strategic planning usually result in a sterile, routine exercise of filling in the mandated forms and preparing the required statements.

When organizations are required by external fiat to engage in strategic planning, it is easy to fall into the trap of viewing this demand as an unavoidable imposition to be disposed of with the least effort. But it is possible and desirable to view this requirement as a significant opportunity to influence the body that requires the formal planning. For example, in 1974 the National Health Planning and Resources Development Act was passed. This act created the National Council on Health Planning and Development, which worked with the secretary of what was then the Health, Education, and Welfare (now Health and Human Services) Department to develop national guidelines for health planning. The act also created health systems agencies that, among other responsibilities, were to develop plans and priorities for health services and facilities needed in their areas to approve or disapprove each use of Federal health funds in their areas (*Health Policy Making in Action* 1975). Furthermore, the act created state health planning and development agencies that, in addition to other activities, were to certify the need for new health facilities and to evaluate all institutional health services at least every five years.

The implications of this act are clear. Organizations may not necessarily perceive the act as a mandate to engage in strategic planning; nevertheless organizations that fail to institute a system of strategic planning would be doing little or nothing to ensure their continued viability in the context of the reviews every five years. New health institutions without a strategic understanding of their role in the territory served would find it difficult to obtain the necessary certification of need.

Apart from the primary incentive of survival, strategic planning can be viewed positively as a means of influencing the strategic thinking of the regulatory and planning agencies. A health organization with a carefully developed, strategic understanding of its mission in society and a well-thought-out approach to fulfilling this mission could substantially influence the thinking of the executives in these agencies. Humana, Inc.'s highly publicized venture into artificial hearts could not have been approved by the various agencies involved if the organization had been unable to articulate a strategic vision of its role, competence, and long-term contribution in the area of terminal heart disease.

The influence exerted by well-prepared strategic plans can, as the Humana example suggests, have an immensely favorable impact on the climate in which the organization is reviewed, its needed resources generated, and its future regulated. Thus strategic planning can assist not only in ensuring an organization's survival but can also help secure a successful existence, with its role widely accepted as being of considerable importance to its milieu.

SPS Components

The SPS has five major components:

1. *Process* or sequence of activities involved.
2. *Linkages* between the SPS and other systems of planning and control.
3. *Administration* or management of the SPS and, in particular, the process.
4. *Timing* considerations or decisions pertaining to temporal characteristics of the SPS.
5. *Output* or documentary results of the process.

These five components lend themselves to the acronym *PLATO,* which serves as a rather appropriate mnemonic. When designing the SPS, I have found it useful to work in reverse order, starting with the output and proceeding through timing, administrative, and linkage decisions to the design of the process itself.

Factors Influencing SPS Design

An extraordinarily large number of factors can influence the design of the SPS. Common sense suggests, however, that the most parsimonious list of key factors is probably the most helpful in terms of guiding systems design. The combined, and possibly conflicting, impact of a large number of factors might confuse rather than guide the SPS designer. I shall therefore limit the discussion to those factors that experience, observation, and research suggest are the most powerful and understandable influences on SPS design.

The first, and most obvious, set of factors is the formal purposes that the SPS is expected to serve. Earlier discussion suggests that there could be creativity-oriented requirements and coordination- or control-oriented requirements that tend to be conflicting in nature. The creativity-control balance, as it has been called, has been studied for over fifteen years, and some clear guidelines as to how to orient the SPS toward one end of the spectrum or the other have been developed. Four of the five purposes of the SPS are considered in determining the desired orientation toward either end of the creativity-control spectrum. In addition, SPS design can respond to the desired emphasis on management development as one of its purposes. The design features and characteristics that promote management development are substantially independent of those pertinent to the creativity-control balance. Finally, the SPS's role as a communication device, particularly across hierarchical levels, can influence the design of the system. Thus, when considering the impact of the purposes of the SPS on its design, it is useful to recognize the preferred position in the creativity-control dimension, the desired emphasis on management development and the communication that needs to be fostered.

The second set of factors influencing SPS design is the aspirations and values of the organization's management. While the SPS helps identify and articulate the objectives of the organization, the a priori biases of top management toward growth and diversity versus stability and focus will inevitably affect the design and outcome of the SPS.

The third set of factors that drives the design of the SPS is the characteristics of the organization. Here again the list of possible factors can be very long, but many of these factors are dominated by a few. For instance, the size of the organization in terms of revenues or assets is often cited as a factor.

However, the SPS for a small, complex organization with multiple product lines and customer types would be more different from the SPS of a small, simple organization with a simple product line than would be the SPS of a large, simple organization.

Two other characteristics that strongly influence SPS design are the climate in the organization and the competence of its managers. With regard to climate, the attitude toward innovation and risk taking promoted by top management is crucial. The perceived competence of the managers will greatly influence the extent and nature of their participation in the planning process, thus affecting the SPS design.

The fourth, and final, set of factors relates to the nature of the environment in which the organization is perceived to function. Here again there is a plethora of value-laden objectives that are commonly employed to describe the environment. Recent research (Veliyath 1985) has shown that in practice, only two characteristics of the environment display a significant relationship with planning and control activities in business organizations: the dynamism and the complexity of the environment in which the business operates.

Other characteristics such as hostility, which are popularly viewed as important, show no significant association with planning and control systems. This is understandable because *hostility* is a value-laden, highly subjective word. While most organizations view governmental regulation as a hostile aspect of the environment, other very successful organizations such as Federal Express and FMC view regulation as a means of creating a defensible, manageable niche. Perceptions in this regard are vital. Witness the bounty hunter, who on waking up to find himself surrounded by twenty desperate, wanted criminals, all armed to the teeth with pistols cocked and trigger fingers twitching, exclaims, "Wow! I'm rich."

Dynamism and complexity, however, do display a strong relationship with the nature of planning and control activities. Dynamism demands a future orientation as opposed to plans based on experience. Research has shown that a future or feed-forward orientation strongly correlates with superior performance, particularly in the context of dynamic environments.

The complexity of the environment in which an organization operates is very much a matter of choice. By choosing to be a multiproduct, multiterritory company, management inevitably has to cope with a complex environment. A limited, homogeneous product line, sold in a limited area to a particular customer segment results in a much less complex environment.

In summary, four factors are important to the design of the SPS:

1. The purposes that the system is expected to serve.
2. The preferred strategic posture of top management.
3. The organizational characteristics.
4. The environmental context.

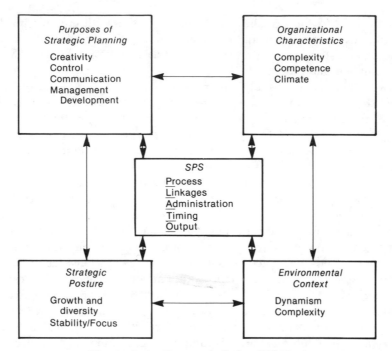

Figure 4–1. Framework for SPS Design

The framework for design suggested by the preceding discussion is illustrated in figure 4–1.

Although the discussion, for the sake of simplicity, addresses the impact of the four sets of factors on SPS design, reality is more complex and dynamic. For instance, although an organization's competence and climate might suggest the initial SPS design, the implementation of the SPS will surely affect the organization's characteristics. These changes in characteristics might not only warrant modification of the SPS design but might also change the organization's preferred strategic posture, which in turn could affect the environmental context and the purposes of the SPS, and so on. In short, the framework is dynamic in nature rather than static. SPS designers must not only define the form of the system that is immediately appropriate but also project changes that should take place as the framework evolves.

References

Health Policy Making in Action. Publication 41-1600. New York: National League for Nursing, 1975.

Veliyath, Rajaram. "Feedback and Feedforward in Strategic Management: A Contingent Framework." Ph.D. dissertation, University of Pittsburgh, 1985.

5
The Output of the Strategic Planning System

T he strategic plan that emerges as the output of the SPS should embrace a range of managerial concerns. A recent study (Calingo 1984) strongly suggests that the SPSs that comprehensively encompass the set of concerns listed below are likely to be perceived as more effective than systems that cover a more limited set of factors. The key statements in the strategic plan of a simple, functional organization should articulate:

1. The organization's mission.
2. Its long-term objectives.
3. Its competitive strategy.
4. Organizational policies.
5. Needed resources.
6. Key assumptions.

The Organization's Mission

In the early 1980s, Federal Express Corporation (FEC) made a significant and intriguing decision. Some of its managers identified the possibility of using FEC planes during the morning and afternoon hours to service passenger traffic. The corporation's jets were idle during these hours, the pilots could legally and safely fly a few extra hours, and the planes' interiors had been designed to facilitate quick changes between cargo- and passenger-carrying configurations. With little incremental expenditure, the revenue-generating potential appeared enormous. FEC's top management, renowned for its aggressiveness, surprisingly chose not to take advantage of this opportunity. Their decision was based on the fact that passenger services were not consistent with FEC's mission, which was limited to the reliable, swift transportation of small packages. Top management believed adherence to this mission was more important to FEC's success than the possibility of higher profits in the short run, obtained by diluting the organization's concept of business.

✗ The organization's mission, often viewed as a tenuous, amorphous abstraction, can be the most powerful of factors in organizational decision making. The uncertainty posed by the infinite complexity of the universe of possible opportunities available to a business can be dealt with only by defining a subset of this universe, a niche in which the organization will function. This niche, defined by the organization's mission or concept of business, must be specified in terms that reflect management's values and preferences. ✗ It is most important that management choose between a mission that is market driven or technology driven, and between a broad statement or a very narrow statement.

Head Ski, when founded by Howard Head, adopted a limiting, technology-driven concept of business. Its mission was to manufacture and sell the best-designed metal skis available. This narrow definition later broadened to include other ski equipment, thus stimulating diversification into new products. Following its acquisition by AMF, Head Ski shifted to a market-driven concept of business—sports equipment—which led to the introduction of products such as tennis rackets that had nothing to do with skiing. AMF's mission was clearly market driven and even broader and more stimulating: to service the leisure industry. These four concepts of business can be usefully placed in a matrix, as shown in figure 5–1.

The strategic orientations implicit in mission statements falling in each of these four cells are quite different. Technology-driven organizations tend to be more internally focused in contrast to the external focus of market-driven organizations. In both cases, limiting statements of mission make for stability, while stimulating statements encourage growth and diversification.

Although the matrix in figure 5–1 is useful and powerful, it does not fully capture the complexities and significance of the mission statement. At one

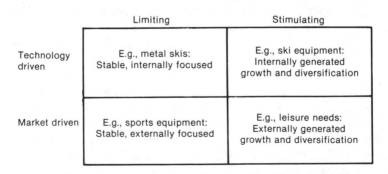

	Limiting	Stimulating
Technology driven	E.g., metal skis: Stable, internally focused	E.g., ski equipment: Internally generated growth and diversification
Market driven	E.g., sports equipment: Stable, externally focused	E.g., leisure needs: Externally generated growth and diversification

Figure 5–1. Characteristics of the Mission Statement

and the same time, a statement of mission can be vague and directive, limiting and stimulating, a reality of the present and a vision of the future. This complexity is perhaps best explained by means of examples.

An organization that is engaged in the production of polypropylene film can state its mission or concept of business as the production of petrochemicals or as the manufacture of packaging materials. Either of these statements is a possible concept of business. The first statement is vague in that petrochemicals is a broad and continually widening area, yet it is directive in that it demands a technological, chemical- and petroleum-engineering orientation and competence. It is limiting in that the hotel industry and education are not possible areas of diversification, but at the same time, it stimulates thinking about different end products that are possibly derived from the same basic raw materials. It is a reality of the present in that the organization is already in the petrochemical industry and is also a vision of the future of diversification and expansion in a technologically creative field. If the same organization had defined itself as being in packaging, it would develop different capabilities and different customers and have a different set of aspirations.

A health organization engaged in providing eye-care services can describe itself as fulfilling the mission of examining eyes and writing prescriptions for corrective lenses or the mission of protecting and improving human vision. The first statement is essentially a description of activities in which the organization is engaged. It does not permit or provoke the addition of other services or activities. The second statement, in contrast, identifies consequences rather than activities and thus leads to the identification of such possibilities as opening clinics where eye surgery is carried out, engaging in the development and possibly the manufacture of devices for rectifying faulty vision, and running programs for educating the public about the proper care of eyes.

A final illustration of the critical importance of the statement of mission is the March of Dimes organization, which originally expressly devoted itself to the eradication of polio. When the development of the Salk vaccine led to this mission's becoming irrelevant, the organization had to identify and adopt a new mission, eliminating birth defects, in order to provide a basis for its continued existence.

A statement of mission should clearly define and limit the areas that the organization wishes to consider, thus reducing the complexity of its environment to manageable dimensions. At the same time, the statement should be broad enough to allow for activities other than the present ones if diversification is desired. If growth is important to management, the statement should be flexible enough to allow for creative alternatives and yet precise enough to guide and stimulate the generation of such alternatives. It should reflect what the organization is but gains in significance by serving as a vision of the long-term form and focus of the organization.

The simultaneously abstract and powerful nature of the mission statement makes it a most important facet of the output of the SPS. It offers a challenge that must be faced and an opportunity that can be exploited.

Long-Term Objectives

Objectives are long-term, enduring ends that drive the organization's efforts. These objectives are a determination, possibly in quantitative terms, of the desired consequences of the organization's endeavors to fulfill its mission. Quantitative goals could include statements about the desired rate of growth in sales, the market share to be maintained, the desired level of return on investment, and the desired rate of growth in profit. Nonquantitative expressions of objectives could include maintenance or achievement of leadership in technology, product quality, or customer satisfaction. For instance, a nonquantitative expression of the objectives of a health organization might be "to increase the percentage of senior citizens receiving needed professional nursing care at home."

The distinction between objectives and goals must be borne in mind. Goals are normally time bound, quantitative in nature, and particularly relevant to the exercise of management control. Objectives, on the other hand, might be timeless in character in that they are relevant over the foreseeable future. The relationships between objectives and goals are important in terms of the linkage between strategic planning and management control. Goals represent the translation of objectives into targets that have to be met within a specified time period. For instance, in the case of the health organization in the example, this objective could be translated at the management control level into a quantified, time-bound goal statement, such as, "To increase by 15 percent within five years the number of citizens in this region over the age of sixty-five receiving needed professional nursing care at home."

The distinction between goals and objectives is important because of the limited time horizon normally encompassed by goal statements. If the strategic plan too has a similar horizon, then goal statements might also serve as appropriately quantified objective statements. Often, however, strategic planning horizons extend over a greater number of years than the horizon mandated by management control requirements. Consequently time-bound quantified objectives might not serve the purpose of guiding strategic decision making if they are not carefully constructed so as to have continuing relevance over the period embraced by the horizon of the strategic plan.

In business organizations, continuing relevance without temporal limitations is often built in to statements of objectives by the device of stating quantitative objectives in terms of growth rates. Thus a business organization might state its strategic objectives by affirming its intention to ensure and provide for an annual growth of x, y, and z percent, respectively, in profits, sales, and investments.

Competitive Strategy

The path that the organization intends to follow in achieving its objectives is in essence its competitive strategy. For business organizations, competitive strategy usually means an understanding of the kind and quality of products or services they intend to provide and to whom. Manufacturing and selling inexpensive, generic antibiotics to middle-income families located in rural areas could be a statement of a viable competitive strategy in the context of a pharmaceutical business in a developing country. Such a competitive strategy would be expected to fulfill, for instance, the financial objectives of the pharmaceutical business. In addition to specifying the product-market combination, the preferred approach to financing the operations of the business is often significant enough to warrant explicit specification in the statement of competitive strategy. Other considerations that are also seen as vital in the context of a particular business would appropriately be included in this statement of competitive strategy. For instance, if the quality of the product, advertising, technological superiority, and the range and level of customer services to be provided are vital to the survival and success of the business, the statement of competitive strategy should include these important dimensions.

In short, a well-formulated statement of competitive strategy relates and integrates the organization with its environment. It is a positive, proactive, directive statement that guides the operationalization of the organization's mission and delineates the approach to accomplishing its objectives. It determines the service-client or product-market posture of the organization. It provides guidance as to the desirability and necessity of the various programs or businesses that might constitute the organization's portfolio.

An alternative approach to delineating the organization's competitive strategy merits consideration. Within each functional area or major responsibility center of each business, critical choices have to be made that guide managerial decisions and actions. For instance, key choices have to be made in most organizations in the areas of human resources, marketing, manufacturing, finance, and engineering. If the organization is service and not manufacturing oriented, other functional areas, such as government relations or logistics, become significant in place of manufacturing and engineering. In each of these functional areas, certain fundamental choices has to be made. Table 5–1 identifies some of the options that managers engaged in strategy formulation need to consider.

Consistent choices made in the context of each of the key functional areas

Table 5–1
Illustrative Key Functional Choices

Finance

Sources of funds
Short-term versus long-term debt
Debt versus equity
Stock issues versus retained earnings
Off balance sheet versus asset restructuring

Dividend payout
High versus low
Flexible versus fixed

Growth orientation
Internally generated projects versus acquisitions
Low risk versus high risk

Manufacturing

Flexibility
Special-purpose versus general-purpose equipment
Automated versus manual
Single versus multiple locations
In-house versus subcontracted

Market orientation
Standard versus customized design
Fixed versus flexible design
Integral versus modular design
Process versus product R&D
Loose versus tight quality control
Low versus high inventory
Located near raw materials versus located near markets
Efficiency oriented versus delivery oriented

Technology orientation
Leader versus follower
Basic R&D versus applied R&D
High risk versus low risk

Human resources

Management style
Participative versus authoritarian
Cooperative versus confrontational labor relations
Turnover discouraged versus turnover encouraged
High versus low salary levels
Low versus high proportion of incentives

Structure orientation
Line oriented versus staff oriented
Hierarchical versus egalitarian
Formal versus informal communication

Developmental orientation
Formal education versus on the job
In-house versus outside training
Formal manpower planning versus ad hoc responses
Promotions to insiders versus induction of outsiders

Table 5–1 *(continued)*

Marketing

Focus
Broad versus limited product lines
Broad versus limited geographic scope
Multiple versus limited market segments
Multiple distribution channels versus single channel
Intensive versus selective distribution

Aggressiveness
Price competitive versus overpricing
Flexible credit or lease terms versus no credit or financing
Competitive versus complementary distribution channels
Direct selling versus selling to wholesalers or jobbers
Market share enhancement versus primary demand generation

Image
High versus low profile
Brand emphasis versus commodity
High versus low promotion or advertising
Multiple media versus single medium
Pull oriented versus push oriented

are, in effect, an indirect determination of the organization's competitive strategy. Although this set of choices is not as explicit an articulation of the competitive strategy as is a statement of the product-market posture of the organization, it possesses the merit of being highly action oriented and providing meaningful guidelines to functional managers. Consistent choices made in the areas of human resources, marketing, finance, and manufacturing lead to effective, competitive postures.

Either approach to articulating and communicating competitive strategy is appropriate. In this book, we will not address in detail the content of competitive strategy in various contexts; excellent guidance is available from other sources such as Porter (1980). Given the systems orientation of this book, it would be inappropriate to attempt an exhaustive analysis of the appropriate content of competitive strategies. Nevertheless, some outstanding examples of successful competitive strategies might provide useful insights. The successes of Air Products and Chemicals, Inc., and Marks and Spencer can be substantially attributed to their competitive strategies.

The competitive strategy adopted by Air Products & Chemicals, Inc. (APCI) in its early years, besides proving to be immensely successful and a marvelous work of art, provides fundamental guidelines regarding effective strategies. First, APCI's competitive strategy represented not only consistent but synergistic choices across functional areas such as finance, manufacturing, and marketing. Second, its strategy responded to emerging market needs by utilizing distinctive organizational resources. Third, its strategy was innovative and represented a major departure from accepted industry practices based on superior insights regarding economics of operation, customer requirements, and technological possibilities.

The production of industrial gases, oxygen in particular, had been dominated by the Linde division of Union Carbide until the emergence of APCI in the 1960s. Linde produced oxygen in plants that served many customers and shipped the gas in cylinders and special vehicles to its customers. In keeping with the Union Carbide philosophy, equity rather than debt was the preferred source of financing.

Recognizing the emerging need for high volumes of gas for new technologies such as the basic oxygen furnaces for steel making and responding to the reality that required raw materials (air) that were literally freely available everywhere, APCI obtained long-term contracts from major customers to supply large volumes of gas from local plants using new processes that its engineers had developed. With these contracts in hand, APCI obtained cheap debt financing, thus permitting even lower prices to its customers as an incentive to them to purchase the commodity that it already produced cheaper than Linde because of much lower, in fact, negligible, transportation costs. This insightful, internally consistent meshing of environmental developments and APCI's competences resulted in the powerful competitive strategy that is diagrammed in figure 5–2.

Another example of the consistency and insight that make for effective competitive strategies is provided by the giant British department store chain, Marks and Spencer. In the first half of this century, this successful firm grew into a national institution based on two fundamental values adopted by its

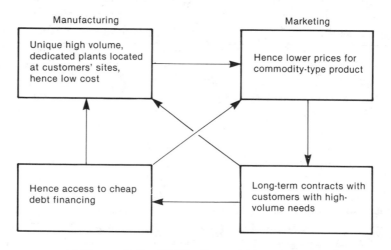

Figure 5–2. APCI's Competitive Strategy

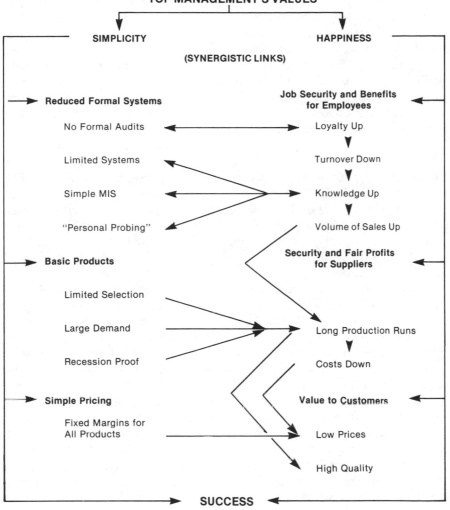

Figure 5–3. Marks and Spencer's Competitive Strategy

tightly knit top management: promoting the well-being or happiness of the firm's stakeholders was of paramount importance, and simplicity in everything it did was an essential virtue. These two values were the foundation of a mutually supportive set of decisions and practices that formed the essence of the firm's competitive strategy, diagrammed in figure 5–3.

The emphasis on simplicity led to a limited use of management information systems (MIS) and control systems and a great reliance on personal probing, as they called it, by top management. This approach to systems required and was supported by the competent, knowledgeable, and dedicated work force that developed because of management's concern for their well-being, which was reflected in innovative and generous benefit and welfare programs. These knowledgeable salespeople could brief top management about needed products and customer preferences. They were also very effective with customers, thus increasing sales volume.

The emphasis on simplicity led to a focus on a limited selection of basic, recession-proof clothing and food products of the highest quality constantly monitored by a top management that personally used these products. The choice of basic, limited product lines led to a highly appreciative cadre of carefully selected suppliers who were pleased by the opportunity to produce stable, large quantities of simple products for the fair price that Marks and Spencer was particular about offering. Because of the high volume, production costs were reduced. The limited product line also permitted careful attention to quality.

The lower costs, higher quality, and the firm's concept of fair profits led to fixed margins on all product lines and low prices, a combination that promoted the customers' well-being by providing the certainty of excellent value.

The simplicity of fixed margins led to simple pricing decisions and simple product mix decisions. All that was needed to increase profits was to sell a greater volume of all products or any product, which the competent and dedicated sales force was able to do well.

The Marks and Spencer saga reinforces the importance of consistency in the creation of an effective competitive strategy. Consistency of choices within functional areas and across functional areas is crucial. Consistency of practices and programs with management's values and stakeholders' priorities is needed. Consistency of the organization's competences and the environmental imperatives addressed is essential. Finally, for a strategy to work, it should possess consistency over time. The highly publicized, painful experiences of J.I. Case before its takeover, when four different CEOs adopted four different, individually justifiable strategies in the period of a few years, strongly suggests that no strategy may be better than strategies that are changed before their benefits can be realized.

Organizational Policies

Organizational policies are statements that define desirable and unacceptable management practices. In large organizations, they are particularly important as a means of ensuring strategic coherence and mobility of resources. For instance, without common accounting, personnel, and credit practices, an organization will not be able to make synergistic use of the resources of its various subunits.

Policies are also a means of operationalizing the values of management and ensuring that the essential requirements of the organization's stakeholders are met. For example, policies might define the organization's attitude toward the quality of its products or services; its approach to dealing with customers and clients, suppliers, and creditors; its orientation to the needs of the community in which it is located; and so on.

Although policies flow from statements of mission and strategy, they are quite different in character. Strategy statements are intended to stimulate and encourage the generation of creative alternatives. Policies, on the other hand, although they may be expressed in affirmative terms, are essentially negative or limiting in nature. They prohibit certain kinds of behavior or practice by explicit negation or by strong affirmation of the preferred alternatives. In essence, they limit managerial discretion at lower levels in the hierarchy and define the feasible space in terms of managerial practices and decisions at these levels.

Needed Resources

A tentative assessment of the magnitude and kind of resources—human, financial, and physical—available to managers responsible for implementing the organization's strategy and achieving its objectives is essential. This statement is necessary to provide broad guidance as to the level of activity and kinds of programs that are feasible in terms of the resources likely to be available. If major subunits of the organization develop and define their own programs or businesses within a charter approved by top management, then the statement of resource availability should provide a breakdown by subunit of the likely level of resources that will be allocated. In functional organizations, subunits tend to be functionally oriented departments that have responsibility for marketing, finance, and human resources. In more complex organizations, such subunits could be independent businesses of major proportions.

The allocation of resources to these subunits should reflect the strategic importance that management ascribes to each of these units in fulfilling the total organization's mission. Clearly the nature and magnitude of resource needs expressed by each of these subunits will also be a major consideration in terms of making these resource allocation decisions. The requirements expressed by the subunits would be viewed in the context of the perceived potential and relevance of the individual subunits to the organization's mission, objectives, and competitive strategies. The ongoing resource allocation process in organizations forms a key link between the SPS and the MCS.

Key Assumptions

A statement of key assumptions is necessary for at least two major reasons. First, management control activities performed at levels below top management require this statement in order to ensure consistency with the strategic plan. If different assumptions about the likely environment of the organization or likely developments within the organization are made at different levels in the organization, not only will any apparent consistency between strategic planning and management control be pure happenstance, but severe problems will be encountered later when implementing and reviewing strategic plans. The operational plan that drives operating managers' actions and decisions can be consistent with the vision that the strategic plan represents only if both are built on the foundation of similar assumptions. If the assumptions are different and if actual performance deviates from plans, top management and lower levels of management will inevitably find themselves at odds about responsibility for deviations, the causes of deviations, and the most appropriate remedial action. It is imperative, therefore, that the key assumptions made by top management in defining the organization's mission, objectives, and competitive strategy be formally stated and communicated to lower levels in the organization.

Second, the statement of assumptions is necessary in order to assess the continuing relevance of strategic plans. If environmental developments or happenings within the organization do not take place as anticipated, it would be necessary to modify the strategic plan. The key assumptions would constitute the fundamental basis for developing contingency plans to respond to events or happenings that may not be consistent with the basis on which the strategic plan was developed.

Thus, in order to serve as a link between strategic planning and management control and also to provide a basis for contingency planning, the statement of key assumptions is of great importance.

Conclusion

An important distinction between the first three outputs of strategic planning—mission, objectives, and competitive strategies—and the last three outputs—policies, resources, and assumptions—bears mention. The first three have a strongly creative orientation. Effective statements of mission, objectives, and competitive strategy demand creativity in their formulation. Statements of mission, objectives, and competitive strategy can stimulate creativity by triggering thought about innovative alternatives. Thus these three outputs demand creativity as an input and result in a climate conducive to creativity if they are well formulated.

In contrast, the last three outputs have an orientation more closely allied to control. Policies, for instance, are intended to place boundaries around the possible courses of action of lower-level managers. Resource availability places limits on what programs are feasible. Formal statements of assumptions are intended to ensure consistency in thought at lower levels in the organization. Such statements are also intended to facilitate the analysis and review of actual performance so as to control effectively the implementation of strategic plans.

These markedly different orientations are important in designing the process of strategic planning. The relative emphasis that an organization may wish to place on increasing creativity and facilitating control would lead to the design of processes that result in added emphasis on the first three outputs or the last three outputs of the strategic planning system.

References

Calingo, Luis Ma.R. "Tailoring Strategic Planning Systems Design to Corporate Strategy." Ph.D. dissertation, University of Pittsburgh, 1984.

Porter, Michael, *Competitive Strategy*. New York: Free Press, 1980.

6
The Process of Strategic Planning

The process of strategic planning, or the specification of who should do what and when to develop the strategic plan, is perhaps the most important component of the design of the SPS. Decisions regarding the process will substantially affect the quality of output, contribute to the linkages with other management systems, determine the nature of administration of the SPS that is required, and clarify the timing aspects of the SPS design.

The design of the process poses a particularly significant challenge in that it is an important means by which rational, economic analyses can be integrated effectively with behavioral, political realities. The design of the process can be viewed from three critical perspectives:

1. The rational perspective of what should be analyzed.
2. The behavioral perspective of who should conduct the analyses and make decisions.
3. The timing perspective of when and how often to conduct analysis so as to integrate most effectively the rational and behavioral perspectives.

Analytic Bases of Strategic Planning

The process of strategic planning requires careful analysis of the organization's internal and external aspects.

The activities of scanning and analyzing the environment are carried out formally or informally in every organization. Our interest here is to suggest how to formalize these activities as part of the process of developing a strategic plan and of continually monitoring the effectiveness of the plan from the point of view of identifying needed modifications.

External Environment

In defining the external environment, two dimensions are of importance: the question of what factors are of importance and the level at which the factors are monitored. In analyzing the external environment, I have found it useful to partition the total environment into two components: the general environment and competition.

General Environment. In identifying the relevant factors in the general environment, it is useful to run through a checklist of the broad categories that pertain to every organization. First, there are social factors. The values and preferences of people in general or the immediate community are not static and clearly affect the organization. For instance, the importance placed on filial. virtues would affect organizations working with the elderly. Attitudes regarding financial security, family life, the work ethic, community service, and so on are vitally important in terms of the services demanded, the quality and character of the work force, and the availability of financial resources.

For measuring and analyzing such social factors, quantitative or objective parameters are hard to come by, so surrogates may have to be employed. For instance, community involvement and attitudes may be indicated by such surrogate measures as the magnitude of contributions to welfare activities and organizations, the prevalence of religious or other social organizations, the pattern of blood donations, and the number of child care centers.

A qualitative understanding of attitudinal changes might be developed by monitoring opinions expressed by groups and by the media. Attitudes and opinions could be measured more precisely and objectively by a formal poll or survey, but such efforts demand an investment of time and money and require technical expertise.

Demographic developments are the second set of factors to be considered. Demographic indicators, which are of value in themselves, are also useful as measures of changes in attitudes or values. Examples of such indicators are the following:

Population.

Population growth rate.

Population density.

Population age profile.

Population per hospital bed or ambulance.

Population per telephone, car, or television set.

Life expectancy.

Infant mortality.

Number of deaths from road accidents, murders, or suicide.

Proportion of marriages at various ages.

Number of divorces.

Number of reported instances of child abuse.

Number of students in higher education or high schools.

Daily newspaper circulation.

Proportions of agricultural and industrial employment.

Unemployment by age, race, or profession.

Proportion of welfare recipients.

Third are regulatory factors. These are easier to identify than social factors but often harder to interpret than demographic indicators. The body of governmental and professional regulations that affect the operations of an organization certainly needs to be tracked. Of great importance are the nature and likelihood of new, emerging, and changing regulations of strategic significance. In most cases, the regulatory environment can be adequately tracked by obtaining the appropriate publications of the relevant governmental or professional bodies. The importance of tracking these regulatory factors cannot be overemphasized. The deregulation of industries such as airlines, telecommunications, and banking has resulted in revolutionary changes. Even apparently minor developments such as the banning of cyclamates could prove to be traumatic to particular industries. Federal regulations have changed the nature of the workplace and the basic economics of many industries and given birth to entirely new industries.

Fourth are technological factors, which are important to all organizations that utilize physical equipment or technical expertise to any significant degree. Monitoring the technological state of the art in a specified field is not overly difficult. Professional and academic journals, meetings, and seminars should provide the needed information. What is difficult to identify and monitor are developments in apparently unrelated fields that are likely to affect an organization's operations. Instances of technological spinoffs that affect quite unexpected areas are numerous. They range from the mundane (cookware based on heat shields for spacecraft) to the exotic (surgical instruments based on laser technology). Such instances are not restricted to hardware. Developments in mathematical statistics, for example, could affect experimental psychology and subsequently the services rendered by organizations that offer hospice services.

It is impossible and certainly wasteful of effort for an individual organization to attempt to organize a formal monitoring system to track all developments that might ultimately prove relevant. Thus a few groups of organizations and trade associations have set up systems whereby members are assigned selected areas and particular journals and report items of possible interest to a coordinating committee, which analyzes and disseminates information to member organizations. In addition, in recent years computer-accessible data bases that attempt to track technological developments have proliferated. In their simplest form they often consist of annotated bibliographies accessed by a system of key words. Such developments make the task of identifying relevant new technologies much easier.

Political factors are the fifth set of elements that need to be analyzed. Political developments are either directly or indirectly significant to most organizations. Changes in the political persuasion of those in power would have a direct effect on the nature and magnitude of governmental support and regulation. Indirectly political instability or changes could be instigators or consequences of social and attitudinal changes of strategic relevance. The election of Ronald Reagan to two terms as president of the United States is a dramatic example of the importance of such factors.

For organizations that confine their activities to a limited geographic region, local politics can be of great importance. Political changes and their implications therefore need to be monitored by maintaining an awareness of the pronouncements of major political parties, the efforts and concerns of organized interest groups, and significant changes in social indicators.

Sixth, economic indicators are always of interest to any organization concerned about its long-term viability. Most of the economic indicators of importance to a particular organization would depend on the territory served, the kind of customer or client, and the product or service being provided. In addition to such specific indicators, broad macroeconomic measures such as the growth in gross national product, price indexes, per capita income, and disposable personal income will have an influence on an organization's strategic stance, affecting the magnitude, quality, or nature of products and services it chooses to offer.

Thus six major sets of factors in the general environment merit monitoring and analysis; we shall now consider the question of the levels at which these factors are to be analyzed. It has been suggested, for instance, that the environment of any organization should be classified into three levels: the internal environment, the operating environment, and the general environment (Thomas 1974). The internal environment is that which is within the organization's official jurisdiction; the operating environment is composed of the suppliers and other interest groups with which the firm deals; and the general environment is the national and global context. Although this classification certainly has merit, an alternative, which is not very different, might facilitate the identification of relevant factors. Four levels are proposed: industry, regional, national, and global.

Combining the two dimensions of factors and levels gives rise to the matrix illustrated in figure 6–1. The value of using such a matrix to aid in identifying environmental aspects that merit monitoring and analysis is considerable. To illustrate by analogy, employing such a matrix is similar to a pilot's checklist before take-off. The value of such a matrix would be self-evident if one attempts a simple test. First, list as comprehensively as possible

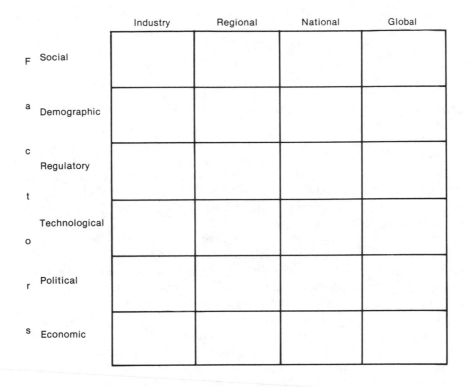

Figure 6-1. Matrix for Environmental Analysis

all the factors that one might consider relevant to one's organization. Then repeat the exercise trying to be comprehensive about factors that pertain to each of the twenty-four cells in figure 6-1. The utility and power of the matrix will be apparent when comparing the list of factors identified without the aid of the matrix and when using the matrix. For instance, following the matrix step by step might lead an organization to identify the following social factors:

1. Employees are professionals who owe allegiance to professional norms and value external professional recognition. (Industry level).

2. The state places priority on and is setting aside funds for community development projects. (Industry level).

3. Nationally a tendency is seen toward stable and growing innercity populations; the government is committed to reinforcing this tendency (National level).

4. Countries with relatively higher levels of industrial development have experienced a significant increase in urban population, followed by an exodus of the economically privileged, which ultimately stabilizes or even reverses. (Global level)

The implications of these social factors or trends for the strategic posture of the organization may be evident. If certain of the factors are critical enough to warrant monitoring, appropriate measures can be identified. For instance, external recognition of professional employees might be monitored by keeping track of positions held in professional bodies, publications in professional journals, citations of such publications, and research grants received. Regional characteristics could be periodically reviewed by monitoring population and income statistics, real estate values, crime statistics, and community development programs.

The utility of the matrix should be evident; however, it has limitations. It is unlikely that it would lead to an exhaustive identification of all possible relevant factors. Sometimes even critical but readily obvious factors are overlooked. This limitation should not lead to discarding the matrix because it certainly does increase the likelihood of identifying critical factors.

Using such a matrix could have helped the manufacturer of diesel pumps for irrigation sets in a developing country. This manufacturer unfortunately did not track governmental plans for rural electrification. With electricity available, farmers would be strongly inclined to use electric motors for irrigation in order to do away with the trouble of obtaining supplies of diesel fuel from relatively far-away depots. In one of its five-year plans, the government of this country decided to give high priority to electrification of rural areas. This resulted in an unanticipated and dramatic drop in sales for the manufacturer and almost resulted in the organization's going under. The use of the kind of matrix illustrated in figure 6–1 could have increased this organization's chances of identifying potential killing variables.

A possible problem in constructing a matrix is to select an excessive number of factors. There are limitations to how much the mind can meaningfully comprehend. Consequently, although the initial effort should be to develop an exhaustive list of factors to analyze and parameters to monitor, subsequently considerable discretion must be exercised in selecting a limited number of the most pertinent and important factors and parameters for detailed analyses and for monitoring on a continuing basis.

Competition. This facet of the external environment is both significant and discrete enough to warrant separate consideration. Competition from a strategic and generalized perspective has at least three dimensions: input, process, and output. The most commonly held perception of a firm's competitors may be appropriate from the marketing manager's viewpoint but not the general manager's. Most companies see their competitors as other firms that sell the same or similar products. Some firms go further, including competitors who do not produce similar products but compete for the same customer dollar. This broader definition would suggest that firms making giant-screen television sets compete with firms that make above-ground swimming pools. A family that invests in one of these very dissimilar products probably will not be able or willing to buy the other for a significant period of time.

Although this definition of competition is broad, it is inadequate because it addresses only one of three possible dimensions of competition. The product-market-based definitions discussed so far recognize only the output dimension of competition.

A second and important dimension of competition is the process dimension, which relates to the nature of the technology employed by the company. For example, a firm that produces hand-held calculators and one that produces missile guidance computers do not compete along the output or product-market dimension, although both employ electronics technology and may possess the competence to manufacture the other's products. Thus firms that compete along the process or technology dimension could eventually compete along the more obvious output or product-market dimension. Recognizing this technological dimension of competition is vital because developments in technology can make a company's product obsolete. Electronic facsimile transmission, for example, may make overnight letter delivery less important, undercutting what is now a major, growing business.

Even firms in the service industry experience competition along the technology dimension. Banks or employment agencies that employ a more efficient process (use a superior technology) would certainly have a distinct competitive edge, for example.

The firm that identifies the potential sources of its obsolescence and exploits these sources before its competition does so is likely to survive and grow. If makers of wooden skis had foreseen the development of superior metal skis, they would have added them to their product lines. Similarly the manufacturer of metal skis should have anticipated and exploited the application of fiberglass and carbon technology in the manufacture of even better skis.

A third and equally important dimension of competition is the input or resources dimension. Firms that compete for finances from the same sources are excellent examples. They could be in totally different industries and employ different technologies, yet they may compete for the same managerial, labor, and financial resources.

Any firm that competes successfully along the input/resource dimension is also well situated to initiate more direct competition along the process/technology and output/product-market dimensions. Apart from that potential threat, companies that have to accept resources of lesser magnitude or poorer quality might plunge into a declining spiral, leading to reduced profits and possible extinction.

The first step in analyzing competition is to identify the three or four most important competitors in relation to each of the three dimensions. Too many competitors makes the analysis too demanding, perhaps superficial, and certainly difficult to appreciate fully. Too few could result in overlooking important insights. After selecting approximately ten to twelve firms, it is possible to conduct a useful and in-depth analysis that should include traditional financial analysis and a more qualitative examination. (It is perhaps useful to recall that we are focusing on organizations that are functional in nature and consequently highly focused in terms of strategic posture.)

A conventional analysis of published or otherwise available financial statements of the competitors is the first step in terms of understanding their strategies. It is essential that trends in financial figures and ratios over a period of at least three years be examined in order to ensure a truly meaningful appreciation of competitors' performances. Table 6–1 lists key figures and ratios.

Most of the ratios and numbers included in the table are well known and need no explanation. Some are, however, relatively uncommon. For example, the ratio of capital expenditures to depreciation suggests how much importance the firm's management places on maintaining or improving productive capacity. Also, the ratio of net fixed assets to gross fixed assets is a measure of how modern or recent the company's plant and equipment are.

Table 6–1
Financial Analysis of Competition

Profits growth rate
Earnings per share growth rate
Sales growth rate
Profits/sales
Sales/capital employed (equity plus long-term debt)
Profits/capital employed
Profits/labor cost (or number of employees)
Net fixed assets/number of employees
Sales/number of employees
Sales/inventories
Accounts receivable as days of sales
Current assets/current liabilities
(Cash + marketable securities + receivables)/current liabilities
Long-term debt/equity
Total debt/total assets
R&D expenses/sales
Sources and uses of funds
Capital expenditures/depreciation
Net fixed assets/gross fixed assets

In addition to the financial analysis, it is essential also to conduct qualitative analyses of the competition. Employees of one's organization who are in direct contact with competitive firms are prime sources of qualitative information. Field sales personnel can obtain information about competitive activities from distributors or customers who have dealings with those competitors. Manufacturing and R&D personnel may interact with competitors' personnel at professional meetings or conventions.

In addition, all publications of the competitors—annual reports, press releases, price lists, brochures, in-house newsletters, and even advertisements—can provide signals about business intentions. Sales and distribution practices, credit policies, product development plans and progress, pricing policies, and personnel and hiring practices are areas of importance in the competitive arena.

It is useful to designate specific individuals to collect, filter, and disseminate information about competitors. Over time, these individuals will develop valuable sources and insights about the competitors whom they have been assigned to analyze.

Internal Environment

In terms of analyzing one's own organization, the internal situation can be usefully partitioned into two components. First, the past performance, accomplishments, and failures of the firm must be understood so that it is possible better to predict and influence its future. Second, the existing core skills, distinctive competence, and key shortcomings of the firm must be comprehensively identified to permit exploiting the strengths and remedying the weaknesses.

The initial step in understanding the past is to conduct a detailed financial analysis. Much more information should be available about one's own organization than about the competition. Consequently a more thorough analysis is feasible than that suggested in table 6–1. The financial analyses that are likely to be found useful are listed in table 6–2.

The trends indicated by such analyses are the key pieces of information. Trends that are at variance with expectations or are out of line with other numbers should receive particular attention.

The last two items listed in table 6–2 are especially valuable. An examination of the trend in the magnitude of strategic dollars allocated to each functional area or department and identification of the purpose of these strategic expenditures leads to an enlightening appreciation of the implicit strategic emphasis. For instance, it is not uncommon to find organizations that believe that they have emphasized marketing as the core of their strategy, but examination of the proportion of strategic dollars committed to marketing might reveal that technology or production has been given even greater

Table 6–2
Financial Analysis of the Organization

Profits and growth rate in profits
Earnings per share and growth rate in EPS
Sales and growth rate in sales
Profits/sales
Sales/capital employed (equity + long-term debt)
Profits/capital employed
Sales growth rate/market growth rate
Profits/labor cost
Profits/number of employees
Net fixed assets/number of employees
Sales/number of employees
Sales/inventories
Accounts receivable as days of sales
Current assets/current liabilities
(Cash + marketable securities + receivables)/current liabilities
Long-term debt/equity
Total debt/total assets
R&D expenses/sales
Sources and uses of funds
Capital expenditures/depreciation
Net fixed assets/gross fixed assets
Cost of goods sold as percentage of sales
Materials cost as percentage of sales
Labor cost as percentage of sales
Rate of change in prices
Product mix changes, (total and by region)
Proportion of capital expenditures allocated to each department (trend)
Market share by product line and region (trend)

importance. More in-depth analysis, such as identifying the purpose of the expenditures in each department in each year, might prove worthwhile. A consistent pattern of emphasizing, for example, distribution within the marketing department might be observed or, on the other hand, inconsistent attention to various other aspects within the marketing department might be noticed. The gap between the strategy that is intended and the strategy that is actually implemented is often very wide but not explicitly recognized. These analyses can identify the gaps between intention and reality.

In addition to the quantitatively oriented analyses suggested in table 6–1, it is necessary to analyze the internal situation further by identifying the core skills, distinctive competences, and key shortcomings of the firm. What has the firm relied on as its primary strength in making profits? What does the firm do better than its competitors? What have been its principal weaknesses?

In developing answers to these crucial questions, it is often necessary to rely on qualitative analysis. For instance, much of the information that affords useful insights may be in the form of anecdotes or stories about particular experiences. The events or experiences that are recounted are important because they often overtly or subtly influence key strategic decisions. A well-known example is the long-held reluctance of Federated Department Stores to engage in retailing through discount stores because of one bad experience.

A somewhat counterintuitive but important phenomenon is that it is ordinarily easier to develop insights by looking at experiences where the organization has been unsuccessful. And instances where the organization has been successful might in fact prove to be a hindrance to future effective strategy development. The economic landscape is littered with organizations that have continued to rely on past patterns that have been successful instead of recognizing that new responses are demanded by environmental changes.

It is often useful to examine two extreme experiences or perceptions relating to particular activities or issues to identify what led to the different experiences. For example, one organization that utilized teams of executives to develop operating plans for its product lines compared the experience of the most conspicuously successful team with that of a less successful team. It then developed guidelines to improve the effectiveness of its management teams. Those guidelines included clear-cut directions for improvements relating to the process followed, the involvement of senior management, and the definition of the responsibilities of its teams. Studying just one experience would not have been as meaningful and could have resulted in a biased understanding.

The organization's management system should be a major part of the study. It is not uncommon to find managerial audits focusing primarily (if not solely) on tangible areas such as products, markets, distribution channels, and manufacturing capabilities. Although these areas are obviously important, the organization's management systems can be a major resource or an insurmountable impediment in the context of alternative strategic options. ITT's growth and success during the Geneen era could be traced substantially to its systems of management control and management of human resources. A thorough managerial audit should especially address the topics listed in table 6–3.

Two caveats are appropriate in the context of these analyses. First, it may be desirable to assign responsibility for such analyses to individuals who are not defensive about the past or about the status quo. If one is studying manufacturing, one may want to employ sources other than, or in addition to, the manufacturing management. Often managers of departments or functions who have close interactions with the department or function being studied will have useful insights to offer. The second caveat is of particular importance: strengths and weaknesses of an organization can be assessed only in relation to environmental opportunities that are of interest. What is a

Table 6–3
Scope of Management Audit

Organizational structure
   Appropriateness of responsibility centers
   Allocation of responsibility and authority

Planning and control systems
   Long-range or strategic planning
   Budgeting
   Reporting
   Review and follow-up
   Transfer pricing
   Materials management
   Accounting and billing

Policies
   Personnel
   Credit
   R&D
   Product
   Customer service

Marketing
   Pricing
   Products
   Advertising
   Market research
   Distribution
   Inventories

Manufacturing
   Production planning and control
   Inventories
   Maintenance
   Capacity utilization (bottleneck areas)
   Human resources
   Product diversification capabilities

Personnel
   Recruiting and selection
   Training and development
   Records management
   Performance review

Finance
   Sources and uses of funds
   Relationships with sources
   Cash management

Research and development
   Investment
   Success rate
   Financial impact
   Human resources

Management
   Climate
   Competence, capabilities
   Turnover
   Age, experience
   Development of second line

strength in one context may be a weakness in relation to another possible market definition. For instance, an organization based in the northeastern United States may find this location to be a strength in the context of one scenario: expansion in the Northeast where attractive government-sponsored investment incentives are available. In another scenario, this locational advantage may prove to be a weakness if expansion is planned in the southwestern United States, where less militant unions might be encountered.

Integrating the Analyses

It is critical to integrate externally and internally focused analyses. The study of external environmental factors and competition should result in a list of practical issues, which can be categorized in terms of their relative importance and the urgency of response required (Grant and King 1982). The resulting four-way classification diagrammed in figure 6–2 ranges from important issues that require immediate action to unimportant issues that do not require an immediate response. This classification offers two benefits: it prioritizes the issues and enables managers to focus on those that require swift response, and it facilitates the identification of patterns that lead to the development of scenarios used to guide the formulation of appropriate stategies. This matrix will later be referred to as the importance-imminence (I-I) matrix. For example, R&D projects may have to be initiated immediately to respond to the anticipated product development activities of the competition. The location of major growth markets might dictate setting up a new plant in a distant location. Investment incentives in a different state combined with labor problems in existing locations might also suggest a need for movement away from existing locations.

Developing such scenarios will produce an improved classification of the issues. For instance, relationships within the investment community might take on importance in the context of a likely need for funds for new plants in different locations.

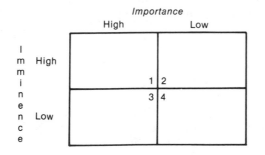

Figure 6–2. Importance-Imminence Matrix

Although the external analyses can give rise to issues that can be classified in the importance-imminence matrix, it is important to analyze closely the organization itself in order to arrive at a good understanding of its distinctive competences. What capabilities does the organization possess that give it an edge over its competition? Broadly, the competitive edge can be in terms of facilities, access to markets (distribution channels), access to raw materials, labor availability and cost, financial resources (magnitude and cost), technology, or management (personnel and systems).

The identification of distinctive competences will influence the selection of environmental opportunities for exploitation. For example, if finances are an organization's distinctive competence, then perhaps unrelated diversification becomes a possibility. If manufacturing in terms of low cost and high quality are an organization's distinctive competence, then perhaps it should prepare to compete on price to maintain or increase its share of the existing market.

The other side of the coin, which also needs to be identified, is best viewed in terms of identified inconsistencies rather than weaknesses. Organizational characteristics are strengths or weaknesses only in the context of particular environmental scenarios. Thus, inconsistencies essentially alert one to possible weaknesses. The kinds of inconsistencies that need to be identified are usually readily apparent following the managerial audit described in table 6–3. Inconsistencies over time in the allocation of capital funds to departments should be given careful attention. Are the organization's departments or functional areas set up to be consistent with each other's capabilities and requirements? For example, are the distribution and warehousing capabilities consistent with the manufacturing facilities possessed by the organization? Perhaps the organization has ignored or inadequately developed its ability to service existing customers despite top management's identification of production quality and customer service as the key elements in the strategic posture of the organization.

Having conducted the external and internal analyses, created the importance-imminence matrix with regard to external issues, and identified the distinctive competences and apparent inconsistencies in practices on the basis of the internal analyses, we are now ready to attempt the critical exercise of translating these analyses into a strategic vision for the organization.

Dimensions of Strategic Choice

The process described here is of considerable significance for a variety of reasons. It determines the value and utility of all the previous analyses that may have been carried out. Unless these analyses lead to the creation of an effective strategic plan, they would essentially be exercises in futility. This stage in the process is important because it is a novel and powerful approach to a step in strategic planning that traditionally has been viewed as an intuitive and cerebral exercise. What is being offered is a way of structuring the transition from analysis to strategic vision. The suggested process is also of value in that it greatly facilitates the later, much-needed, and difficult transition from strategic aspirations to managerial actions. Also, the process results in the identification of criteria that can be used to evaluate subsequent incremental modifications to the chosen strategy.

The result of this process is not necessarily the optimal strategic plan for the organization; nevertheless, it has demonstrated its value as a way of structuring creative steps in strategy formulation.

Step 1

The first step entails listing the issues belonging to the first quadrant (important and immediate) of the I-I matrix along with the key competences and the identified inconsistencies. For purposes of illustration, we shall employ the example of American Instrument Manufacturers (AIM), a firm manufacturing electrical meters. Figure 6–3 shows an environmental scanning matrix for AIM.

In the case of AIM, the two major issues were (1) the threat of electronics-based products and (2) the high cost of debt financing. The distinctive competences AIM possessed were (1) adequate management experience; (2) excellent manufacturing and marketing (distribution) capability; (3) good working relationships with financial institutions; and (4) a record of profitability in the previous five years. The inconsistencies identified in the case of AIM were (1) an aging work force, (2) ineffective planning and control systems, and (3) a lack of capability with regard to computers and electronics technology.

Step 2

The second step in the process is to match competences and inconsistencies with each of the important issues identified. For example, against the issue of high borrowing rate, the corresponding strengths and inconsistencies are that the firm possesses not only excellent relationships with the financial institutions but also a record of profitability. These play an important role when negotiating with financial institutions for future cash needs. In contrast, the issue of electronic flow meters serving as a more efficient and effective substitute product, when matched with the inadequate capability of AIM in the new technology, indicates significant cause for concern.

Step 3

The third step entails developing alternative programs to respond to each of the issues requiring attention. A possible I-I matrix for AIM is illustrated in

	Levels			
	Firm	Industry	Regional	National
Social	Loyalty to company declining as alternative employment opportunities emerge	Preference for high-technology firms will affect new recruitment	Movement away from single-family housing to apartment complexes and condominiums	Increased mobility, reduced commitment to traditional family structure
Demographic	Percentage of elderly in local population will continue to increase	No significant developments	Movement of population from Northeast to Southwest and West	Tendency toward zero population growth continues
Regulatory	Occupational safety regulations will be enforced	No significant developments	Pollution control emphasis likely to increase in West and Southwest	Continued emphasis on health, environmental and safety standards
Technological	Local computer service bureau permits increased computer applications in manufacturing	Electronic flow meters of improved performance characteristics and reduced cost are becoming available	No significant regional differences	Explosion in CAD/CAM capabilities
Political	Local taxes likely to increase to fund new welfare program	Industry association will open office in capital	Investment incentives in Northeast will increase in response to movement of capital to Southwest and West	New party in power will emphasize business and industry's role in national development
Economic	Credit will be available but at 13 percent or higher interest rates	Marginal firms likely to go bankrupt	Southwest and West will experience significantly more investment in new plant than Northeast and Midwest	Recession expected to continue. Interest rates will remain high. Housing starts will decline further. No increase in investment in new plants

Figure 6–3. AIM Matrix for Environmental Analysis

figure 6–4. Two major alternatives (set A) for the first issue of high borrowing rates are:

1. Postpone all borrowing until interest rates decline, selectively reduce working capital, and postpone capital expenditure.

		HIGH	*Importance*	LOW
I m m i n e n c e	Immediate Action Required	High (13%) borrowing rate Electronic flow meters being offered by competition		Local taxes likely to increase Industry association location in capital
	Delayed Response Adequate	Computer service bureau facilities improvement CAD/CAM applications increasing Political climate increasingly favorable to business		Increasing proportion of elderly in local population Loyalty of employees declining Investment incentives in Northeast likely to increase

Figure 6–4. AIM I-I Matrix

2. Capitalize on the past record of profitability and good working relationships with financial institutions to negotiate additional favorable credit and make appropriate changes in customers' credit policies and inventory management.

Similarly, two alternatives (set B) can be identified for the second issue, the threat from new technology:

1. Continue the existing product line of mechanical meters and focus on efficiency and productivity in order to remain profitable, even if the total market demand declines.
2. Participate in the new technology to manufacture electronics-based meters, recruit personnel with the required expertise, and strengthen formal planning and control systems to implement the new activity.

Step 4

Having accomplished a preliminary identification of the key alternatives for each of the significant issues, the fourth step is to identify the major dimensions of difference between the alternatives. For instance, the alternatives identified in set A are quite different in terms of financial policy, growth orientation, profit orientation, and risk. In the alternatives in set B, the dimensions of difference include the diversification orientation, the character of the management systems, and the orientation toward technology. Table 6–4 identifies the different strategic postures that AIM can adopt in the context of these key dimensions of difference.

Table 6–4
Dimensions of Strategic Choice

Dimensions	Strategic Orientation		
Profit orientation	Short term	⟷	Long term
Growth orientation	Status quo	⟷	High growth
Diversification orientation	Status quo	⟷	Diversity
Management systems	Informal	⟷	Formal
Financial policy	Conservative	⟷	Aggressive
Technology orientation	Status quo	⟷	New
Risk	Low	⟷	High

These dimensions of strategic choice are very much dependent on the nature of each organization and its environment. Additional dimensions are location, potential for product differentiation, personnel characteristics, corporate image, competitive reaction, and possibility of erecting barriers to entry. Although the number of dimensions of strategic choice can be considerable, it is useful to limit them to five to ten. The importance of these dimensions is made evident by considering the character of AIM if it chooses to position itself at one or the other extreme in terms of strategic orientation with regard to each dimension. AIM could become an organization focusing on short-term profits, with no intention of growing or diversifying, employing informal management techniques, adopting a conservative financial policy, and utilizing the existing technology. Or it could become a growth- and diversification-oriented organization willing to take risks in anticipation of long-term profitability, employing formal management systems to support decision making and emphasizing aggressive financing combined with an emphasis on new technology. Although neither of these extremes is necessarily desirable or feasible, the positioning of an organization along its dimensions or strategic choice is obviously the critical decision to be made by top management in the context of strategic planning.

Step 5

The fifth step in the process is to classify the identified alternatives with regard to the dimensions of strategic choice. A variety of approaches can be used to accomplish this step. One possibility is to develop a table such as that shown in table 6–5. Another is to diagram the strategic orientation implicit in each of the alternatives being considered. Thus it would be possible to arrive at a strategic profile as diagrammed in figure 6–5. A third possibility (and one I have found to be particularly effective) is to employ recently developed techniques for responding to complex problems. A particularly appropriate

Table 6–5
Classifying the Alternatives

Dimensions	Set A		Set B	
	1	*2*	*1*	*2*
Profit orientation	Short term	Long term	Short term	Long term
Growth orientation	Status quo	High growth	Status quo	High growth
Diversification orientation	Status quo	Status quo	Status quo	Diversity
Management systems	Informal	Informal	Informal	Informal
Financial policy	Conservative	Aggressive	Conservative	Less conservative
Technology orientation	Status quo	Status quo	Status quo	New
Risk	Low	High	Low	Medium

technique is the analytic hierarchy process (Saaty and Kearns 1985). Although it is relatively more difficult to implement than the two previously described approaches, the outcome perhaps justifies the added effort. This technique enables one to rank the alternatives being considered in relation to one another. Such rankings can be arrived at from the point of view of individual key decision makers, as well as groups of key executives. A version of the technique that is available for use on personal computers is called Expert Choice. Whatever approach is adopted, it will be possible as a result of this step in the process to make consistent choices from within each set of alternatives, thus ensuring cohesive, synergistic packages of programs. Top management can then select the package most closely allied with their values and aspirations. The selected programs would in a sense represent the strategic posture of the organization.

Process Benefits

The process described offers several significant advantages. First, it results in an explicit understanding of the present and emerging strategies adopted by the organization. Too often this understanding is implicit or taken for granted and subsequently fades into oblivion, with obvious undesirable consequences. Second, it provides a strong foundation for integrating strategic planning and management control. The linkage between strategic planning and management control where it substantially depends on the capital budgeting process is made more meaningful as will be described in a later chapter. Third, the evocative character of the dimensions of strategic choice is perhaps evident. These dimensions, when identified, trigger creative new programs and also lead to an understanding of distinctive competences and possible competitive tactics. Fourth, the strategy that is represented by the chosen set of alterna-

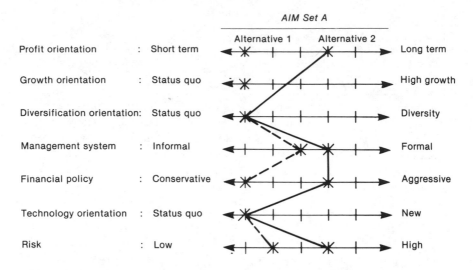

Figure 6–5. Strategic Profiles of Alternatives

tives possesses the great merit of being action oriented. The strategic posture is in essence a consistent set of possible actions, which when fleshed out will constitute the actions and operational plan of the organization. Strategic visions that do not possess this action orientation remain abstractions rather than operational reality. Fifth, the process recognizes and responds to top management's values. When selecting among alternatives that reflect different strategic postures, top management in essence is implicitly, yet concretely, articulating its values.

Although it may be argued that formalizing a creative process such as the formulation of strategies might result in the inhibition of creativity and innovation, it does not appear that the process proposed here suffers from this drawback. On the contrary, it is a demonstrably feasible and stimulating approach to structuring a step in the creation of strategy that has traditionally been difficult.

Timing Decisions

Three time-related decisions must be made in the context of designing the process of strategic planning:

1. The horizon of the strategic plan has to be identified. This decision relates to how far in the future management needs to attempt to plan.

2. The span of the planning process needs to be defined. This decision relates to the number of weeks or months over which the planning process is to be conducted.

3. The frequency of strategic planning needs to be set.

With regard to the planning horizon, two key considerations are involved. First, the time horizon should be long enough to encompass the consequences of operating decisions and actions of managers. The operating cycle of the business or industry will provide a good indication of this time. In the garment industry, for example, operating cycles cannot exceed six months because of the influence of fashion and seasonal changes. In the shipbuilding industry, the operating cycle is usually two to three years. In most manufacturing firms, the operating cycle is less than a year. At the minimum, the strategic planning horizon should encompass the time period beyond the operating cycle that would be affected by decisions made at the end of the operating cycle. Thus a firm with an operating cycle of, say, two years should not conduct strategic planning analyses that do not encompass at least four years.

The second determinant of the horizon of the strategic plan is somewhat more judgmental in character. The strategic planning horizon should cover the period necessary to enable an organization to move efficiently out of an existing business into a new business. Although new strategic postures can be adopted overnight, the cost of such urgent and dramatic changes can be enormously high. The more lead time there is for making such changes, the lower will be the associated cost. Restructuring the organization's capital assets can be particularly difficult in basic and heavy industries. On the other hand, service industries that rely on the skills of their personnel will have to make a judgment of the time period required for effective and ethical outplacement of existing employees who may not fit into future plans.

The guidelines for the span of time over which the strategic planning process should be conducted in an organization is difficult to define precisely. My experience suggests that three to six months is usually suitable for most organizations that are functional in character. Less than three months often does not provide adequate time for thorough analyses and involvement of the personnel who could contribute. On the other hand, a planning exercise that takes more than six months is likely to suffer from a loss of momentum and commitment and probably result in a less effective plan than could have been accomplished in a shorter period of time. It should be borne in mind that the longer the time span involved is, the greater is the probability that assumptions made at the start of the process will be obsolete by the time the final plan is arrived at.

The third and final time-related decision to be made—the frequency with which the strategic planning process should be repeated—is of great impor-

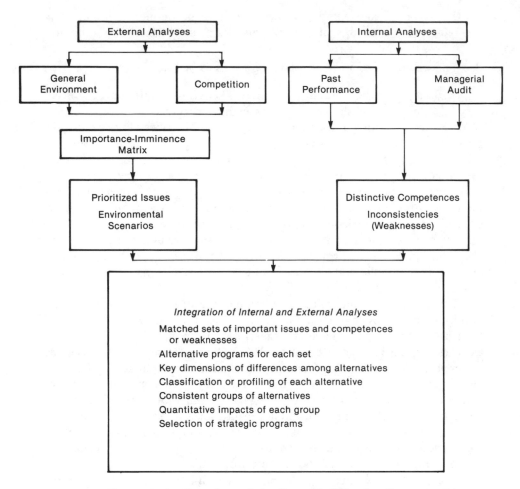

Figure 6–6. Overview of the Strategic Planning Process

tance. Traditionally designers of planning systems tend to recommend an annual repetition of the strategic planning process. I strongly recommend against an annual process. To reexamine the organization's mission, to restate its long-term, enduring objectives, to reshape corporate strategy, and to modify functional policies on an annual basis is counterproductive. Creativity, the acknowledged essence of strategic planning, will be stifled by the monotony of routine. Reaping the benefits of a strategy often requires lead times of several years. Too frequent a change of strategic direction, too frequent a requirement to scan the environment for strategic discontinuities, could lead to a lack of managerial motivation and to an insensitive, lethargic planning climate.

Comprehensive exercises involving large numbers of executives, such as the process described in this chapter, can be conducted meaningfully only on a triennial or quinquennial basis. It must be recognized, however, that the intervening years could require strategic responses to unexpected developments. In order to ensure that the needed strategic changes are made in the intervening years between formal comprehensive exercises, an annual review of strategic assumptions is important. In addition, the strategic issue management system described in a later chapter should provide adequate mechanisms for incremental changes in the strategic posture that may be required in the three- to five-year period between comprehensive strategic planning exercises.

Figure 6–6 provides an overview of the strategic planning process described in this chapter.

References

Grant, John H., and King, William R., *The Logic of Strategic Planning*. Boston: Little, Brown, 1982.

Saaty, Thomas L., and Kearns, Kevin P., *Analytical Planning: The Organization of Systems*. Oxford: Pergamon Press, 1985.

Thomas, Philip S., "Environmental Analysis for Corporate Planning." *Business Horizons* (October 1974).

7
Managing the Strategic Planning System

S trategic planning systems require careful management to ensure effectiveness. The required administrative support can be provided by managers whose primary responsibility is the organization's planning system or by other executives who are assigned responsibility for a planning system as one of several functions that they perform. Regardless of whether the SPS is the sole responsibility of a planning executive or a subsidiary concern of line or staff managers with other responsibilities, these executives will need to perform certain tasks. In understanding the tasks that are the responsibility of the manager of the SPS, it is useful to look at the range of roles that can be adopted.

Role Dimensions

The spectrum of possible roles is very wide and has not been particularly well defined in the literature. Some designers of planning systems have defined the possible roles of the planning executive in terms of those that focus on the process of planning and those associated with decision making regarding the output of planning. Instead I offer a framework that facilitates the identification of the knowledge and skills that are required for the planning manager to be effective.

Some of the roles that managers of the planning system have to play are relatively technical in nature, and others are more decision oriented and managerial. Technical roles emphasize the responsibilities of planning managers in establishing schedules for the implementation of the planning process, applying specific techniques such as forecasting, providing analyses for use by other managers in planning decisions, and so on. Managerial or decision-oriented roles highlight activities, such as the integration of the viewpoints of various functions and hierarchical levels in the organization. Technical roles tend to be associated with the process of strategic planning, while managerial roles tend to be related to the output or content of the plan.

In addition to the distinction between managerial and technical roles, it is possible to visualize the roles of planning managers in terms of their being passive or active in nature. The distinction between passive and active roles stems from the extent of responsibility that planning managers assume in initiating analyses, actions, or decisions. In passive roles, planning managers respond to requests for technical or analytical assistance from line and staff managers engaged in the planning process. In active or catalytic roles, the planning manager influences the analyses and decisions relating to the corporate plan.

Related to this passive-active classification is the extent to which planning managers act in an advisory capacity as opposed to a decision-making capacity. In fact, in visualizing the spectrum of possible roles that planning managers play, roles that are technical, process related, passive, and advisory in character are likely to be at one end of the spectrum, while at the other end one would find roles that are managerial, output related, active, and decision oriented.

Role Options

Six distinctive roles can be identified. First, the planning manager can act as a coordinator, monitoring the execution of the planning process and consolidating the elements of functional, subunit plans into an organizational plan. This role exists in all organizations where formal planning is undertaken. A recent survey of planning practices in over two hundred organizations shows clearly that this is an important role in every situation. As one would expect, however, the larger or more diverse the organization is, the greater is the importance of the coordinating role. The coordinating role is intrinsically process oriented. It is substantially technical in character in that consolidation of subunit plans is often a required activity. This role is largely passive and advisory in character.

A second role that the planning manager often plays is that of an analyst, typified by such activities as financial forecasting and routine environmental scanning. Technical capabilities appear to be paramount here, and the role is essentially passive and advisory in nature.

A third role is that of consultant. Here the planning manager serves as a corporate resource, offering expertise in process and output to organization subunits requiring assistance. This role is also somewhat passive in nature in that the planning manager responds to requests for assistance, as opposed to initiating interactions with other managers.

In larger organizations, a fourth role, that of integrator, takes on importance. In this role, the planning manager serves as a channel of communication between the different levels of management and between departments. This role is very managerial, active, and output oriented since the planning manager seeks to bring about a meeting of minds on appropriate organizational goals or courses of action.

The fifth role that is occasionally encountered in practice is that of instigator, where the planning manager acts as an idea generator, identifies significant managerial issues, and may even be a corporate gadfly. This is clearly an active, managerial, output-related role that can significantly influence the content of managerial decisions.

Sixth, the planning manager can take on the role of decision maker. In this role, the planning manager is actively involved in decision making regarding organizational goals or plans of action. Although this role is rarely adopted and is often criticized by academics and practitioners, it is an option that may be appropriate.

These six roles have been identified in a particular order. The initial roles described are technical, process related, passive, and advisory; the later roles are increasingly managerial, output related, active, and decision oriented.

Planning Managers' Profiles

The different characteristics of each role means that a different combination of capabilities, style, experience, and academic training is needed in order to perform the various roles effectively. It is obvious that an advisory, passive, technical role demands one kind of person and a decisive, active, managerial role a different kind.

The demands of each role in terms of appropriate capabilities can be broadly outlined. Active, decision-oriented roles clearly require a self-starter inclined to confrontation as a means of conflict resolution, qualities not crucial to the performance of other, more passive, advisory roles.

Broadly speaking, the "compleat" planning manager would at the very least possess:

Familiarity with such disciplines as econometrics, operations research, accounting, information systems, and planning and control.

Knowledge of environmental situations and the capability to predict trends.

Familiarity with and systematic understanding of the organization's operations.

Interpersonal and communications skills.

Some of these requirements are based on knowledge acquired through the study of specific academic disciplines, and others reflect skills developed through business or organizational experience. Academic knowledge is more suited to technical, advisory, passive roles; experience and interpersonal skills are demanded by active, managerial, decisive roles.

These differences have several implications. If roles are specified, broad but critical indications of the kind of person best suited for each role are available. If the planning department is large, the internal structure of the department is clearly suggested. Responsibility centers based on the roles assigned to each subunit of the planning department can be created. There could be a group or responsibility center concerned with the provision of analyses and forecasts, for example, and another concerned with formats, timetables, and general coordination. The profile of the manager of the planning department should be consistent with the roles that are of the greatest importance. And the need for more than one planning department might emerge. Figure 7–1 provides a guide to the requirements suggested by the nature of each of the roles identified.

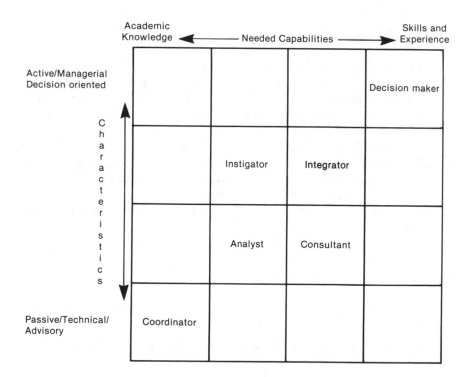

Figure 7–1. Planning Managers' Roles and Related Requirements

Selecting the Appropriate Roles

The appropriate roles for the planning manager to emphasize in a particular organization are dependent on the strategic orientation of the organization in terms of growth and diversification and its size and complexity. The larger and more complex the organization is, the greater the need there is to play coordinating and integrating roles.

When the organization's emphasis is on more efficient management of the existing business, the roles likely to be most suitable for the planning manager are the technical, advisory, passive ones of analyst, coordinator and consultant. When the emphasis is on growth through expansion of the existing business, the technical, advisory, passive roles continue to be appropriate. Line managers in these contexts will have to perform the managerial, decision-oriented, active roles as part of their responsibilities.

When the organization emphasizes growth through diversification and acquisition, the appropriate roles for the planning managers are the managerial, decision-oriented, active roles of instigator, integrator, and decision maker. In order to respond to the different roles that are appropriate in the context of planning for new businesses, it may be necessary to partition the planning manager's roles through assignment of responsibility for the ongoing business to a different individual or group than the individual or group to whom responsibility for new business oriented planning is assigned.

Industry Practices and Perceptions

We are fortunate in having access to information regarding the roles of planning managers in organizations as they existed in the late 1960s (Camillus 1978) and similar information obtained from over two hundred organizations in the mid-1980s (Ramanujam, Camillus and Venkatraman 1984). The general patterns remain the same over the fifteen-year period spanned by these two studies. All organizations, in both the late 1960s and the mid-1980s, require that planning managers assume a coordinating role. Active, decision-oriented roles were not assigned to planning managers in a substantial (25 percent) number of organizations in the late 1960s. The trend in the mid-1980s seems to be to continue this deemphasis of active, decision-oriented roles.

Although the size of planning staffs and the occurrence of decision-oriented roles have lessened over the last fifteen years, organizations have at the same time given increasing importance to the planning activity. Planning has become more and more a line function as opposed to a staff activity in organizations. Interestingly, and not surprisingly, planning managers tend to prefer active, managerial, decision-oriented roles, a preference that may not at times be consistent with organizational requirements.

The framework developed in this chapter can be used to define the appropriate roles for planning managers in the context of specific organizations and to identify suitable individuals to fulfill these roles. Also the framework could assist in structuring the planning department so as to maximize the contribution that those responsible for managing the planning function can make to overall organizational effectiveness.

References

Camillus, John C., "Planning Managers' Roles: An Operational Framework." *Vikalpa* (April 1978): 99–109.

Ramanujam, Vasu, Camillus, John C., and Venkatraman, N., *The Design and Use of Strategic Planning Systems: Some Key Issues for the Eighties*. Monograph, Weatherhead School of Management, Case Western Reserve University, 1984.

Part III
Management Control in Functional Organizations

8
The Structural Foundations of Management Control

The key prerequisite to effective design of the management control system is to recognize the different characteristics of the various subunits that comprise functional organizations. The input-process-output model of organizations described in chapter 2 can be employed to categorize and highlight the differences among the various subunits of each organization. An organization can be visualized as a mechanism or process that converts inputs such as money, human effort, and raw materials into desired outputs such as profits. The manager of the organization exercises control or authority over the inputs and process and is responsible for generating the desired output. This view of the organization is diagrammed in figure 8–1.

Most modern organizations large enough to consider the introduction of a formal management control system are usually too complex and diverse in their operations to allow a single manager to make all the decisions needed to convert inputs efficiently and effectively into profits. Consequently the firm is divided into simpler, more homogeneous subunits or functions or departments, each of which can be viewed as a process of converting inputs into desired outputs. Thus, the manufacturing department converts raw materials and power into finished goods, the marketing department converts these finished goods into dollars of revenue, the personnel department converts job applicants into machinists and salespeople, and so on.

Each department is very different from the others, and these differences are important from the point of view of planning and control. The planned work load of some departments, such as manufacturing, is based on the desired output. The work load in other departments, such as legal or maintenance, is based on inputs, such as lawsuits or job requisitions. The outputs of certain departments are tangible and readily measurable. The outputs of other departments are hard to describe, let alone objectively measure. It is necessary therefore to classify the subunits into categories that permit appropriate approaches to the exercise of management planning and control.

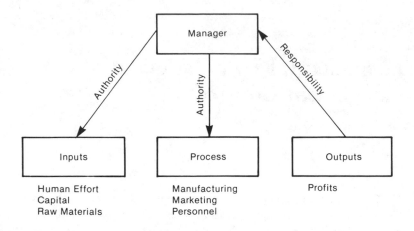

Figure 8–1. Input-Process-Output Model of the Firm

Process-Output Matrix

In describing each subunit of functional organizations from the point of view of designing appropriate planning and control mechanisms, perhaps the most important attribute of each subunit or department is whether its outputs are quantifiable and measurable. In the manufacturing and the marketing departments, the outputs (units of production and dollars of revenue) are readily measurable. On the other hand, the accounting and finance department and the personnel and industrial relations department generate outputs (managerial information and industrial harmony) that are often intangible and difficult to quantify and measure.

The second major distinguishing characteristic of various types of departments is whether the processes they employ are well defined and understood. Assembly operations in manufacturing are representative of well-defined, well-understood processes. Creating advertising copy and designing a new product are relatively undefined and not clearly understood processes in most situations.

Employing these two major considerations, we can identify four types of departments as indicated in the process-output matrix in figure 8–2. Type I departments, where the process is known and the outputs are measurable, are the easiest to manage and evaluate. They can be tightly controlled, and efficiency (the relationship between inputs and outputs) becomes the primary focus of budgeting systems for these departments.

Type II departments, where the process is unknown but outputs can be measured, require control mechanisms that focus on the extent to which

Process
Known   Unknown

Type I   Type II

	Type I	Type II
Measureable	Most manufacturing departments (focus on input-output relationships—efficiency)	Some staff departments such as legal, some marketing departments (focus on outputs)
Not Measurable	**Type III** Some staff departments such as personnel (focus on process—procedures and practices)	**Type IV** Some R&D departments (focus on inputs—resource allocation)

Outputs

Figure 8–2. Process-Output Matrix

desired outputs are achieved. The functional organization as a whole would possess the characteristics of type II units. The many and complex processes and decisions involved in managing the organization may not be totally understood or clearly defined, but the end result or outputs appear in black and white on financial statements.

Type III departments are extremely difficult to manage well. Although one can focus on whether accepted practices and procedures are carried out carefully and in a timely manner, it is often impossible to ascertain whether the desired results are being obtained. Personnel departments are a good example of this type.

Type IV departments are typified by R&D units oriented toward basic rather than applied research. Since both process and outputs are unclear, the best that can be done is to manage the quantity and quality of inputs or resources provided to these departments.

Applying the Matrix

In order to demonstrate the application of the classification scheme, we shall again employ the firm American Instrument Manufacturers (AIM), which manufactures two product lines, water meters and gas meters. All manufacturing activities are carried out in one plant located on the East Coast of the United States. The plant is run by a manufacturing manager and consists of four major departments: foundry, machining, assembly, and maintenance. Sales are the responsibility of the marketing manager, who has two product managers reporting to him. The product managers are responsible for residential and industrial sales, respectively. The president and general manager directly supervises the manufacturing manager and marketing manager. In addition, the chief accountant and the personnel manager report to the general manager. The organization chart for AIM is provided in figure 8–3.

Manufacturing Responsibility Centers

The term *responsibility centers* refers to subunits that have a manager or supervisor with well-defined authority and responsibility. Three of the four responsibility centers in the manufacturing area—foundry, machine shop, and assembly shop—are clearly type I units. Their inputs (raw materials,

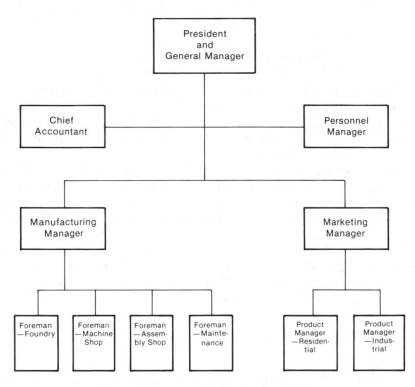

Figure 8–3. AIM Organizational Chart

components, supplies, labor, utilities) and outputs (components, finished goods) are well defined and readily measurable. Moreover, the processes by which the inputs are converted into outputs are well defined and understood. As a consequence, it is possible to determine objectively the amount of inputs that should be used in order to generate a required amount of outputs. In other words, the efficiency (output ÷ input) with which these three departments should operate can be specified.

There is one more important characteristic of these three responsibility centers: the inputs that they require (raw materials, components, supplies, labor, utilities, and so on) are measurable in monetary terms. Thus the dollar value of all the inputs these responsibility centers require can be determined.

It is difficult to assign a monetary value to their outputs, however. Cost accountants might offer their understanding of the cost of producing a machine component, for instance, but such cost figures are very misleading because they usually include arbitrary allocations of costs and represent one of several possible methods of attaching costs to products rather than an objective, defensible, economic valuation of the products. The outputs of these three manufacturing responsibility centers are, however, easily measured in physical, quantitative terms such as kilograms or number of units.

To summarize, the important characteristics of these three manufacturing responsibility centers are as follows:

1. Their inputs are objectively and easily measurable in monetary (dollar) terms.
2. Their outputs are objectively and easily measurable in quantitative, physical (but nonmonetary) terms.
3. The processes by which they convert inputs into outputs are well defined and understood.
4. The optimal relationship between inputs consumed and outputs generated can be specified.
5. They basically belong to the type I category of the process-output matrix.

Designers of planning and control systems use the term *engineered expense center* to describe responsibility centers with these characteristics. It is useful to keep this term and what it means in mind because the budgeting systems for all engineered expense centers are remarkably similar, regardless of whether they belong to the manufacturing, marketing, or finance function.

Systems designers use the phrase *expense center* to mean responsibility centers where the inputs are measured in monetary (dollar) terms and the outputs are measured in physical and quantitative but nonmonetary terms. *Engineered* is added to indicate that the optimal relationship between inputs and outputs can be objectively determined.

The maintenance shop is different from the other three responsibility centers reporting to the manufacturing manager. Depending on the nature of breakdowns that have to be rectified, repairs that need to be made, and preventive maintenance activities that are specified, the functions and processes employed by the maintenance shop change. The relationship between inputs and outputs cannot be easily specified because the demands on the maintenance shop cannot be known in advance.

The maintenance shop shares one basic similarity with the other three responsibility centers in the manufacturing area: all are expense centers in that their inputs are measured in dollar terms, and their outputs are measured in physical terms. The optimal relationship between inputs and outputs cannot be readily and objectively determined in the case of the maintenance shop, however. Thus it is not an engineered expense center. It is what is called a discretionary expense center and will be considered again later in this chapter along with other discretionary expense centers such as the personnel department.

Marketing Responsibility Centers

The two product managers reporting to the marketing manager deal with different types of products and customers and have different responsibilities. The product manager of residential products sells a standard line of water and gas meters for household use to plumbing and building supply distributors throughout the country but primarily on the East Coast. Six sales representatives report to this product manager. Wholesale list prices are set by the marketing manager, and the price list is usually updated annually. The sales representatives visit the distributors and obtain their orders, which are transmitted back to the product manager, who initiates the packing and shipping activity. The product manager maintains personal contacts with and often visits the major distributors.

The product manager of industrial products operates in a very different fashion. Sales in this area are made directly to end users. Orders are usually obtained through a competitive bidding process. Meters often have to be custom tailored to the client's specifications. No formal price list is printed because the number and type of variations in design specifications are almost infinite. Brochures describing the types of meters that AIM can make are printed and distributed to former customers. In addition, advertisements in industry and trade journals trigger inquiries from prospective customers.

The product manager of industrial products determines the price quotations that are made to prospective customers. Every few months, the marketing manager reviews the prices quoted but otherwise leaves the pricing decisions entirely to the judgment of the product manager.

The product manager of industrial products has three senior, technically qualified salespeople reporting to him, stationed in the Southwest, West, and Midwest. The product manager and these three salespeople often try to get in touch with the purchasing and technical personnel of prospective clients in order to explain the superior technical characteristics of AIM's meters.

These two marketing responsibility centers are clearly quite different, requiring different approaches to budgeting. Let us consider the residential products center first. Here the product manager has no authority over pricing. The responsibility is to generate the maximum amount of unit sales within the constraints of the output of the manufacturing function. The manager's outputs are therefore dollars of sales revenue, and the inputs are the efforts that the manager and the sales force invest in their dealings with the distributors and the meters provided for sale. Their salaries can be viewed as a measure of their efforts, but this has obvious shortcomings; the goods provided for sale can be valued at cost, which is arbitrary, or at list price, which is inappropriate since the manager has no margin for profit.

We therefore have a responsibility center that is a mirror image of the expense centers seen in manufacturing. Here the inputs are not readily measurable in monetary terms, and the outputs are best expressed in dollars of revenue. This kind of responsibility center is called a revenue center. Revenue centers are type II subunits in that their outputs are measurable, but the process by which the outputs are generated is not well defined. The planning and control system for such revenue centers would therefore focus on the level of output generated, with only secondary attention to the relationship between inputs and outputs.

The product manager of industrial products has one important managerial decision to make that results in his or her responsibility center's being very different from the residential products center. The fact that this manager controls the pricing decision means that he or she can influence the dollars of revenue generated by manipulating two factors: price and volume. The product manager of Residential Products could affect revenue by manipulating only one factor — volume — because the pricing decision was made by the marketing manager.

The control of price and volume makes the industrial products center more complex than a revenue center. Should advertising expenditures be increased if additional revenue can be generated by increased prices that are made possible because of a better image? If 10,000 units of a meter can be sold at $15 apiece and 15,000 units can be sold at $10 apiece, what is the right decision?

The product manager of industrial products has to balance inputs and outputs to arrive at the most profitable combination of selling price, marketing and production costs, and units sold. To evaluate this responsibility center purely or primarily on revenue generated would be undesirable. We have to determine the contribution to the organization's profits made by this responsibility center. In order to do this, we have to place an appropriate value on the meters supplied to this department. Thus we get a type of responsibility center called a contribution center, where both the inputs (marketing expenses, goods provided for sale) and outputs (revenue generated) are measurable in monetary terms. In such a center, the contribution it makes to the organization's profits is calculated as the difference between the revenue generated and the cost incurred, including the cost of the meters supplied by the manufacturing department.

In chapter 11, we shall discuss how to specify the cost of the meters so that the firm's profits are maximized by the decisions taken by the product manager of industrial products. The correct determination of the transfer price of meters from manufacturing to the contribution center is relatively simple, but in my experience, most firms that employ contribution centers set the transfer price in ways that lead to incorrect decision making by the managers of these contribution centers.

To summarize, the important characteristics of a revenue center are the following:

1. The inputs are objectively and easily measurable in quantitative, physical (but nonmonetary) terms.

2. The outputs are objectively and easily measurable in monetary (dollar) terms.

3. The process by which inputs are converted into outputs are not very well defined, and individual salespeople can employ subtly or radically different methods.

4. The focus of planning and control is on the outputs (revenue) generated, in the context of a given quantity of goods being available for sale.

5. The center basically belongs to the type II category of the process-output matrix.

The important characteristics of a contribution center are the following:

1. It is basically a revenue center where the inputs are converted to a monetary value by the use of an appropriately determined transfer price for valuing the goods provided by manufacturing to the center.

2. The focus of planning and control is on the difference between the revenue generated and the costs incurred (that is, the contribution to the organization's profits made by the contribution center).

3. It is basically a type II subunit as defined by the process-output matrix.

Staff and Service Responsibility Centers

The maintenance shop under the manufacturing manager, the personnel department, and the accounting department are in the nature of type III subunits. Their outputs are difficult to measure, but the activities or processes they are expected to carry out are fairly well defined. For all of them, however, their inputs are readily measurable in monetary (dollar) terms. They are therefore expense centers.

An important difference between these expense centers and the three other expense centers (foundry, machine shop, and assembly shop) is that the relationship between inputs and outputs in the case of staff and service units is a matter of judgment. The amount of money that the personnel manager should spend on salaries and wages, supplies, and other expenses cannot be determined by means of a formula. Managerial discretion has to be exercised—for instance, regarding the caliber and quality of people to be hired. Consequently these expense centers (where the amount of inputs consumed in order to generate the desired, often intangible outputs is a matter of judgment) are called discretionary expense centers. They have the following characteristics:

1. Their inputs are objectively and easily measurable in monetary (dollar) terms.
2. Their outputs are difficult to measure, often intangible, and cannot be measured in monetary (dollar) terms.
3. The process by which inputs are converted into outputs is usually not well defined.
4. The optimal relationship between inputs and outputs cannot be specified objectively.
5. They usually belong to the type III category of the process-output matrix.

Planning and controlling in the case of discretionary expense centers pose special problems. A variety of methods are widely used however, and these are listed and discussed in detail in chapter 11.

The Organization as a Responsibility Center

The organization as a whole has characteristics different from the responsibility centers discussed previously. In essence, the organization is the sum of all the responsibility centers within it. The inputs employed by the organization as a whole are best measured in monetary (dollar) terms. Its outputs are represented by the profit (dollars) that it generates. The organization as a whole is appropriately labeled a profit center. It is essentially a type II unit in that the process by which profits are generated is complex and cannot readily be optimized, while the outputs are quantifiable and measurable.

The key to designing a budgeting system for a profit center lies in designing a process that

> Identifies the range of alternatives available to the organization and selects the alternative that represents the optimal matching of the organization's resources and environmental opportunities.

> Precisely defines what is expected of managers of responsibility centers so as to ensure that each supports the other in the implementation of the chosen alternative.

> Recognizes and responds to shortcomings within the organization or changes in its environment so that midcourse corrections that are needed are made.

> Accomplishes the above while recognizing that human beings with a variety of motivations and capabilities are involved.

Designing such a process for profit centers is the essence of management control. Before embarking on the design of the operational plan or the profit or master budget that is the linchpin of management control in functional organizations, we shall quickly review the design of the information systems and the management planning and control practices appropriate to expense centers, revenue centers, and contribution centers.

To summarize the classification scheme and its application to AIM, each responsibility center must have a manager in charge and should be significant enough to have a material influence on the organization's profit picture. The responsibility centers are classified in figure 8–4.

The initial classification of responsibility centers is necessarily tentative. Experience with the system of management control will soon indicate whether more responsibility centers need to be created or whether what is currently a revenue center should be converted into a contribution center, and so on. The classification, though it requires judgment, is important; appropriate planning and control techniques for these responsibility centers have to be selected based on whether they are engineered expense centers or discretionary expense centers, revenue centers or contribution centers. The responsibility centers in AIM are identified and classified below in table 8–1.

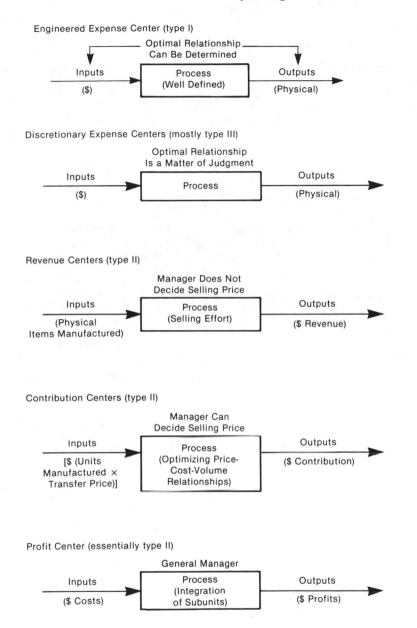

Figure 8-4. Responsibility Centers

Table 8–1
Classification of AIM's Responsibility Centers

Responsibility Center	Manager	Classification	Type
Foundry	Foreman	Engineered expense center	I
Machine shop	Foreman	Engineered expense center	I
Assembly shop	Foreman	Engineered expense center	I
Maintenance	Foreman	Discretionary expense center	III
Manufacturing	Manufacturing manager	Primarily engineered expense center with discretionary elements	I/II
Residential sales	Product manager	Revenue center	II
Industrial sales	Product manager	Contribution center	II
Marketing	Marketing manager	Contribution center	II
Accounting	Chief accountant	Discretionary expense center	III
Personnel	Personnel manager	Discretionary expense center	III
Total organization	General manager	Profit center	II

9
The Design of the Information System

The management control system relies on the information or reporting system in the same way as the body relies on the central nervous system. Effective management control requires well-designed reporting systems.

An information system cannot and should not be designed to meet an organization's total information needs. When designing information systems for corporations in the public sector in India, I frequently used to be asked whether the management information system (MIS) would enable the corporation to answer questions asked by members of Parliament. To try to anticipate the range of possible questions stemming from the variety of motivations of members of Parliament would have meant systems of inordinate complexity and cost.

In identifying a feasible and appropriate focus for the MIS, it is useful to keep in mind three characteristics of the information required to manage the organization: the information can be quantitative and objective or qualitative and subjective; it can be required routinely and regularly or nonroutinely and unpredictably; and it can be derived from internal or external sources.

The first characteristic—whether the information is quantitative or qualitative in nature—is important in that quantitative information is easier to verify, aggregate, and handle with electronic data-processing equipment. Whether the information is routine or nonroutine is important because including nonroutine information of unpredictable value in the system is difficult and expensive. Finally, internal information can be more easily fashioned to meet the organization's requirements in terms of content, frequency, and timing of availability.

These three important characteristics can be employed to classify the information into eight categories, as illustrated in figure 9–1. Although all eight categories are undoubtedly important, the most important one from the point of view of the formal MIS required for management control (as distinct from strategic planning) is the quantitative, routine, internal information. This key category is the hatched cell in figure 9–1.

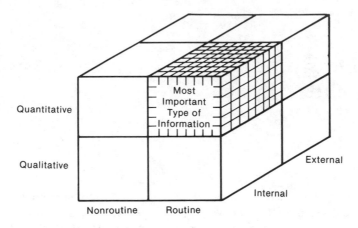

Figure 9–1. Key Characteristics of Information for Management Control

Qualitative information is perhaps best handled through oral communications and, possibly, semistructured letters at specified intervals from managers. For instance, at AIM, qualitative information can be communicated from subordinate to superior at performance review meetings. Senior salespeople reporting to the product manager of industrial products could be required to write monthly or quarterly letters to the manager, in addition to the routine weekly or monthly quantitative reports. These letters could focus on prospective new customers, expected requests for quotations in the next month or quarter, competitors' activities, customers' reactions to advertisements, product design and quality, and any other developments that may be of value in planning the manufacture and marketing of industrial meters.

Nonroutine information should normally be excluded from the formal data base of the MIS. Most nonroutine information is required during the course of strategic planning or annual operational planning exercises or when unexpected problems or opportunities arise, and it can be obtained as needed. To include all conceivable information requirements in the formal MIS is highly undesirable and violates basic design principles.

Identifying Information Requirements

In order to identify the quantitative, routine, internal information needed to control the organization's operations, the input-process-output model of the organization and its responsibility centers is of great value. The design of the MIS is best initiated in the context of any one of the lowest levels of responsibility centers. For instance, for AIM, we can select the foundry or machine shop or either of the product managers. In selecting the first responsibility center to work with, it is best to choose a center with whose operations one is most familiar.

In order to describe fully the operations of a responsibility center, it is necessary to identify the following measures or indicators of performance:

1. Input measures: These measures track the resources consumed or costs incurred by the responsibility center.

2. Work-load measures: These relate to the level of activity or the amount of effort invested in the operations of the responsibility center.

3. Output measures: These are the amount of goods, services, or revenues produced or provided by the responsibility center.

4. Effectiveness measures: These assess the extent to which the goals of the responsibility center are achieved. In some responsibility centers (such as production units), effectiveness measures and output measures are similar (number or value of items produced); in others they may be different. For instance, in a contribution center, sales revenue is an output measure, and dollars of contribution to the organization's profits is an effectiveness measure.

5. Efficiency measures: These are the ratio of outputs and effectiveness to input and work-load measures.

These five types of measures adequately describe the operations of any responsibility center. It is useful to keep this framework in mind because it can be applied systematically to ensure an adequate reporting system. Without it, we would have to rely on experience and familiarity with operations to develop rules of thumb regarding appropriate measures. For instance, without this framework, one would have to operate with guidelines developed on experience such as, for production units, keeping track of costs, quality, delivery performance, and volume. Often such guidelines are not available and are sometimes not comprehensive. Lists of typical measures for various types of responsibility centers follow:

Measures for Engineered Expense Centers
(Production Units)

Input
    Costs: Direct material; direct labor (regular and overtime); overhead (indirect labor, regular and overtime; supplies; other expenses, such as utilities); estimates of inventory (raw material and work-in-process) carrying charges.

Resources: Labor hours, machine time, Inventories (raw material, work-in-process).

Work load
Total number of units worked on (assuming units are comparable).
Standard cost of work-in-process, rejected work, and finished goods (where multiple products are made).

Output
Number of units of finished goods (in single-product situations).

Effectiveness
Delivery delays.
Backlog of work orders.
Rejects or rework (in units and dollars).
Absenteeism.
Employee grievances (number of and disposition).
Personnel turnover rates.
Customer complaints traceable to this responsibility center.
Accidents (number of and severity indexes).

Efficiency
Cost variances: Materials (price, quantity or yield), labor (rate, efficiency), overhead (controllable, volume).
Idle time: Labor (by reasons), machines (by causes).
Capacity utilization.
Inventories (expressed as days of production): Raw materials, work-in-process.

Measures for Discretionary Expense Centers (Staff and Service Units)

Each discretionary expense center requires unique measures of performance. Input and work-load measures usually pose no problem, but care must be taken in developing output and effectiveness measures. Outputs such as people recruited and trained (personnel); letters, briefs, and court cases handled (legal); and new designs and blueprints (design), although readily identifiable, may be misleading because no indication of quality or timeliness is implicit or explicit in these measures. Effectiveness measures are important but hard to develop. Often one will have to rely on negative indicators of effectiveness such as complaints from the users of the outputs of these responsibility centers. A variety of special approaches to managing discretionary expense centers will be identified in chapter 11.

Measures for Revenue Centers (Sales Units)

Input
> Units of goods for sale.
> Marketing expenses: Salaries, commissions, distribution and freight, advertising and promotion.

Work load
> Number of calls on customers.
> Number or weight of units transported.
> Freight costs.

Output
> Sales revenue.
> Units sold.
> Order backlog.
> New customers.

Effectiveness
> Sales revenue.
> Units sold.
> Repeat customers.
> Returns and allowances.
> Customer complaints.
> Market share.

Efficiency
> Marketing expenses as percentage of sales.
> Receivables expressed as days of sales.
> Inventories expressed as days of sales.
> Returns as percentage of sales.
> Sales ÷ salespersons
> Sales ÷ customers
> Sales ÷ customer calls

Measures for Contribution Centers (Marketing Units)

These are similar to the measures for revenue centers, with the following additions:

Inputs: Value of production provided for sale.

Work load: Number or value of quotations or bids made.

Output: Number and value of quotations or bids accepted.

Effectiveness: Contribution (sales revenue − marketing costs − transfer price of units sold).

Efficiency: Orders obtained as percentage of number and value of quotations or bids made.

Measures for Profit Centers (Firm as a Whole)

Profit centers usually incorporate expense and revenue or contribution centers. Many measures could be selected from among those already identified for these expense and revenue and contribution centers.

Inputs
  Aggregate of costs incurred by subunit responsibility centers.
  Corporate overhead.

Work load
  Selected measures from individual subunit responsibility centers.

Outputs
  Sales revenue.
  Unit sold (number).
  Order backlog.
  Units produced or standard cost of production.
  New customers.

Effectiveness
  Profits (in dollars and growth rate).
  Market share (current and growth rate).
  Personnel and morale: Absenteeism, turnover, overtime, disputes or grievances, accidents.
  Stock price-to-earnings ratio.
  Weighted average cost of capital.
  Debt coverage.
  Capital expenditure-to-depreciation ratio.
  R&D-to-discretionary-expenses ratio.
  Capital projects audit (estimated time and cost to complete).

Principles of Design

The preceding framework suggests the kinds of quantitative, routine, internal information that should be part of the MIS. Experience has suggested a few vital guiding principles to increase the effectiveness with which this information is reported and acted upon. The guidelines deriving from these principles can be used to assess quickly the quality of existing information systems.

The first principle is that information gathering and dissemination should be kept to a minimum, for two reasons. The obvious reason is that information is expensive not only in terms of the time and effort devoted to collection, analysis, and presentation but also in terms of the time wasted by executives on unimportant and trivial information. To the extent that management attention is diverted from the most appropriate priorities, irrelevant or less important information results in great cost to the firm. In addition, information must be kept to a minimum to ensure that managers can fully comprehend the material. Human capabilities are limited; the mind cannot readily absorb and understand large amounts of information. Thus the MIS designer would be doing an inadequate job if insufficient attention was paid to ensuring that the outputs of the MIS can be understood and acted upon by the concerned executives.

Too much information is often almost as bad as no information at all. For instance, in a large telecommunications organization, the chief executive received about three hundred reports from each of fifty geographic units. It was impossible for the chief executive to assimilate, let alone act upon, this mass of information. Everything that the chief executive needed to know was included but difficult to locate. By employing the techniques described in this chapter, we were able to eliminate this overload of information and reduce it to just one two-page monthly report. Later evaluations of the new MIS were extremely positive. For the first time, the chief executive and other managers received key information in quantities that enabled them to identify and remedy problems.

The second guiding principle is that information contained in formal, routine reports should be tailored to the specific requirements of individual recipients. Although the needs of each manager are unique, a well-designed MIS will present characteristics that enable it to be adapted to individual purposes. The content and frequency of reports should show certain trends based on the hierarchical level of the managers. For instance, in AIM, managers of the lowest level (the foundry and machine shop) of responsibility centers would tend to receive reports frequently, say daily or weekly, with much detail focusing on physical rather than monetary measures. Managers at the next level (manufacturing manager, marketing manager) would receive reports less frequently, say weekly or monthly, with more aggregated information and with a greater emphasis on monetary indicators. At the level of the general manager, reports might be prepared monthly or quarterly, with even more financial content and less detail. In a well-designed MIS, the frequency of formal reports should decrease as we go up in the hierarchy, and the content also changes with an increasing bias toward financial rather than physical information.

The tailoring of information to the needs of the recipient might be a demanding exercise but is well worth carrying out and it supports the first principle of MIS design: minimizing the information generated. It is useful to work closely with the recipients in identifying what is important to them.

The third principle of good MIS design is that critical variables and key result areas should be explicitly identified and employed in the design of formal reports. The concept of key result areas is based on the finding that the effectiveness of every firm and every responsibility center is determined by a critical few of its numerous activities. If four or five selected indicators or critical variables can be identified that reflect how these key activities are being performed, then managers can draw reasonable conclusions about their units' effectiveness.

To illustrate, the short-term and long-term effectiveness of a hotel can be readily assessed by tracking just two or three critical variables. The room occupancy rate is the most important and entirely adequate indicator of short-term profitability. Long-term profitability, especially when competition exists, is influenced by the quality of service, which can be measured by the number and kind of complaints from guests and the frequency of repeat visits by guests. In chemical process industries, the yield ratio (output ÷ input) and frequency and duration of breakdowns are the critical variables. In most industries, market share is a key overall indicator of effectiveness.

The identification and use of critical variables reinforces the application of the previous two principles: the amount of information needed to describe performance is minimized, and reports are tailored to the characteristics and needs of each responsibility center.

The three principles serve not only as a guide to design but also as a means of assessing the quality of the design of existing information systems. If the design of the existing MIS does not reflect the application of these principles, then a careful and comprehensive redesign may be required.

A few important technical considerations can greatly improve the value of the MIS for planning and control. Each of these is discussed below.

Multiple Dimensions of Information

Each piece of information that is part of an MIS can possess several dimensions; that is, it can be looked at in many ways. In AIM, for example, let us assume that an expense of $1,000 was incurred. The amount of the expense is one dimension of the information. This expense may have been incurred by and included in the report of the responsibility center headed by the product manager of industrial products. The information now possesses two dimensions: the amount of the expense and the responsibility center that incurred it. The report may also indicate that the $1,000 was spent on travel. The traveling may have been done by the salesperson operating on the West

Coast. We now have three further dimensions: the purpose of incurring the expense, the geographic area in which it was incurred, and the level of the person incurring the expense. A sixth dimension could be the time period (the month in which the expense was incurred). The type of customer being contracted could be a seventh dimension, and so on.

The illustration serves to suggest that the number and type of dimensions for any piece of information is dependent on the analyses needed to manage the responsibility center. The MIS designer needs to determine what dimensions are of importance and should be recorded. If several dimensions are of importance, one might consider the use of electronic data processing so as to facilitate the coding, retrieval, and analysis of the various dimensions of information. In my opinion, this capability of electronic data processing (and computers) is even more important than the potential improvements in timeliness and accuracy of information reporting that result from the use of computers.

Timeliness versus Accuracy

One of the most commonly encountered decisions in the design of the MIS is the choice between timeliness and accuracy of information. It is often possible to approximate performance figures before final, accurate, legally acceptable figures are obtained. I believe that if there is a question as to which figures are to be used in an MIS — approximate, speedily obtained information or accurate, delayed information — the question should be resolved in favor of approximate, timely information. For instance, from a managerial standpoint, obtaining approximate financial statements within a week after the close of an accounting period is more useful than getting accurate statements that will satisfy an external auditor two months later.

Treating dispatches from warehouses as equivalent to sales may be appropriate when designing an MIS for a high-volume, low-margin business, though this practice is unacceptable to traditional accountants. Estimations of changes in work-in-process may be unnecessary for production units where the work-in-process is either stable or small in amount. In such production units, tracking finished goods alone would be an entirely satisfactory estimate of work load or output from a managerial point of view.

The possibility of using early warning indicators should be considered. Most information systems record historical performance. The concept of leading indicators, which has been widely accepted and used in the context of macroeconomics, has received little attention in the context of the performance of individual firms. For instance, monitoring employee grievances and absenteeism may enable managers to recognize and remedy morale problems that might have resulted in debilitating rates of turnover in personnel. Age analyses of accounts receivable might signal emerging cash flow problems before they actually occur. Analysis of increases in customer complaints may reveal quality or design problems that could cause severe profit problems if they are not immediately rectified.

It is possible to identify potential problems and make sure they do not occur if the system is well designed. A subsidiary of a multinational pharmaceutical firm used to base its marketing and sales reports on an analysis of invoices. Thus, sales in April would be analyzed in May, and suitable managerial action would be taken to correct problems that had occurred in April. This practice, which was typical of most other firms in the industry, was changed when their MIS was redesigned. The new marketing and sales reports included analyses based on indents (requisitions) from the firm's distributors, received twice monthly, by the fifth and twentieth day of each month. Production schedules were developed based on these indents, and goods were dispatched by the fifteenth and thirtieth day of each month. With the introduction of the new reports based on the indents received in, say, April, the marketing managers could compare the volume indented by the fifth day to the planned sales for the month of April and take actions in April itself that would influence the second indent received in the month. The sales representatives in each territory were informed of the products they were expected to emphasize, and sometimes product promotions or discounts were speedily initiated so as to influence the second set of indents in April. Thus, a simple change in the MIS enabled the marketing manager to take immediate actions in April to remedy shortcomings. This would have been impossible under the old system, which permitted action only in May, after the problems had occurred.

Tracking Trends

Information about the performance of a responsibility center at a particular point in time or for a single accounting period is undoubtedly of value. If information about trends in performance is available, however, managerial planning and control is greatly facilitated. Keeping track of performance over several reporting periods enables managers more readily to identify causes of good and bad performance. Also, future performance can be more reliably and accurately forecasted if records of past trends are available.

The importance of recording trends cannot be overstated. Random events will inevitably influence performance. To react to every deviation in performance is counterproductive. In ITT, for example, senior managers do not step in to question or remedy the performance of a responsibility center unless a two- or three-month trend indicates a continuing, identifiable, non-random problem.

Information reports therefore should contain information not only about the immediately past period but also year-to-date performance. An even better approach is to include information about the past for a whole year, updated in each report on a rolling basis.

Format Design

The Single Report Approach

It is useful to attempt to provide all the information pertaining to a responsibility center in a report consisting of just one page or at least in a single report. There are two important reasons why there should be a single report incorporating all the indicators of performance for a reporting period, rather than several reports received at various points in time.

The first is that the endeavor to include all relevant information in a single short report requires the identification of critical variables, the tailoring of information to the recipients' needs, and the minimization of the information provided. In short, the three principles of good design mentioned earlier would necessarily have to be followed.

The second, and more important, reason is that providing all relevant indicators of performance in a single report helps the recipient comprehend and integrate the information. For instance, at AIM, valuable information for the assembly shop foreman would be overtime figures in hours and dollars. If the foreman also received absenteeism figures simultaneously, he or she is both enabled and encouraged to assess the extent to which unexpected absenteeism affected the overtime figure. Furthermore, if the level of activity, or work-load figures, is also provided at the same time, each item of information takes on significantly greater meaning than would any one item alone provided in separate reports and generated at a different time in each reporting period. On receiving all three items of information simultaneously, the foreman can analyze the extent to which overtime wages have resulted from worker absenteeism, from the work load, and from inefficiency. Appropriate remedial action can now be reliably identified and taken.

This example illustrates the advantage of providing comprehensive information in a single report. If the foreman received various pieces of information at different times, he or she would have to make a greater effort to gain an overall, integrated view of operations—and perhaps would be unable to do so.

There is one disadvantage to employing a single report: the work load of the department running the MIS can be very great at particular times. If indicators of performance were split into groups and provided by means of staggered reports generated at various times, the work load of the MIS department or personnel would be more stable. The advantages of a single report need to be weighed against this disadvantage. In my opinion, the single report is the preferred method.

Financial and Physical Information

Financial and physical indicators of performance should be separated in a report. Every item of financial information in the firm necessary has to be linked. For instance, the salaries and wages of the responsibility centers under the marketing manager have to be added to those incurred by the responsibility centers under the manufacturing manager, the chief accountant, and the personnel manager in order to obtain the salaries and wages of all personnel reporting to the general manager of AIM. Similarly, every other item of costs and revenues needs to be linked in order to obtain the financial picture for AIM as a whole.

In contrast, physical indicators of performance tend to be relevant to only one or two levels in the organization's hierarchy and to individual functional areas such as marketing or personnel. The number of distributors visited by the sales representatives reporting to the product manager of residential products is not of much value at the level of the general manager. The manufacturing manager would find such information entirely irrelevant.

Therefore, if physical and financial data are kept separate, the linkages between the reports going to the various managers of the responsibility centers of the organization can be more easily designed. The aggregation of financial information in particular is facilitated by this practice.

Applying ABC Analysis

If the amount of detail in a reporting format appears excessive—the number of rows (for instance, account heads) and columns (for instance, products) seem to be too many—the ABC analysis technique can be effectively applied. If, for example, there are twenty headings of accounts in which expenses incurred by the assembly shop are categorized, normally four or five (20 percent) of them will include a substantial proportion (as much as 80 percent) of the expenses. The remaining fifteen or sixteen headings can be conveniently aggregated into a single category. By employing ABC analysis, the reports can be designed to provide all relevant and significant information while minimizing the possibility of information overload.

Exception Reporting

The exception principle or management by exception is fundamental to the effective use of an MIS. Essentially management by exception means that only occurrences that merit managerial concern and action are brought to the attention of managers. In order to identify exceptions, the standard or normal expectation must be identified. The following chapters discuss the appropriate methods for setting standards for individual activities within responsibility centers, specifying performance expectations for the responsibility centers, and developing the master or profit budget for the organizationa as a whole.

The exception principle requires that the reporting formats identify the difference or variance between these standards, expectations, and budgets and actual performance. By scanning these variances, a manager can identify which activities or operations require further analysis and remedial action.

In order to minimize the number of columns in the report, all three pieces of information (actual, budget, and variance) need not be provided. The actual and variance information are sufficient. The budget figures are implicit and can be easily calculated if the recipient so desires.

Routing the Reports

It is not uncommon for managers to request that reports going to all their subordinates be provided to them. The general manager in AIM, for instance, might be inclined to ensure that all reports, including those intended for the foreman and product managers, be provided to him. But this practice is not entirely desirable because it can cause information overload.

Each manager should receive the report specifically designed for him or her and the reports intended for managers reporting directly to him or her—not those for all subordinates. The general manager in AIM should get his or her own report and those intended for the manufacturing manager, marketing manager, chief accountant, and personnel manager but not those for the foremen. The manufacturing manager would get his or her own report and the reports going to the foremen.

This practice reduces the likelihood of information overload. It also recognizes the reality that managers often require more detail about particular aspects of the operations in their charge. Thus, the general manager would have the marketing manager's report available if there are more details about the marketing operations that he or she might want to know in a particular reporting period. The likelihood of the general manager's needing the detail in the reports going to the product manager is remote. Such details are best provided by the marketing manager. To provide the product managers' reports to the general manager would therefore be unnecessary, if not undesirable.

Examples of Reports

In order to illustrate the application of the principles and techniques of design presented in this chapter, two examples of forms that could be used in the AIM context are included. Reporting forms for the manufacturing manager (figure 9–2) and the product manager of industrial products (figure 9–3) provide illustrations relating to different hierarchical levels and functional areas.

MONTH: YEAR:

TOTAL MANUFACTURING				FINANCIAL PERFORMANCE ($ × 000)		FOUNDRY				MACHINE SHOP				ASSEMBLY				MAINTENANCE			
YEAR TO DATE		CURRENT PERIOD				YEAR TO DATE		CURRENT PERIOD		YEAR TO DATE		CURRENT PERIOD		YEAR TO DATE		CURRENT PERIOD		YEAR TO DATE		CURRENT PERIOD	
ACTUAL	VARIANCE	ACTUAL	VARIANCE			ACT.	VAR.	ACT.	VAR.	ACT.	VAR.	ACT.	VAR.	ACT.	VAR.	ACT.	VAR.	ACT.	VAR.	ACT.	VAR.
				LABOR COMPENSATION																	
				LABOR-RELATED BENEFITS																	
				RAW MATERIAL CONSUMPTION																	
				SUPPLIES & SMALL TOOLS																	
				UTILITIES																	
				OTHER OPERATING EXPENSE																	
				TOTAL MFG. EXPENSES																	
				OPERATIONAL (PHYSICAL) INDICATORS																	
				HEAD COUNT	DIRECT																
					INDIRECT																
					TOTAL																
				CAPACITY UTILIZATION (%)																	
				ABSENTEEISM (%)																	
				OVERTIME	$																
					HOURS																
				DOWN-TIME	BREAK-DOWNS																
					LACK OF OPERATOR																
					LACK OF R.M.																
					TOTAL																
				ACCIDENTS	$																
					SEVERITY																
				GRIEVANCES INITIATED																	
				WORK-IN-PROCESS INVENTORY																	
				RAW MATERIAL INVENTORY																	
				PRODUCTION VOLUME																	

Copy to: General Manager

Figure 9–2. Performance Report for Manufacturing Manager

MONTH: _____   YEAR: _____

FINANCIAL PERFORMANCE		YEAR TO DATE TOTAL		TOTAL		PRODUCT TYPE 1		PRODUCT TYPE 2		OTHER PRODUCT TYPES	
		ACTUAL	VARIANCE	ACTUAL	VARIANCE	ACTUAL	VARIANCE	ACTUAL	VARIANCE	ACTUAL	VARIANCE
NORTH-EAST REGION	REVENUE										
	TRANSFER PRICE OF GOODS SOLD										
	CONTRIBUTION MARGIN										
	RELATED REGIONAL EXPENSES										
	ADJUSTED REGIONAL CONTRBN. MARGIN										
MID-WEST REGION	REVENUE										
	TRANSFER PRICE OF GOODS SOLD										
	CONTRIBUTION MARGIN										
	RELATED REGIONAL EXPENSES										
	ADJUSTED REGIONAL CONTRBN. MARGIN										
WEST REGION	REVENUE										
	TRANSFER PRICE OF GOODS SOLD										
	CONTRIBUTION MARGIN										
	RELATED REGIONAL EXPENSES										
	ADJUSTED REGIONAL CONTRBN. MARGIN										
SOUTH-WEST REGION	REVENUE										
	TRANSFER PRICE OF GOODS SOLD										
	CONTRIBUTION MARGIN										
	RELATED REGIONAL EXPENSES										
	ADJUSTED REGIONAL CONTRBN. MARGIN										
TOTAL REGIONAL CONTRIBUTION MARGIN											
PRODUCT MANAGER'S OVERHEAD											
CONTRIBUTION BEFORE MARKETING AND CORPORATE OVERHEADS											

NEXT MONTH REVENUE FORECAST	N.E.	
	M-W.	
	W.	
	S.W.	
	TOTAL	

Copy to: Marketing Manager

Figure 9–3. Performance Report for Product Manager of Industrial Products

SALES PERFORMANCE

	YEAR TO DATE ACTUAL	YEAR TO DATE VARIANCE	CURRENT PERIOD ACTUAL	CURRENT PERIOD VARIANCE
CALLS PER SALESPERSON				
N.E.				
M-W.				
W.				
S.W.				
TOTAL				
SELLING EXPENSES TO SALES RATIO				
N.E.				
M-W.				
W.				
S.W.				
TOTAL				
CONTRIBUTION MARGIN TO SALES (%)				
N.E.				
M-W.				
W.				
S.W.				
TOTAL				
CONTRIBUTION MARGIN VARIANCE DUE TO PRODUCT MIX ($)				
N.E.				
M-W.				
W				
S.W.				
TOTAL				
CONTRIBUTION MARGIN VARIANCE DUE TO PRICE CHANGE ($)				
N.E.				
M-W.				
W.				
S.W.				
TOTAL				
CONTRIBUTION MARGIN VARIANCE DUE TO VOLUME ($)				
N.E.				
M-W.				
W.				
S.W.				
TOTAL				
ORDERS BOOKED				
N.E.				
M-W.				
W.				
S.W.				
TOTAL				

	YEAR TO DATE ACTUAL	YEAR TO DATE VARIANCE	CURRENT PERIOD ACTUAL	CURRENT PERIOD VARIANCE
ORDER BACKLOG				
N.E.				
M-W.				
W.				
S.W.				
TOTAL				
NO. OF EMPLOYEES				
N.E.				
M-W.				
W.				
S.W.				
TOTAL				

ACCOUNTS RECEIVABLE ANALYSIS

AGE	TOTAL	N.E.	M-W.	W.	S.W.
< 31 days					
31–45 days					
46–60 days					
> 60 days					
TOTAL ACTUAL					
VARIANCE					

DISTRIBUTION PERFORMANCE

INDICATORS	YEAR TO DATE AVERAGE ACTUAL	YEAR TO DATE AVERAGE VARIANCE	CURRENT PERIOD ACTUAL	CURRENT PERIOD VARIANCE
TOTAL FREIGHT EXPENSES ($)				
DELIVERY DELAYS (#)				
DELIVERY DELAYS ($)				
FREIGHT AS % OF SALES VALUE				

N.E. = Northeast
M-W. = Midwest
W. = West
S.W. = Southwest

Figure 9–3. Continued

10
Determining Performance Expectations: Standards and Budgets

Management control can be exercised only if benchmarks exist against which actual performance can be assessed. For the organization as a whole, the strategic planning exercise provides the basis for developing performance expectations. The operational plan or master budget derived from and linked to the strategic planning exercise will be discussed in chapter 12. To arrive at such operational plans or master budgets, the performance expected of each responsibility center must also be defined. Performance expectations or benchmarks are based on standards that apply to discrete operations or individual activities within responsibility centers and budgets that recognize the widely varying characteristics of responsibility centers as a whole.

Standard Setting within Responsibility Centers

The first step toward specifying the benchmarks against which actual performance is to be assessed is to set standards for discrete operations or individual activities within responsibility centers. These activities or operations should be repetitive in nature and should possess clearly identifiable inputs and outputs. The process of converting inputs to outputs need not be well defined.

Activities with clearly identifiable inputs and outputs normally occur in engineered expense centers. AIM's foundry, machine shop, and assembly operations are examples of situations where formal standards can and should be specified. In the foundry, the output in terms of number of units to be obtained from a given weight of inputs would be a useful standard. The time needed to carry out various machining or assembly operations in the other two engineered expense centers would constitute a useful set of standards.

Repetitive activities with clearly defined inputs and outputs can be found in other types of responsibility centers too. In the maintenance shop, for instance, standards can be developed that specify the time within which specific preventive maintenance activities should be carried out. Standards can be set for the time and cost of supplies for breakdown maintenance activities that frequently occur. In rayon spinning plants, for instance, the electric motors that operate the spinning machines frequently break down because of acids employed in the process. The time required to replace a motor can and should be specified.

In revenue centers and contribution centers, the presale operations of customer relations, product specification, and quotation preparation are not suitable activities for developing standards. The postsale operations involving packaging, freight, and other distribution-related activities are situations where setting standards is desirable.

Judgment needs to be exercised in discretionary expense centers. Certain activities might be repetitive enough and important enough to justify setting standards for them. For example, standards may be appropriately used in the context of the preliminary screening of applications for junior positions. On the other hand, the management of grievances represents activities that are not readily susceptible to time standards. Similarly it would be meaningless to specify the briefs per workday to be generated by the legal department.

Need for Standards

It is not uncommon for managers to argue that the development of formally stated standards of performance for individual activities within responsibility centers is unnecessary. A plant manager working in a process industry once made this typical comment: "I am not really convinced of the need for standards. Just by walking through the plant, I can very easily tell whether everything is running as it should or not. Why go through all this rigmarole [of developing formal standards] when really it is unnecessary and unlikely to improve the performance of the plant?" Although there is an element of truth in such statements, they fail to recognize the variety of advantages to having formal standards.

First, formal standards contribute to the elimination of implicit, subjective, often unconscious biases. If the expected level of performance is to be formally and explicitly recorded and communicated, then it must be justifiable. Consequently the subjective and unjustifiable expectations of individual managers are more readily identified and hence corrected.

Second, formal standards contribute to the continuity of knowledge in the firm. A particular manager, on the basis of long experience, might have mentally arrived at an understanding of what is acceptable performance for various responsibility center activities. This knowledge might be lost to the firm if the manager leaves the firm or is promoted or transferred unless a written record of the standards has been maintained. Occasionally managers consciously avoid records of their operations so as to make themselves indispensable to the firm. Formal performance standards and records minimize these problems.

Third, formal standards of performance are an important means of communication within the firm. They reflect a common understanding between levels in the hierarchy of what constitutes acceptable performance. Standards also facilitate communication between interdependent departments such as sales and distribution or production and purchasing.

Fourth, standards are essential if management by exception is to be practiced. Deviations from expected performance cannot be identified or highlighted unless a clear understanding exists of what constitutes standard performance.

Fifth, formal standards facilitate the analysis of trends in performance. A manager may be able to assess how well a particular operation or activity is being carried out without formal standards. But in order to assess cumulative performance over a long period, formal records and standards are essential. Performance at a point of time may be the result of random events. Performance trends over suitable periods of time are necessary to ensure true understanding of what has been happening.

Sixth, formal standards can be employed as a motivational device. Standards that are relatively hard to achieve may stimulate greater efforts by individuals in certain firms. In other firms, standards may be consciously set at a low level to encourage new workers.

Seventh, standards are of immense value for planning, in addition to control. Standards of material usage and output per worker-hour, for instance, can greatly assist in the planning of materials purchases and worker recruitment and training.

Characteristics Leading to Acceptance of Standards

Based on an assessment of the benefits to be expected from setting standards, appropriate activities within each of the responsibility centers must be selected as candidates for standards. It will be necessary to go through the reporting formats designed for each responsibility center to determine which of the measures chosen represent repetitive, discrete activities with clearly defined inputs and outputs. Standards will have to be set for each of these measures. Before proceeding to select the appropriate techniques for setting these standards (these techniques are described later in this chapter), however, it is necessary to recognize what makes a standard acceptable or otherwise to the concerned personnel.

The importance of standards being acceptable to the personnel concerned cannot be overemphasized. One that is not acceptable to the individual performing the concerned activity and this individual's superior is perhaps even less desirable than having no standard at all. A standard that is not acceptable contributes to an erosion of commitment and motivation, leads to frequent disagreements, and detracts from the quality of managerial decision making.

The most important characteristic that leads to acceptance of a standard of performance is that it be perceived as fair and reasonable. Unfortunately the understanding of what is fair and reasonable varies depending on whether the person's performance is to be evaluated on the basis of the standard or whether he or she is to specify the standard of performance for a subordinate.

Top management would consider a standard to be fair and reasonable if it is as close as possible to ideal performance. Those being evaluated on the basis of the standard would consider it to be fair and reasonable if it appears to be easily attainable. Reconciling these two points of view is difficult. Any technique that is chosen as a means of developing standards should be applied with sensitivity, recognizing the need to arrive at a reasoned compromise between the conflicting expectations of superiors and subordinates. Some statistical techniques are particularly effective in arriving at acceptable compromises.

Classifying the Techniques

The number of possible techniques for developing standards is limited only by human ingenuity. Essentially the techniques are methods for arriving at an acceptable understanding of the relationships between inputs and outputs that exist under normal conditions when an operation or activity is carried out efficiently and effectively. Normal conditions recognize the resource limitations and other constraints that make actual performance less than the ideal. The relationships between inputs and outputs do not represent ideal performance, nor do they necessarily reflect the lowest acceptable level of performance, but they represent performance that requires a reasonable amount of effort and motivation by subordinates.

The numerous techniques that exist for developing standards can be usefully classified into three categories: theoretical and engineered approaches, historical and statistical approaches, and comparative and subjective approaches. Each of these categories possesses advantages and disadvantages that make them desirable or undesirable in particular contexts.

Theoretical and Engineered Approaches. These approaches assume that optimal input-output relationships can be calculated. Some differences exist between the theoretical approach and the engineered approach. An example of a standard developed by the theoretical approach is the output per hour of a machine, based on the manufacturer's specifications. The theoretical approach also finds ready application in chemical process industries where mass balances can be calculated. In other words, the theoretical approach is based on machine or process specifications.

The engineered approach is applicable to situations where human physical endeavors determine output and is based on industrial engineering techniques such as time and motion study. The engineered approach suffers from more than one disadvantage: it is expensive and time-consuming; it demands special technical expertise on the part of the individual having the responsibility for specifying the standard; and the individuals to be evaluated usually do not readily accept either the process of arriving at the standards or the actual standards specified. Engineered standards are often perceived as being arrived at without the workers' involvement and are consequently viewed with suspicion. This is extremely unfortunate because this approach is particularly applicable to situations where human endeavor primarily determines the level of output.

In situations where an atmosphere of trust and cooperation exists, engineered standards, or a combination of engineered and theoretical standards, would be appropriate. For instance, in the communication industry, the cost of making cable joints can be analyzed in terms of the materials (theoretical) and man-hours (engineered) required, and a standard can be arrived at for the cost of jointing cables of various sizes.

Historical and Statistical Approaches. These approaches find application in situations where input-output relationships cannot be specified on the basis of theoretical and engineered approaches or where theoretical and engineered approaches are unlikely to find acceptance. These approaches, however, assume that historical records of past performance are available.

The historical approach relies on the projection of trends in past performance to arrive at an understanding of an acceptable standard of performance. Not uncommonly, an arbitrary 5 to 10 percent improvement over past performance is also incorporated. This approach has the obvious limitation that unless past performance approximates optimal performance, past inefficiencies will be treated as acceptable. Also, an arbitrary determination of desired improvements in performance is likely to have a demotivating effect.

The statistical approach can be considerably more sophisticated than the historical approach. The well-known statistical quality control technique of setting control limits for a process can be usefully applied to the development of standards in operations where there are considerable variations in performance due to more than one cause.

This method could be used to develop standards of consumption for items such as spares and accessories that are consumed irregularly. Assuming that variations in consumption are primarily due to chance causes, quality of the items being consumed, and assignable causes independent of the first two and assuming that variations due to chance causes are so intractable that the difference between the savings arising out of their identification and the cost of identifying these causes would be insignificant if not negative, then it is a simple matter, if enough data are available, to determine statistically the cally the limits within which consumption would fall if there were no variations in quality. If consumption figures for an item fall outside the determined limits, it can be presumed with a calculable degree of confidence that the quality of the item is at fault.

Another statistical method of developing standards responds so well to the basic problems encountered in specifying standards that it merits careful consideration. Briefly, the steps involved in this method are as follows:

1. The relevant records containing the data for the immediately previous year would be examined thoroughly to identify cases of abnormally good or bad performance. The reasons for abnormal performance would be ascertained and when found to be due to uncontrollable factors (like machine malfunction, breakdowns, unusually poor or good quality of raw material or processing material, excessive loads arising out of rush orders), these readings would be excluded for the purpose of determining standards.

2. After the abnormal readings are eliminated, the remaining readings should be sorted out according to the level of performance achieved— that is, beginning from the highest level of performance downward.

3. The distribution indicated by the first thirty readings in this prioritized list (or a number of readings representing not less than 15 percent of the total sample) would be plotted.

4. If a range of acceptable performance is to be specified, then the highest and lowest readings remaining would define this standard range.

5. If a single value that represents acceptable performance is to be specified, then the average of the remaining readings would be the standard.

An example of this approach appears in tables 10–1 and 10–2. Table 10–1 presents the readings relating to the consumption in a foundry of a fluxing agent (chemical A) that is added to the molten metal to give the castings certain desired characteristics. The consumption of chemical A and the output (castings) are specified in kilograms. In order to arrive at the data presented in table 10–1, the 450 readings of the relationship between the consumption of chemical A and output that were taken over the past year were scanned to identify abnormal readings. Only 17 readings were found to be abnormal, leaving 433. These 433 readings were then ranked; the top 65 (15 percent of 433) are listed in the table.

In table 10–2, these 65 readings are regrouped into 18 categories by an arbitrary procedure that need not be carried out. In order to get an understanding of how these readings are distributed, however, we have found it useful to work with 15 to 20 groups of readings if there are large numbers of readings involved.

Table 10-1
Sixty-five Best Readings of Chemical A (Out of 433 Normal Readings Selected from 450 Readings)
(ratio of Chemical A to Output)

Sl. No.	Total Output (Kgs)	Chemical Consumption (Kgs)	Ratio	Rank	Sl. No.	Total Output (Kgs)	Chemical Consumption (Kgs)	Ratio	Rank
1.	809.8	3.0	0.00370	13	34.	460.2	4.5	0.00978	64
2.	611.3	2.5	0.00409	18	35.	722.5	4.0	0.00554	56
3.	615.0	2.5	0.00407	17	36.	687.5	3.5	0.00509	49
4.	945.4	3.0	0.00317	7	37.	776.7	3.5	0.00451	30
5.	746.3	3.0	0.00402	15	38.	484.3	2.0	0.00413	19
6.	653.6	3.0	0.00459	33	39.	588.5	2.5	0.00425	24
7.	745.1	1.5	0.00201	3	40.	556.6	2.0	0.00359	12
8.	827.3	3.5	0.00423	23	41.	622.6	3.0	0.00482	41
9.	1076.8	3.0	0.00279	6	42.	751.4	4.0	0.00532	54
10.	605.2	2.5	0.00413	20	43.	677.2	3.0	0.00443	25
11.	725.9	3.5	0.00482	40	44.	592.3	3.0	0.00507	48
12.	783.2	3.5	0.00447	27	45.	633.8	3.0	0.00473	38
13.	805.5	3.0	0.00372	14	46.	628.7	4.0	0.00636	58
14.	721.6	3.0	0.00416	21	47.	646.4	4.5	0.00696	61
15.	641.8	1.0	0.00156	1	48.	659.1	4.5	0.00683	60
16.	615.4	3.0	0.00487	44	49.	797.6	8.0	0.01003	65
17.	868.7	3.0	0.00345	9	50.	910.7	3.0	0.00329	8
18.	867.8	3.0	0.00346	10	51.	1049.9	5.5	0.00524	51
19.	629.1	1.5	0.00238	5	52.	637.3	3.0	0.00471	37
20.	660.7	3.0	0.00454	32	53.	783.2	3.5	0.00446	26
21.	652.0	3.0	0.00460	34	54.	892.7	4.0	0.00440	29
22.	470.6	2.5	0.00531	53	55.	559.7	2.5	0.00447	28

Table 10–1 (continued)

Sl. No.	Total Output (Kgs)	Chemical Consumption (Kgs)	Ratio	Rank	Sl. No.	Total Output (Kgs)	Chemical Consumption (Kgs)	Ratio	Rank
23.	477.4	2.0	0.00419	22	56.	722.5	2.5	0.00346	11
24.	482.6	4.0	0.00933	63	57.	638.0	3.0	0.00470	36
25.	664.4	4.5	0.00677	59	58.	993.3	4.5	0.00453	31
26.	530.7	4.0	0.00754	62	59.	719.5	3.5	0.00486	43
27.	704.0	3.5	0.00497	46	60.	719.5	3.5	0.00486	42
28.	538.8	2.5	0.00464	35	61.	709.5	3.5	0.00493	45
29.	688.7	1.5	0.00218	4	62.	800.8	4.0	0.00500	47
30.	505.5	1.0	0.00198	2	63.	761.9	4.0	0.00525	52
31.	629.2	3.0	0.00477	39	64.	708.1	4.0	0.00565	57
32.	577.6	3.0	0.00519	50	65.	831.0	4.5	0.00542	55
33.	620.7	2.5	0.00403	16					
					Total	45168.5	209.5	0.004638	

Table 10–2
Frequency Distribution of Sixty-Five Best Readings

Reading	Number of Times Read					
0.00151 – 0.00200	II					(2)
0.00201 – 0.00250	III					(3)
0.00251 – 0.00300	I					(1)
0.00301 – 0.00350	JHT					(5)
0.00351 – 0.00400	III					(3)
0.00401 – 0.00450	JHT	JHT	II			(12)
0.00451 – 0.00500	JHT	JHT	JHT	JHT	I	(21)
0.00501 – 0.00550	JHT	III				(8)
0.00551 – 0.00600	II					(2)
0.00601 – 0.00650	I					(1)
0.00651 – 0.00700	III					(3)
0.00701 – 0.00750						(0)
0.00751 – 0.00800	I					(1)
0.00801 – 0.00850						(0)
0.00851 – 0.00900						(0)
0.00901 – 0.00950	I					(1)
0.00951 – 0.01000	I					(1)
Above 0.01000						(0)

65 Readings
Average reading, 0.004638
Range of readings, 0.00156–0.01003

The average reading of 0.004638 could serve as the standard. Alternatively, if the standard is to be specified in terms of upper and lower limits of acceptable performance, these limits could be 0.00156 to 0.01003 (in table 10–1, see readings ranked 1 and 65). The advantage of plotting the readings as done in table 10–2 is that it is possible to get a visual understanding of past performance. By looking at table 10–2, one could determine that instead of using the average reading as the standard, the large number of readings falling within the group 0.0045 to 0.005 would indicate that the standard be the midpoint of this group: 0.00475. Alternatively, if determining the range of acceptable readings, one could specify this range to be 0.003 to 0.0055 because 49 of the 65 readings fall within it.

This method has a number of advantages:

1. It is much less expensive and time-consuming than approaches based on time and motion study.

2. The standard arrived at would represent a level of performance that had actually been achieved in the past and would therefore be acceptable from the point of view of feasibility of attainment.

3. It would represent a level of performance distinctly higher than past average performance and would therefore be acceptable in terms of improvement in performance.

4. Once the method is explained and understood, a feeling of participation could be generated on the part of individuals to be evaluated on the basis of the standard arrived at by having them develop the standard themselves.

5. Over time, if actual performance meets the standard specified and the standard is revised, then performance should gradually approach the optimal level.

There are, however, certain disadvantages inherent in the method. For instance, if management control is lax and performance is allowed to deteriorate, the standard, when reviewed, would also fall. Also, the method has no real justification from the statistical point of view and needs to be appreciated purely as a mechanism for arriving at an acceptable standard, which would be independent of the person employing the method.

The suggestion that not less than the best 15 percent of the normal readings be selected is of great importance. If less than 15 percent of the best readings are taken, the standard arrived at would represent a relatively higher level of performance; if more than 15 percent are taken, the standard will be lowered. In fact, if 100 percent of the normal readings are taken, the standard arrived at would represent the average performance in the period considered. Of course, the suggested figure of 15 percent is quite arbitrary, but I have found that it often represents a level of performance that demands extra effort from subordinates and yet is not too high to be discouraging.

Comparative and Subjective Approaches. These approaches are useful only in situations where the theoretical, engineered, statistical, and historical approaches cannot be applied. The comparative approach makes the assumption that the operation or activity for which standards are being developed are identical or very similar to operations or activities being performed in other locations or organizations. Consequently it is presumed that the standards set in these other situations can be applied to the operation or activity under study. The limitations of this approach are obvious. The subjective approach, as the name suggests, is essentially a judgmental, managerial assessment of what the standard should be.

But although these approaches possess severe limitations, they do have some uses. The comparative approach has been used by firms in developing countries when setting up industries that have been in existence in the more developed countries for substantial periods of time. The subjective approach is of value in situations where managerial decisions have to be made about matters such as the level and quality of service to be provided by customers in order to remain competitive. For instance, an airline might make a decision that any telephone call from a potential customer should be responded to within 20 seconds in order to ensure that the customer does not go to a competitor. Such a standard, while undoubtedly subjective and perhaps arbitrary, is of value in that it represents an assessment of the level of service that should be provided in order to remain in business.

It is important to remember that the standard-setting techniques discussed in this chapter are applicable only to activities within responsibility centers. In order to specify the expected performance of a responsibility center as a whole or overall profit performance of the organization, more complex techniques are required. Aggregated standards of performance, however, can greatly contribute to the development of a sound and acceptable budget for a responsibility center.

Budgeting for Responsibility Centers

In order to illustrate the process of budgeting for responsibility centers, we shall focus initially on the production function. The requirements of the various other kinds of responsibility centers will be discussed in chapter 11, although the principles and some of the techniques described in the context of the production budget will also apply in these other kinds of responsibility centers.

Production Budget

The performance reports for the responsibility centers that carry out the production function are a good place to start from when designing the production budget. These reports should identify the critical areas where expectations regarding satisfactory performance need to be stated. For the important individual activities within the responsibility centers, standards would have been set based on the methods suggested earlier in this chapter. For the responsibility center as a whole, particularly with regard to aggregate financial performance, the standard-setting technique discussed earlier in this chapter would be inappropriate.

In order to budget for expected performance during the next year or two (or whatever the chosen budget horizon is), the impact of several sets of factors is important. First, as in the historical and statistical methods of setting standards, the past performance of the responsibility center must be taken into account. Second, factors external to the responsibility center may significantly influence performance. For instance, a shortage of skilled machinists in the labor force could affect the performance capabilities of the machine shop. Third, the amount and kind of resources being made available to the responsibility center can affect performance. If extra lathes or milling machines are added to the machine shop, its aggregate performance capabilities will increase. Fourth, in describing aggregate performance of a responsibility center, the impact of normal changes on demand for the products should be considered. Aggregate performance in the winter months, when housing starts are reduced, would be different for AIM's residential meters compared to the peak activity periods in the spring and summer. Fifth, aggregate performance is affected by the detailed plans of action adopted by the managers of the various responsibility centers. The foreman of the assembly shop may decide to adopt new scheduling practices during the coming budget period. Perhaps additions to the work force will be scheduled at different times than in the past. The response to seasonal changes in the level of activity may be to level the work load of building inventories of residential meters during the winter. The usual lead time between receiving a special order for an industrial meter and making the delivery could perhaps be reduced by increasing the number of items stored in the raw materials inventories. The action plans of the managers are the heart of any budgetary system and need to be carefully developed. Finally, the production budget must be flexible so as to recognize the impact on performance of varying levels of activity caused by factors other than just the seasonality considerations mentioned.

Designing the Production Budget Format

The design of the production budget is not as complex as it might first appear if performance reports have already been designed. For purposes of illustration, we shall consider the machine shop in AIM.

The performance report for the machine shop is given in figure 10–1. To convert this performance report into a form for recording the budget for this responsibility center, the minimum that is needed is given in figure 10–2. The format in figure 10–2 is not recommended, although it is apparently adequate. There are several shortcomings to this format, but before analyzing them, two points need to be made.

First, the format assumes that the appropriate budget period is one year. This may or may not be suitable to every organization. In my opinion, one year is the minimum time horizon that should be considered, but in many situations a longer time period should be used. (The selection of an appropriate time period for each organization will be discussed in detail in chapter 12 in the context of the operational plan or master budget.) Second, operational indicators such as the number and severity of accidents and work orders delayed are not considered in the budget format. The presumption is that there will be no accidents or delays, that is, the budget for these kinds of

	WEEK:	MONTH:	YEAR:

		YEAR TO DATE		CURRENT PERIOD TOTAL		MILLING SECTION		OTHER MACHINES	
		ACTUAL	VARIANCE	ACTUAL	VARIANCE	ACTUAL	VARIANCE	ACTUAL	VARIANCE
FINANCIAL PERFORMANCE ($)									
LABOR	DIRECT								
COMPENSATION	INDIRECT								
	TOTAL								
LABOR RELATED BENEFITS									
DIRECT MATERIALS									
SUPPLIES & SMALL TOOLS									
UTILITIES									
REPAIRS & MAINTENANCE									
OTHER OPERATING EXPENSES									
TOTAL EXPENSES									
OPERATIONAL INDICATORS									
HEADCOUNT	DIRECT								
	INDIRECT								
	TOTAL								
CAPACITY UTILIZATION (%)									
ABSENTEEISM (%)									
OVERTIME	$								
	HOURS								
DOWNTIME	BREAKDOWNS								
(HOURS)	LACK OF OPERATOR								
	LACK OF R.M.								
	TOTAL								
ACCIDENTS	#								
	SEVERITY								
GRIEVANCES INITIATED									
WORK-IN-PROCESS INVENTORY									
PRODUCTION VOLUME									
WORK ORDERS DELAYED									

Copy to: Manufacturing Manager

Figure 10–1. AIM: Performance Report for Machine Shop Foreman

FINANCIAL PERFORMANCE ($)		TOTAL SHOP		LATHE SECTION		MILLING SECTION		OTHER MACHINES	
		ANNUAL BUDGET	Average WEEKLY BUDGET	ANNUAL BUDGET	Average WEEKLY BUDGET	ANNUAL BUDGET	Average WEEKLY BUDGET	ANNUAL BUDGET	Average WEEKLY BUDGET
LABOR COMPENSATION	DIRECT								
	INDIRECT								
	TOTAL								
LABOR RELATED BENEFITS									
DIRECT MATERIALS									
SUPPLIES & SMALL TOOLS									
UTILITIES									
REPAIRS & MAINTENANCE									
OTHER OPERATING EXPENSES									
TOTAL EXPENSES									
OPERATIONAL PERFORMANCE									
HEADCOUNT	DIRECT								
	INDIRECT								
	TOTAL								
CAPACITY UTILIZATION									
NORMAL ABSENTEEISM									
OVERTIME	$								
	HOURS								
WORK-IN-PROCESS INVENTORY									
PRODUCTION VOLUME									

Figure 10–2. Simplest Budget Format for AIM Machine Shop

indicators is zero. Other indicators such as machine downtime due to break-downs may perhaps be budgeted at a level above zero, but this is a matter of choice that is best made in the context of each organization. If it is unreasonable to expect that despite adhering strictly to specified preventive maintenance practices, breakdowns can be avoided, a standard expectation for breakdown hours should be included.

Proceeding to the shortcomings of the format in figure 10–2, there are several. First, the format does not give any indications of how reasonable the budget is in relation to the past performance levels. Second, external factors that significantly affect the performance of the responsibility center are not identified. Third, there is no formal recognition of any changes in the level or kind of resources that will be made available to the responsibility center. Fourth, assuming that performance is affected by seasonal factors, the average weekly performance recorded in the format could be meaningless. Fifth, there is no provision for stating the plans of the foreman for doing things differently or better. Sixth, there is no mechanism through which the impact on financial and operational performance of changes in the level of activity of the machine shop can be recognized and assessed. Finally and fundamentally, the format serves as nothing more than a convenient way of recording budget figures. It does not encourage or require that the managers developing these figures consider and analyze the various factors that are relevant to the development of truly meaningful budget figures.

The design of budgeting forms that force managers to recognize and analyze the factors that will affect the future performance of their responsibility centers can be accomplished by a step-by-step procedure. First, past performance should be taken into account. This can be achieved in the machine shop form in figure 10–2 by adding columns that report the shop's performance in the past two or three years. In order to force the foreman to recognize the trend, a column could be added where the percentage change over the past year is calculated. Including this information may require that more pages be added to the form. Thus the past trend and budget for the total machine shop could be on the first page and details for the lathe, milling, and other sections in subsequent pages.

The second step is to include external factors in the firm—perhaps the past and projected availability of skilled machinists. The product manager of residential products could keep track of housing starts as a powerful indicator of probable sales levels. In addition to such factors that may be external to the firm as a whole, each responsibility center must recognize its obligations and commitments to the other responsibility centers in the firm. For instance, the machine shop's production volume may be dictated by the projected deliveries of various kinds of meters derived from AIM's sales budgets. The foundry's production will be determined by the machine shop's planned schedule for the budget period. (The process of planning to ensure this communication between and integration of the responsibility centers in the firm will be discussed in chapter 12.) In terms of the budget format design, such commitments to the other responsibility centers must be highlighted. The machine shop may accomplish this by emphasizing the critical importance of the production volume estimates in figure 10–2 and by supporting these estimates with more detail about the type of jobs likely to be carried out.

The third step is to identify the levels of availability of key resources in order to recognize the impact of internal top management decisions. For instance, there could be approved capital expenditure plans for adding to the capacity of the machine shop by replacing some old milling machines with a new numerically controlled machine capable of a much greater volume of producton. It would be desirable to include the resource levels in past years so that the impact these resources have had on performance may be more easily or better understood.

The fourth step is to recognize the influence of seasonality. This is not important in all industries, but if there is marked and predictable variation in demand at various times in the year, then the form given in figure 10–2 is entirely inadequate. For soft drink companies, garment manufacturers, and building contractors operating in countries where climatic conditions vary greatly with the seasons, it would be imperative to recognize seasonality. For AIM too, with its demand for residential products being a function of housing starts, seasonality is an important consideration. For AIM it may be adequate to break up the yearly volume figures into quarterly details. For other firms, monthly variations may be significant and predictable enough to require explicit recognition.

The fifth step is to record the major and different actions that the head of the responsibility center plans to take. In fact, these plans of action are the foundation of budgets. Thus the numbers recorded in the budget format should essentially reflect the consequence of taking the actions that are planned. For instance, the foreman of the machine shop must have plans for installing the numerically controlled milling machine. Job training for machinists may be another key program during the forthcoming budget period. These programs or plans of action must be recorded and included as part of the budget with the following details:

1. Description of the action or program.

2. Person responsible for carrying out the action or program.

3. Person responsible for monitoring the effectiveness with which the action or program is executed.

4. Deadlines by which the action or program is to be completed and the scheduled time of completion of major components of the program.

5. Expected impact on performance, financial and operational, of the action or program that is planned.

The sixth step is needed only in responsibility centers that are engineered expense centers (type I). The machine shop in AIM is of this type, and it is desirable to develop flexible budgets for costs that are not readily covered by standards. Material consumption and direct labor costs could be based on standards developed as discussed earlier in this chapter; however, overhead costs may require the development of flexible budgets. Essentially these are budgets for the permissible level of overhead costs at various levels of activity. These flexible budgets are discussed in more detail in the following chapter when the cost accounting inputs to production budgets are considered.

Employing the six-step procedure detailed would result in a much more detailed budget format than the one illustrated in figure 10–2. The new budget format for the machine shop is given in figure 10–3.

The desirability of having a format that does not exceed one page does not apply to budgeting formats. In fact, it is better to err on the side of more detail when designing budget formats. The desirability and usefulness of having action plans and performance expectations spelled out in detail are particularly evident when the time comes to review actual performance in relation to budgeted performance.

Figure 10–3. Recommended Budget Format for AIM Machine Shop

(continued on next page)

	ACTUAL 198X-3 (1)	ACTUAL 198X-2 (1)	ACTUAL 198X-1 (1)	TOTAL BUDGET FOR 198X (1)	% CHANGE (COMPOUNDED) 198X-3 TO 198X-1 (1)	CHANGE 198X-1 TO 198X (1)	FIRST QUARTER TOTAL (4)	FIRST QUARTER AVERAGE WEEKLY BUDGET (4)	SECOND QUARTER TOTAL (4)	SECOND QUARTER AVERAGE WEEKLY BUDGET (4)	THIRD QUARTER TOTAL (4)	THIRD QUARTER AVERAGE WEEKLY BUDGET (4)	FOURTH QUARTER TOTAL (4)	FOURTH QUARTER AVERAGE WEEKLY BUDGET (4)
FINANCIAL PERFORMANCE														
LABOR COMPENSATION — DIRECT														
LABOR COMPENSATION — INDIRECT														
LABOR COMPENSATION — TOTAL														
LABOR RELATED BENEFITS														
DIRECT MATERIALS														
SUPPLIES & SMALL TOOLS														
UTILITIES														
REPAIRS & MAINTENANCE														
OTHER OPERATING EXPENSES														
TOTAL EXPENSES														
EXTERNAL FACTORS/RESOURCES														
ESTIMATED AVAILABILITY OF MACHINISTS (APPLICATIONS?) (2)														
VALUE OF P & E (3)														
OPERATIONAL PERFORMANCE														
PRODUCTION VOLUME (BASED ON SALES BUDGET) (2)														
HEAD COUNT — DIRECT														
HEAD COUNT — INDIRECT														
HEAD COUNT — TOTAL														
CAPACITY UTILIZATION (%)														
NORMAL ABSENTEEISM (%)														
OVERTIME $ / HOURS														
WORK-IN-PROCESS														
WORK-IN-PROCESS INVENTORY														

SECTION-WISE BUDGET		LATHE SECTION											
			FIRST QUARTER		SECOND QUARTER		THIRD QUARTER		FOURTH QUARTER				
FINANCIAL PERFORMANCE		ANNUAL TOTAL	TOTAL (4)	AVERAGE WEEKLY BUDGET (4)	TOTAL (4)	AVERAGE WEEKLY BUDGET (4)	TOTAL (4)	AVERAGE WEEKLY BUDGET (4)	TOTAL (4)	AVERAGE WEEKLY BUDGET (4)			
LABOR	DIRECT												
	INDIRECT												
	TOTAL												
LABOR—RELATED BENEFITS													
DIRECT MATERIALS													
SUPPLIES & SMALL TOOLS													
UTILITIES													
REPAIRS & MAINTENANCE													
OTHER OPERATING EXPENSES													
TOTAL EXPENSES													
EXTERNAL FACTORS/RESOURCES													
ADDITIONAL MACHINISTS (2)													
VALUE OF EQUIPMENT (3)													
OPERATIONAL PERFORMANCE													
PRODUCTION VOLUME (2)													
HEAD COUNT	DIRECT												
	INDIRECT												
	TOTAL												
CAPACITY UTILIZATION (%)													
NORMAL ABSENTEEISM (%)													
OVERTIME	$												
	HOURS												
WORK-IN-PROCESS INVENTORY													

Figure 10-3 Continued

SECTION-WISE BUDGET

MILLING SECTION

		ANNUAL TOTAL	FIRST QUARTER		SECOND QUARTER		THIRD QUARTER		FOURTH QUARTER	
			TOTAL (4)	AVERAGE WEEKLY BUDGET (4)	TOTAL (4)	AVERAGE WEEKLY BUDGET (4)	TOTAL (4)	AVERAGE WEEKLY BUDGET (4)	TOTAL (4)	AVERAGE WEEKLY BUDGET (4)
FINANCIAL PERFORMANCE										
LABOR	DIRECT									
	INDIRECT									
	TOTAL									
LABOR—RELATED BENEFITS										
DIRECT MATERIALS										
SUPPLIES & SMALL TOOLS										
UTILITIES										
REPAIRS & MAINTENANCE										
OTHER OPERATING EXPENSES										
TOTAL EXPENSES										
EXTERNAL FACTORS/RESOURCES										
ADDITIONAL MACHINISTS (2)										
VALUE OF EQUIPMENT										
OPERATIONAL PERFORMANCE										
PRODUCTION VOLUME (2)										
HEAD COUNT	DIRECT									
	INDIRECT									
	TOTAL									
CAPACITY UTILIZATION (%)										
NORMAL ABSENTEEISM (%)										
OVERTIME	$									
	HOURS									
WORK-IN-PROCESS INVENTORY										

Figure 10-3 Continued

SECTION-WISE BUDGET													
OTHER SECTIONS													
			FIRST QUARTER				THIRD QUARTER				FOURTH QUARTER		
FINANCIAL PERFORMANCE		ANNUAL TOTAL	TOTAL (4)	AVERAGE WEEKLY BUDGET (4)	TOTAL (4)	AVERAGE WEEKLY BUDGET (4)	TOTAL (4)	AVERAGE WEEKLY BUDGET (4)	TOTAL (4)	AVERAGE WEEKLY BUDGET (4)	TOTAL (4)	AVERAGE WEEKLY BUDGET (4)	
LABOR	DIRECT												
	INDIRECT												
	TOTAL												
LABOR—RELATED BENEFITS													
DIRECT MATERIALS													
SUPPLIES & SMALL TOOLS													
UTILITIES													
REPAIRS & MAINTENANCE													
OTHER OPERATING EXPENSES													
TOTAL EXPENSES													
EXTERNAL FACTORS/RESOURCES													
ADDITIONAL MACHINISTS (2)													
VALUE OF EQUIPMENT													
OPERATIONAL PERFORMANCE													
PRODUCTION VOLUME (2)													
HEAD COUNT	DIRECT												
	INDIRECT												
	TOTAL												
CAPACITY UTILIZATION (%)													
NORMAL ABSENTEEISM (%)													
OVERTIME	$												
	HOURS												
WORK-IN-PROCESS INVENTORY													

Figure 10–3 Continued

FLEXIBLE OVERHEAD BUDGET (6)

BUDGET ITEM		85% OF NORMAL CAPACITY (PRODUCTION VOLUME: --)				90% OF NORMAL CAPACITY (PRODUCTION VOLUME: --)				95% OF NORMAL CAPACITY (PRODUCTION VOLUME: --)				100% OF NORMAL CAPACITY (PRODUCTION VOLUME: --)				105% OF NORMAL CAPACITY (PRODUCTION VOLUME: --)			
		TOTAL	LATHE	MILL-ING	OTH.	TOTAL	LATHE	MILL-ING	OTH.	TOTAL	LATHE	MILL-ING	OTH.	TOTAL	LATHE	MILL-ING	OTH.	TOTAL	LATHE	MILL-ING	OTH.
INDIRECT LABOR	WAGES																				
	BENEFITS																				
	TOTAL																				
SUPPLIES & SMALL TOOLS																					
UTILITIES																					
REPAIRS & MAINTENANCE																					
OTHER OPERATING EXPENSES																					
TOTAL EXPENSES																					

Figure 10–3 Continued

ACTION PLAN DOCUMENTATION (5)					IMPACT ON PERFORMANCE	
SERIAL NO.	ACTION/PROGRAM DESCRIPTION	EXECUTIVE RESPONSIBILITY	MONITORING RESPONSIBILITY	COMPLETION DEADLINE AND SELECTED MILESTONES	PRIOR TO ACTION/PROGRAM	AFTER COMPLETION

Note: Numbers in parentheses refer to how the format responds to six considerations: 1, consider past performance trends; 2, analyze external factors; 3, identify the level of resource available; 4, recognize the impact of seasonality; 5 articulate the underlying action plans or programs; 6, develop flexible budgets for overhead costs.

Figure 10–3 Continued

11
Line and Staff Budgets: Special Characteristics

T
he discussion of the production budget in the preceding chapter identifies the basic approach to budgeting for responsibility centers within functional organizations. But each type of responsibility center has unique problems, requirements, and design options that merit recognition.

Cost Accounting Systems and the Production Budget

The cost accounting system in most organizations is the source of much of the accounting information that is contained in production budgets and reports. Cost accounting systems are supposed to serve at least three major purposes:

1. Valuation of production and inventories, particularly work-in-process and finished goods inventories, so as to provide the cost of goods sold figures for the income statement and inventory values for the balance sheet.
2. Control of costs, particularly manufacturing costs, both direct costs and overheads.
3. Planning of revenue-related decisions such as pricing and product mix.

From the managerial standpoint, the last two purposes are much more important than the first. Unfortunately the valuation of inventories was the initial purpose of cost accounting systems and still continues to be the primary consideration determining the design of these systems. As a result, most systems tend to be poorly suited to the needs of budgeting and managerial control. Some of the most common major flaws in the design of cost accounting systems can be identified.

Accounting for Direct Material

The system for accounting for direct material is relatively easy because tangible items are involved. Depending on whether a job-costing or process-costing system is appropriate, the issue of raw materials to specific work orders or departments can be easily tracked through the mandatory use of requisition slips with the necessary details. The cost accounting system should identify at least two reasons for variances from budgeted or standard consumption of materials: the variance due to a difference in the price paid from the standard or budgeted price (the price variance) and the difference in the quantity of material consumed compared to the budgeted or standard quantity (quantity or usage variance). The price variance is often wrongly generated or wrongly interpreted and used, however.

The first common error in relation to the price variance is the point in time at which it is generated. Let us assume that in AIM the manufacturing manager's office carries out the purchasing function. Figure 11–1 illustrates two systems for generating the price variance and identifies the better method. The first method generates information on a timely basis regarding changes in material prices from the standard price. The second method is much inferior because the price variance is generated at the time the material is issued to the production shop. Moreover, the price variance is generated piecemeal in that the quantities issued at a time may be much smaller than the quantity purchased at one time. The second method is, however, more than adequate and indeed is often viewed as preferable from the point of view of facilitating the allocation of actual material costs to the products that are manufactured.

The importance of generating price variances at the time the material is purchased cannot be overemphasized. On occasion, the time period between purchase and issue of the material may be so long as to make the variances generated by the second method meaningless.

Price variances are intended to trigger managerial action. Perhaps purchase requisitions are not being generated early enough to give the purchasing officer enough time to pick the sources offering the lowest price. Perhaps the efficiency of the purchasing section needs to be improved. Perhaps the price at which the products that use these raw materials are sold should be changed. Or perhaps management should seek alternative sources, substitute materials, different product designs, or different products. The timely generation of the material price variances is of importance in effecting the needed changes expeditiously.

The second common misunderstanding about price variances is that they are not worth the effort involved in generating them. Two reasons are frequently advanced to support this point of view. First, there are too many different materials and components to be purchased, and developing price

Method 1: Recommended

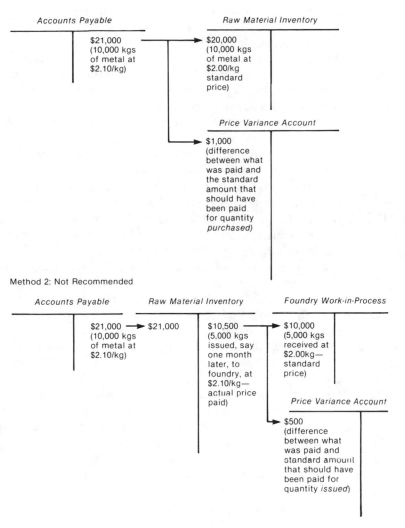

Figure 11–1. Systems for Generating Price Variances

expectations and calculating price variances is too demanding a task. Second, the purchasing managers cannot in most cases be held responsible for price variances because the causes of these variances are uncontrollable. Both of these reasons are unacceptable and irrelevant.

It is unnecessary and undesirable to develop price standards and price variances for all the different materials purchased by the organization. The technique of ABC analysis (mentioned previously in relation to the design of reporting formats) was developed in the context of materials management in order to respond to the problem of too many different items. Standards and variances should be developed only for the A items that are purchased. These A items are the 20 percent of total items that in most organizations account for 80 percent of the money spent on materials. The B and C items in inventory, which constitute by far the largest number, can be safely excluded from consideration and their actual prices treated as standard.

The argument that purchasing managers cannot normally be held responsible for price variances is irrelevant. Price variances are needed not so much to find fault with the purchasing manager but to trigger needed remedial actions such as changing sales prices, vendors, materials, or product designs. Unless a standard materials price is set on which decisions regarding sales prices, product mix, and so on can be based, there is no meaningful way an organization can plan or budget its profits or identify situations where these decisions need to be modified. Moreover, the exercise of setting price standards for the A items forces purchasing executives to evaluate and plan sources, timing, and quantity of purchases. Price standards are also necessary so that the responsibility of the production departments can be appropriately identified. Barring exceptional circumstances, the production departments cannot be held responsible for the impact of price variances on the cost of producing goods. By extracting price variances and charging the standard price for materials issued to the production departments, only quantity variances are included in their reports. The separation of price and quantity variances greatly facilitates performance review and the identification of appropriate remedial action.

Tracking and recording usage variances is a much simpler task. In fact, an effective method is to issue only predetermined standard quantities of raw materials for each work order. Additional requests for materials for a work order already serviced would be charged to the materials usage variance account for the concerned responsibility center. Also, if the output of the responsibility center does not conform to the quantity specified in the work order, the standard quantity of materials that is needed to produce the difference would be charged to the concerned responsibility center.

Cost accounting textbooks often spend an inordinate amount of time discussing the interrelated character of material price and usage variances and stress the fact that different methods would give rise to different figures for these two components of the total materials variances. In my opinion, this controversy is of little or no significance to practicing managers. The method that I recommend—calculating price variances at the time of issue—is clearly the best from the point of view of triggering needed managerial action. Further refinements are quite unnecessary and possibly inappropriate.

Accounting for Direct Labor

Labor costs that can be directly traced to the products being manufactured should, just like direct material costs, be analyzed in terms of two variances: the labor efficiency variance and the labor rate variance, which is analogous to the material price variance.

Generating these labor variances poses no unusual problems. Time cards to be filled in by each worker or his or her superior identify the job numbers or work orders on which their time was spent. The accounting office can add data regarding standard time for the work carried out, standard wage rates for the responsibility center, and actual wages paid to the worker. From these data, the rate and efficiency variances for the responsibility center can readily be calculated.

Accounting for Overhead

Overheads (costs that cannot be directly traced to the products or that are individually not significant enough to warrant a system that could directly attach them to the products) have been consistently growing as a proportion of total costs in most industries. Unfortunately the overhead budgeting techniques that are widely used are more oriented toward allocating overhead costs to the products rather than providing ways to plan and control these increasingly significant costs. Several studies and experience have shown that most overhead budgeting systems are unnecessarily complex, resulting in a variety of variances that are usually not understood by managers receiving reports on this information. In the interest of brevity, only the most significant concerns regarding the budgeting of overhead costs will be considered here. First, in order to control overhead cost, it is necessary that the cost accounting system distinguish between overhead costs relatable to a responsibility center and those allocated to the responsibility center. For instance, in the AIM machine shop, supplies and small tools are relatable overhead. The cost of the supplies and small tools consumed by the machine shop is directly identifiable from records. These supplies and small tool costs are overhead costs rather than direct material costs because the proportion consumed by each job order, work order, product line, or product cannot be physically tracked and has to be allocated to the products on some presumably rational basis. Although they are clearly overhead costs, they are very different from other overhead items, such as the proportion of the manufacturing manager's salary that may be allocated to the machine shop by the cost accountant as a first step toward attaching a reasonable proportion to each product or product line.

Relatable overheads are usually subject to the control of the manager of the responsibility center; allocated overheads are not. The accounting system should distinguish between these two types of costs. In fact, it is often desirable to exclude allocated overheads in performance reports intended for control purposes.

The second major set of concerns relating to the overhead budget is that too many variances are generated. In one large firm, the accounting system generated five overhead variances: volume, seasonal, calendar, spending, and efficiency. These fine distinctions were confusing rather than helpful or informative. The redesigned performance reports ignored the volume, seasonal, and calendar variances because the information they provided was more simply and directly provided by the variance of actual production volume from budgeted production volume. And although the distinction between spending and efficiency variances is meaningful, the redesigned reports combined these into a single controllable variance derived by comparing actual overhead costs to the costs budgeted for the actual level of production. The step chart approach to flexible budgets for overheads is simpler to understand and more informative than the more complex aggregated methods where volume, spending, and efficiency variances are generated from budget equations that assume costs are either fixed or variable and that aggregate all fixed costs and all variable costs. The variances generated by the use of budget equations do not identify which items of overhead were responsible and can also be criticized as being more theoretical than realistic.

An example of a step chart for the flexible overhead budget is given in figure 10–3. The variances between the actual costs incurred for each of the items listed and the standard figures at the appropriate capacity level drawn from the step chart, combined with the production volume variance, give all the information that the more complex systems provide. Moreover, these variances can readily be understood, can be related to actual happenings, and can swiftly point to needed remedial action.

Characteristics of the Sales Budget

In most organizations, the sales budget is the basis of other budgets, such as the production budget. There are exceptions, such as organizations where production constraints influence the sales and other budgets. However, even in countries where governmental regulations and licensing practices control capacity expansion, continued shortages of production capacity normally trigger investments to increase this capacity. Developing the sales budget is therefore particularly important.

Developing the sales budget is more difficult than developing the production budget because the uncertainties are greater and the alternatives usually more numerous. The production budget applies primarily to engineered expense centers (type I units where the process and outputs are known and measurable). Technological considerations often limit the available alternatives. Sales budgets apply to revenue and contribution centers. Both are type II units where the process is not well defined though the outputs are measurable. The interaction with the external environment of the firm is explicit and extensive. The variables that can be manipulated by the managers of revenue and contribution centers are more numerous and less well understood than the variables available in engineered expense centers.

These considerations reinforce some basic conclusions. The firm must pay careful attention to the process of development of the sales budget. Creativity must be encouraged, and perhaps greater discretion must be allowed to the managers of revenue and contribution centers compared to the managers of engineered expense centers.

A critical decision influencing the nature of the sales budget is whether the concerned responsibility center should be treated as a revenue center or a contribution center. This issue was discussed in chapter 8 using the examples of the product manager of residential products and the product manager of industrial products in AIM. It was pointed out in chapter 8, and bears mention again, that the key criterion on which this determination of the nature of the sales responsibility center should be made is whether the manager of the responsibility center should have control over the price at which the products he or she deals with are sold. In the case of the manager of residential products, the determination was made that the marketing manager appropriately and effectively decided on this price. Consequently the residential products responsibility center was defined as a revenue center. Because a revenue center is simpler to budget for than a contribution center, we shall first discuss the characteristics of budgets in revenue centers before taking up the design of budgets for contribution centers.

Budgets for Revenue Centers

The product manager of residential products is responsible for generating the maximum amount of unit sales within the constraints of the capacity of the manufacturing function. Also, he or she has to operate with the selling prices determined by the marketing manager. The available resources or inputs are the six salespeople. Other inputs to this responsibility center include the residential meters produced by the manufacturing department.

The performance report for this revenue center, designed in accordance with the guidelines in chapter 9, is the starting point for developing the budget format. The step-by-step procedure incorporates past performance, external factors, resource availability, seasonality trends, and action plans or programs.

The flexible budgets suggested in the case of overhead costs in production units are usually inappropriate for revenue centers. Presale marketing costs cannot be said to vary necessarily in a particular fashion with sales levels. Postsale distribution costs can be controlled with the use of standards. Perhaps the best approach here is to specify the inputs—personnel, products—that will be made available to the revenue center. Following the tentative determination of feasible resource levels, the possibilities for revenue generation can be analyzed, and a fixed figure for revenues to be generated should be budgeted. An iterative procedure that examines the relationship between sales potential and needed inputs to achieve this potential is desirable.

Because the step-by-step procedure was demonstrated in detail in the context of the production budget, it will not be repeated here since the procedure is identical. The emphasis on and importance of external factors is greater in the case of revenue centers than in production units, and it may be necessary to analyze external sales possibilities in a detailed and structured fashion.

A useful matrix for directing the analysis of sales potential is the product-market matrix diagrammed in figure 11–2. This matrix not only categorizes the possibilities for increasing revenue in a manner that encourages consider-

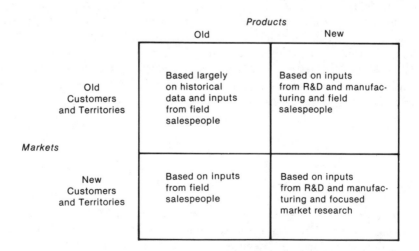

Figure 11–2. Product-Market Matrix

ation of all possibilities, but it also can serve as a useful basis for developing the action plans and programs that express and structure the manager's plans for the budget period. The personnel who should be involved in the process of identifying sales potential in each of the four categories are identified in the matrix. Action plans based on this matrix and the involvement of the appropriate personnel can greatly facilitate the identification of causes if actual revenues are different from those budgeted and can also aid in the speedy determination of needed remedial action.

In short, revenue centers require very simple fixed budgets for revenues to be generated and expenses to be incurred based on the projected availability of products from the manufacturing department matched with the perceived potential for sales of both old and new products to old and new markets.

Budgets for Contribution Centers

In contrast to the budgets for revenue centers, the budgets for contribution centers are relatively complex. As was discussed in chapter 8, because the product manager of industrial products has the authority to decide the price at which industrial meters are to be sold, evaluating this person on revenues generated would be inadequate and inappropriate. In order to recognize the interrelatedness of prices, costs, and volumes, an artificial profit figure must be developed as a basis for evaluating sales units where the manager has control over the pricing decision. A drop in units sold might not mean that performance is bad in such a unit as the increased price at which this reduced number of units is sold might affect positively the organizations profits. The cost to the organization of manufacturing the products is a key consideration in determining price because marginal pricing based on incremental costs may be a relevant consideration, particularly in competitive bidding situations.

Contribution centers, unlike revenue centers, have to be made to pay a price for the products provided to them. The contribution to overheads and profits made by the contribution center would then be determined as follows:

	Revenues generated	$100
Less	Transfer price of products sold	(45)
Less	Costs directly relatable to the center	(25)
Equals	Contribution	$30

The figure of contribution arrived at is the key effectiveness measure. Revenues generated are easy to measure. Also costs that can be directly related and not allocated to the contribution center can be objectively determined. The specification of the transfer price is therefore the critical decision that has to be made in calculating the contribution.

Transfer Pricing for Contribution Centers. Although there are several ways in which this transfer price can be specified, there are basically only two alternatives underlying all of the apparent variations. The first alternative is to specify the full cost of manufacturing the product as the transfer price. This cost would include the direct material, direct labor, and an allocated proportion of manufacturing overheads. Although this is the most widely used approach, with variations that include a markup on the full costs, this method is undesirable because it leads to wrong decisions on the part of the manager of the contribution center.

The second alternative is to specify that the transfer price should be the variable manufacturing costs relatable to the products. This seems at first to be an inferior method but in practice leads to the right profit-maximizing decisions by the manager of the contribution center. The superiority of this alternative can be demonstrated by means of the example given in table 11–1, which illustrates the different decisions that transfer pricing based on full costs and on variable costs can give rise to in the same firm.

The example is simple. Line 1 gives the variable (marginal) cost of manufacturing one unit of product. The $20 variable cost is the same under both methods. We are assuming a reasonable and limited range of volume; hence this figure is a constant. Line 2 gives the total fixed costs, again assuming a limited range of volumes being considered. Line 3 indicates the planned volume. Line 4 is obtained by dividing the total fixed costs of line 2 ($20,000) by the budgeted production in line 3 (2,000 units). The full cost or absorption cost of a unit of the product is given in line 5 ($30) and is obtained by adding the variable cost per unit of line 1 ($20) and the fixed cost per unit of line 4 ($10).

The transfer price (line 6) is the crucial difference between the two methods. Under the full-cost alternative, the transfer price is the full cost calculated on line 5. Under the variable-cost alternative, the transfer price is the variable cost indicated in line 1.

Lines 7 through 13 reflect the point of view of the manager of the contribution center. When calculating the variable (incremental or marginal) cost to the contribution center of selling one more unit, the costs that the manager would take into account are the transfer price (line 7) and the relatable marketing costs (line 8) that are incurred per unit by the contribution center. Under the full cost alternative, this cost (line 9) works out to $40; under the variable-cost approach to transfer pricing, it works out to $30 because the transfer price is less. This difference under the two methods affects subsequent calculations. When calculating the contribution per unit (line 11) by subtracting the variable cost (line 9) from the selling price per unit of $50

Table 11–1
Comparison of Transfer Pricing Alternatives

	Assumptions[a]	*Alternative 1:* *Full Cost*	*Alternative 2:* *Variable/Marginal* *Cost*
1	Variable cost per unit of product	$20	$20
2	Fixed costs, total	$20,000	$20,000
3	Budgeted production	2,000 units	2,000 units
4	Fixed costs per unit	$10	$10
5	Full cost	$30	$30
6	Transfer price	$30	$20
	Variable costs per unit		
7	Transfer price	$30	$20
8	Relatable marketing costs	$10	$10
9	Total	$40	$30
10	Selling price per unit	$50	$50
11	Contribution per unit	$10	$20
12	Decision if an increase in marketing costs of $100 is expected to increase unit sales by six units	Do not increase marketing costs [($10 × 6) − $100 = loss]	Increase marketing costs [($20 × 6) − $100 = profit]
13	Correct decision (because contribution to firm's profits is [$50 − $30] × 6 units, less $100 = $20)	Increase	Increase

[a]Assumptions in lines 1–6 are for the manufacturing department. Those in lines 7–12 are for the contribution center.

(line 10), the figures vary depending on the method chosen. Consequently managerial decisions will be different as indicated in line 12, despite the fact that the actual economics of the situation are the same under both systems. The different decisions result from changes in the accounting system, not because the costs and revenues are different.

The decision given for illustrative purposes (line 12) is whether to incur an additional marketing expense of $100 if sales will increase by six units as a result. Under the full-cost alternative, the manager of the contribution center calculates that the increased contribution ($60) resulting from the additional sales will not cover the expense of $100. The calculations indicate a decrease in reported contribution of $40 if the expense is incurred and six additional units are sold.

Under the variable-cost alternative, the increase in contribution resulting from an increase in sales of six units ($120) more than covers the additional expense of $100. The reported contribution would increase by $20 if the expense is incurred and six additional units are sold.

Clearly both methods of transfer pricing cannot be right because each leads to a different decision. The correct decision is made when variable costs are the basis of transfer prices because the contribution figure on which the manager of the responsibility center bases decisions is the correct one from the perspective of the firm. *Contribution* in economic theory is the difference between selling price and variable costs. The contribution figure is the same from the points of view of, say, the general manager of AIM and the product manager of industrial products if variable costs are the basis of the transfer price.

There are several reservations or doubts that managers often express about the recommended method of transfer pricing. First, there is the valid argument that the apparent profitability of such contribution centers will be very high because manufacturing fixed costs are ignored. This could possibly lead to misunderstandings about the relative importance of the manager of the contribution center. One way of responding to this psychological—not economic—problem is to deduct a fixed amount approximately equal to manufacturing fixed cost before reporting the center's contribution figure. Care must be taken to avoid deducting a fixed cost per unit because this would convert the transfer pricing system into the undesirable full-cost method.

The second major concern is whether the manufacturing department should also be converted into a profit center by crediting it with revenues equal to the transfer price debited to the contribution center. I have on one or two occasions designed such artificial profit centers for manufacturing, essentially to respond to the feeling on the part of production executives that they are otherwise seen as generating only expenses, not profits. Experiences with this practice have been mixed. On balance, I would recommend not creating artificial profit centers out of manufacturing departments because of the ease and appropriateness of managing them as engineered expense centers.

The third concern is about the accounting problem created by this artificial cost charged to contribution centers if the manufacturing departments are not to receive a balancing credit. The technical response is simple: the marketing manager's report or the general manager's report (preferably the latter) could have a counterbalancing entry that would eliminate the problem. Of course, care must be taken to explain to the general manager the nature of the entry and its technical rather than managerial character.

The fourth issue often raised is about the accounting and economic justification of the transfer pricing practice. Fortunately the philosophy behind the design of planning and control systems makes a theoretical justification unnecessary. The control system is attempting to ensure that subordinate managers make the decisions and take actions that superior managers would wish them to take. The transfer pricing system based on variable manufacturing costs ensures that the managers of contribution centers make the right decisions from the point of view of the firm as a whole. Any alternative system, mechanism, or technique that would accomplish the same end would be acceptable from a planning and control standpoint, though accounting purists and economists may find reasons to be critical.

Relative Contribution Approach. The importance of creativity in developing sales budgets was stressed previously. The discussion of the multiple dimensions of information in chapter 9 has particular relevance to the design of budgeting formats for contribution centers because these multiple dimensions are important in directing the analysis of alternatives in a creative and comprehensive fashion.

Sales are generated by products, in territories, and from customers. Each or all of these sources of revenue may be fruitfully analyzed in the case of contribution centers so as to determine the most profitable products, territories, and customers. The relative contribution generated by categories within each of these dimensions is a valuable input to developing the optimal contribution budget.

The relative contribution figure is calculated by deducting from the contribution generated by each product line, territorial location, or customer type those fixed costs that would no longer be incurred if the revenues were sacrificed. An example based on territories is given in table 11–2.

Table 11–2 indicates an apparently profitable marketing department. The department contributes $270,000 to manufacturing fixed costs, corporate overheads, and profits. The $270,000 contribution figure may or may not result in profits for the firm as a whole depending on the magnitude of manufacturing fixed costs and other corporate overheads. What is important to recognize, however, is that looking at the territorial (regional) dimension of information in detail reveals that the Midwest region, if eliminated, could increase this contribution figure to $280,000. Without calculating the relative contribution of each region, this possible avenue for improving profits may not have been identified by the marketing department. Similarly, it might prove worthwhile to calculate the relative contribution along other dimensions, such as customer types and product lines.

In conclusion, the design of budget formats for contribution centers is not the primary problem faced by the systems designer. The simple step-by-step procedure discussed for revenue centers holds here also. The major issue to resolve in the context of contribution centers is the transfer pricing system for products received from manufacturing. Also, as in the case of revenue centers, the quality of analysis that goes into generating and evaluating creative alternatives for improving profitability is crucial. The relative contribution approach is of great value in this regard.

Table 11–2
Relative Contribution Approach

	Total	Northeast Region	Midwest Region	Southwest Region	West Region
Sales revenue	$6,850,000	$1,750,000	$600,000	$2,000,000	$2,500,000
Variable costs (including transfer prices)	5,480,000	1,400,000	480,000	1,600,000	2,000,000
Contribution before relatable costs	$1,370,000	$350,000	$120,000	$400,000	$500,000
Relatable regional costs (avoidable if region is dropped)	800,000	200,000	130,000	220,000	250,000
Relative regional contribution		$150,000	($10,000)	$180,000	$250,000
Remaining marketing costs	300,000				
Relative marketing contribution	$ 270,000				

If Midwest Region Is Dropped, Impact on Marketing Contribution:

1 Reduction in Revenues	=	($600,000)
2 Reduction in Variable Costs	=	$480,000
3 Elimination of avoidable costs	=	$130,000
4 Net Impact	=	$ 10,000 (positive)

Characteristics of Staff Function Budgets

Most staff departments fall into the category of discretionary expense centers, where the relationship between the inputs (dollars) and the outputs (physical) is a matter of judgment. They can be either type II or type III units where, respectively, the process or outputs are not well defined, though usually they are type III units. In developing budgets for staff departments, it is important to understand the character of each department so that appropriate planning and control techniques can be selected.

Purchasing Department

Purchasing departments lend themselves to a variety of techniques. Standards can be applied for routine activities such as the processing of purchase requisitions leading to the placing of an order. Effectiveness measures are very important in the case of purchase departments. For instance, raw material stockouts due to delays caused by the purchasing department would be an important measure of how effectively the department is functioning. If most purchases made are of a routine nature, the department increasingly takes on the character of an engineered expense center, and efficiency measures become meaningful. The number of purchase requisitions handled and the dollar amount of purchases made serve as measures of the output; the costs and number of personnel in the purchasing department are the input measures when calculating efficiency. The purchase price variance is of great value to the purchase department as a basis for planning improved purchasing practices. The price variances as a control device to evaluate the purchasing department must be employed with caution because of the likelihood of uncontrollable factors affecting price.

To summarize, in purchasing departments, budgets should:

1. Have standards for routine, repetitive activities.
2. Focus on effectiveness (stockouts, quality, and price variances).
3. Add efficiency measures if large numbers of routine purchases are made.

Maintenance Department

From a planning and control perspective, maintenance departments are similar to purchasing departments. If there are repetitive jobs, either preventive or breakdown, standards should be developed. Subjective or theoretical standards for major jobs that involve substantial production volume implications may be useful, though the frequency of occurrence or repetition may be low. Effectiveness measures such as downtime due to poor maintenance or delays in maintenance are important but difficult to develop and apply because they require subjective assessments of the quality of the work done by the department. Such assessments of quality are often a source of discord and conflict. In contrast, efficiency measures are easier to develop and apply because they focus on the time and cost of completing specific jobs and require less subjective assessments of quality.

To summarize, in maintenance departments, budgets should:

1. Have standards for repetitive maintenance activities, both preventive and breakdown.
2. Focus on efficiency measures (time and cost to complete jobs).
3. Add effectiveness measures (downtime due to poor or delayed maintenance) when resonably objective assessments of the quality of the maintenance work can be made.

Computer Services and Accounting Departments

Computer services and accounting departments tend to be somewhat more difficult to manage than the previous two types of staff departments. Often it has proved best to limit the measures employed to the timeliness with which promised services are provided by these departments to other responsibility centers. If there are repetitive, routine activities that are of significance within each of these departments, the development of standards becomes desirable. Standards could be set, for instance, for the number of punched cards to be processed or entries to be made. The best way of controlling these departments is to make the right decisions about the kind and caliber of personnel and equipment for these departments. Although such input controls are important in any discretionary expense center, they become even more important when the process and outputs are undefined or difficult to measure.

To summarize, in computer services and accounting departments, budgets should:

1. Have standards if and where applicable.
2. Focus on effectiveness measures (timeliness of reports and services).
3. Emphasize making careful decisions about key inputs such as personnel and equipment.

Personnel Department

The personnel department is different from the previous types of staff departments considered in that the appropriate focus of planning and control is on the process and work load rather than the inputs and outputs. The number and type of training and development activities conducted, the personnel reviews carried out, the recruiting and selection activities performed, grievances investigated, and so on can be planned and measured. Standards may be applicable to certain routine activities such as updating personnel files. To assess the results and quality of these efforts is, however, difficult. Effectiveness measures that are of any practical significance tend to be indirect. For instance, training programs can be evaluated by the participants, but the true results will show up only on the job and possibly much later.

To summarize, in the personnel department, budgets should:

1. Have standards if and where applicable.
2. Focus on process measures (work load).
3. Attempt to develop indirect or surrogate measures of effectiveness (unfilled positions, ratio of promotable to promoted, and so forth).

Research and Development Departments

Research and development departments that emphasize applied research, where specific results are expected within given deadlines, can be managed with the use of output and effectiveness measures. Project planning and control techniques are usually most appropriate. For each research project or program, reports should be generated at specified intervals or when specified milestone events occur. These reports should include information about time spent, costs incurred, and progress made to date. In addition—and this is very important—these reports should include revised estimates of time and cost to complete the project. These updated estimates are vital because the key management decision is whether to continue with or drop the project.

If the R&D department engages in basic research, where the objective is to increase knowledge without any specific purpose in mind, project planning and control techniques have little value. The key decisions to be made are the amount of money to be allocated to basic research and to whom this money will be allocated. Essentially input controls are all that are feasible.

To summarize, for R&D departments, budgets need the following:

1. For applied research, use project planning and control techniques with time- and milestone-triggered reports that include revised estimates of additional time and costs to complete the projects.
2. For basic research, emphasize input controls.

Summary

The discussion of the various staff departments commonly encountered should provide adequate guidance when assessing the character of individual staff departments. Essentially the attempt should be to identify activities where standards can be applied and to determine what combination of input, process or work load, output, effectiveness, and efficiency measures make sense and are feasible.

In designing the budget formats for staff departments, the same step-by-step procedure recommended for production and marketing departments can and should be applied. It must be recognized, however, that unlike in production and marketing departments where the desired outputs (and in some case, the process also) are clear-cut and measurable, the highly discretionary character of staff departments and the intangible nature of most of their outputs demand special planning and control techniques. A variety of techniques have been developed and employed by organizations seeking to manage their staff departments better.

Special Techniques for Staff Departments

Many of the special techniques that have been developed for discretionary expense centers are based on the fact that in all such responsibility centers, the inputs can be measured objectively and in monetary terms. Consequently, it is possible to specify expense or appropriation budgets for these responsibility centers.

Appropriation budgets are spending limits specified for each of the accounts under which expenses incurred are recorded. For instance, the personnel manager in AIM would be informed through the appropriation budget how much could be spent on salaries and wages, travel, supplies, and other areas. In contrast to performance budgets (the flexible overhead budget for the production department is a good example) where inputs and outputs are linked through efficiency measures, appropriation budgets attempt to convert the plan for the responsibility center into a determination of suitable expenditure levels. No attempt is necessarily made to link inputs with desired outputs, unlike the case of engineered expense centers.

Appropriation budgets must reflect a plan and must be based on some kind of analysis of the operations of the responsibility center. The simplest form of analysis is to compare the proposed spending levels to those budgeted and incurred in the previous year. Such incremental analyses are a simple but powerful tool to bring to bear some measure of judgment about appropriate spending levels. If the personnel manager in AIM requests a substantial increase in the appropriation budget, it would be his or her responsibility to identify and justify the changes in level or kind of activities that make the requested increase necessary.

The key assumption in incremental analysis is that the level of spending in the previous year was appropriate. Consequently it becomes necessary to examine only the proposed changes in spending levels and the reasons for these changes. This assumption is highly questionable, however. There is good reason to believe that the previously approved spending levels may not be appropriate. Zero-based budgeting techniques that facilitate the analysis of the total budget rather than just the increases therefore become important.

The initial approach adopted by the proponents of zero-based budgeting was what has come to be known as sunset analysis. Sunset analysis presumes that the responsibility center does not exist. Starting from this zero base, the function that the responsibility center should serve is identified, and a new responsibility center is designed to fulfill these functions. Although sunset analyses are a mandated exercise for certain government agencies at intervals of five years, experience has shown that it is a difficult procedure to carry out, even infrequently. Variations on this comprehensive but difficult analytic technique have been developed, some of them better suited to business firms.

A variation that has been widely adopted, with considerable success, is sensitivity analysis. Here the manager of the responsibility center is asked what activities or functions will be affected, added, or dropped if authorized spending levels are increased or decreased by 10, 15, or 20 percent. Thus, the personnel manager at AIM might identify training programs that could be added or dropped if the budget was changed. The general manager can then make a more meaningful judgment about the appropriate level of spending for the personnel department.

Another variation, which is more demanding but has been used with great success by many companies, including Texas Instruments, is the decision-package approach. The managers of responsibility centers are required to break down and group their activities into discrete, stand-alone packages, each of which can be added or dropped without affecting the other packages. This is a more comprehensive approach than the sensitivity analysis technique. Although it demands greater effort the first year it is implemented, the decision-package approach offers benefits of flexibility and comprehensiveness that usually justify the added effort.

In addition to these analytic techniques, it is useful to review and specify to the extent possible the standard operating procedures for discretionary expense centers. A good example is an insurance company that employs mortgage examiners who review the legal aspects of mortgages being purchased from other financial institutions. When economic downturns reduce the number of mortgages being offered for sale, it is standard operating practice for these mortgage examiners to shift to handling foreclosures, which increase under such economic conditions. Another example could be in the personnel department in AIM, where clerical workers may be assigned to the accounting department for certain days at the beginning of each month to assist in the preparation of performance reports. The specification of standard operating procedures would ensure that the resources assigned to discretionary expense centers are employed more efficiently.

Another possibility that should always be thoroughly explored but cautiously implemented is the use of surrogate or indirect measures of effectiveness. The quality and availability of services that a particular responsibility center is expected to provide to other responsibility centers could, for instance, be assessed by the recipients. In particular, complaints about the availability and quality of service should be recorded and analyzed as a basis for improved planning and control of the operations of discretionary expense centers.

Allocation techniques can bring about an awareness and questioning of the cost of operating the organization's discretionary expense centers. An effective approach is to allocate the cost of each discretionary expense center to the responsibility centers receiving its services. If the amount of the allocation of the personnel department's costs to the manufacturing department increases for the coming budget year compared to the allocation for the previous year, the manufacturing manager is sure to raise questions unless an increase in services is anticipated. Such allocations ensure incremental analysis. A precaution to be observed if this practice of allocation is adopted is to ensure that in performance reports, the amount of allocation reported to, say, the manufacturing manager should always be the same as the budgeted amount. Any variation between actual and budgeted amounts should not normally be considered the responsibility of the manufacturing manager, and to report such variances in allocations would result in wasted time and unnecessary explanations during performance reviews. In short, the practice of allocations is useful when planning the budget but undesirable when comparing actual and budgeted performance.

Many companies (Ford, for example) focus on personnel as the key to planning and controlling for discretionary expense centers. In most such responsibility centers, personnel is the most important resource. By carefully planning and strictly controlling the number and types of personnel employed by discretionary expense centers, organizations can easily and effectively manage the level of expenses incurred by these centers. Thus, human resource management practices are an important determinant of the cost and quality of staff departments.

The preceding techniques focus on internal practices in the firm. Some companies use information from trade and industry associations as a basis for identifying staff departments that appear to merit particularly careful analysis. For instance, if the accounting departments in other organizations similar to AIM employ, on the average, 6 percent of the personnel in the organization and if AIM's accounting department employs 8 percent, perhaps there is reason to examine whether the difference is justified. Industry comparisons should be used with care because there might be excellent reasons to deviate from the industry norms.

Finally, it must never be forgotten that discretionary expense centers in general, and staff departments in particular, almost always include activities that are amenable to the application of standards. It is often worthwhile to seek out the activities that are in the nature of engineered expenses and develop standards that can serve as a basis for planning and control.

The techniques discussed have been found to be effective in practice. It is not desirable, though, to rely solely on such techniques to control the cost of staff departments or discretionary expense centers in general. The managers of these staff departments should exercise close personal supervision over their subordinates. Also, during reviews of actual costs and performance against budgeted costs and performance, probing questions about the variances will motivate managers to pay close attention to their operations. Such close attention is particularly necessary in staff departments where the appropriate level of expenditure is a matter of opinion. Without demonstrated top management concern, the costs of these departments will inevitably increase. To summarize, the wide differences among staff departments make it necessary to emphasize the careful selection of the appropriate planning and control focus from among the following possibilities:

Focus primarily on effectiveness. (Purchasing, computer services, accounting)

Focus primarily on efficiency. (Maintenance)

Focus primarily on the work load or process. (Personnel)

Focus on projects and project planning and control techniques. (Applied research and development)

Focus primarily on the inputs or resources employed. (Basic research, legal)

In addition to developing budget formats as recommended in the previous chapter, the range of techniques available for planning for and controlling the staff departments should be examined and suitable techniques selected for each staff department. These techniques include the following:

Using appropriation budgets.

Employing incremental analysis.

Applying sunset analysis.

Trying sensitivity analysis.

Identifying decision packages.

Specifying standard operating procedures.

Developing surrogate or indirect measures of effectiveness.

Implementing allocation techniques.

Instituting suitable personnel practices.

Making industry comparisons.

Identifying engineered expense elements and applying standards.

12
The Master Budget and Operational Plan Formulation and Review

The master budget and operational plan is more than just the aggregation of the standards and budgets developed in the context of the responsibility centers that comprise the organization. Obviously, though, there is a strong linkage in both directions between the master budget of the organization and the budget of the responsibility centers.

Perhaps the most important perspective to maintain in this context is that the master budget is much more than a control mechanism. It is very much a planning mechanism, which is why I emphasize that it is the master budget and operational plan. Being both a planning and control mechanism creates special problems in terms of balancing efficiency and effectiveness, control and creativity, risk taking and caution. The impact of the budget and the budgeting process on managerial behavior can be most significant.

Three particularly significant elements of the master budget affect managerial behavior: the degree of difficulty or reach implicit in the benchmarks set, the extent of managerial participation in the formulation of the budget, and the nature of the review of actual performance in relation to the budget.

One final point must be recognized. The master budget constitutes perhaps the most important device by which the various parts of the organization can be brought together or integrated. The functional organization emerges as a response to the need for specialized expertise in such key areas as production, marketing, finance, and human resources. The need for integration that results from this inevitable differentiation can be responded to in a truly synergistic manner by the budgeting processes and the budget. This critical function of the master budget and operational plan has a major influence on the design of the system.

Key Characteristics of the Master Budget

Two characteristics in particular distinguish the master budget recommended here from the conventional budgets that are developed in most organizations.

First, the time horizon (number of years into the future) that the master budget will be designed to cover will be carefully selected in keeping with the characteristics of each firm. The conventional choice of a one-year or two-year horizon is essentially arbitrary. The choice of a horizon of one year stems from the traditional financial emphasis of budgets. The one-year horizon undesirably reinforces the financial orientation of the budget unless the horizon is in line with the operating characteristics of the firm. The action orientation of the master budgeting system recommended here requires the choice of the time horizon to be consistent with the nature of of the actions and decisions typical of the firm.

The second major difference between the proposed master budgeting system and conventional budgets is the scope and focus of the content of the master budgeting system. Traditional budgets focus on financial statements. The proposed system will focus on action plans that are carefully and logically developed to respond to the issues identified by the strategic planning system and therefore be consistent with the environmental opportunities and internal capabilities of the organization. The quantitative goals that will be employed to define the organization's direction and measure its accomplishments will include financial and nonfinancial indicators of performance. In addition, in the light of the range of uncertainties that have a bearing on the organization's performance, suitable contingency plans will be included as part of the documentation of the master budget.

Defining the Horizon

The master budget must respond to the nature of the organization's activities. Each firm usually has an obvious operating cycle if all of its products belong to a single industry. An operating cycle is the length of time it takes to manufacture and sell a typical product. In the garment industry, operating cycles cannot exceed six months because of the influence of fashion and seasonal changes. In the shipbuilding industry, the operating cycle is two to three years. In many manufacturing firms, the operating cycle is less than a year.

The time horizon of the master budget must be linked to the operating cycle, as indicated in table 12–1. The reasoning that is the basis for the recommended time horizons is simple. The time horizon of the master budget cannot be less than one year, regardless of how short the operating cycle is. Forecasted financial statements for at least one year into the future are necessary to plan cash management, negotiate with financing agencies and unions, and so on. The financial community operates on an annual cycle, and the firm has no option but to comply with this convention.

Assuming that master budgets are rolling plans developed on an annual basis, the time horizon should be designed to capture the implications of

Table 12–1
Master Budget Time Horizon and the Operating Cycle

Operating Cycle	Recommended Time Horizon
Less than 6 months	1 year
6 months to 1 year	2 years
More than 1 year but less than 2 years	3 years
More than 2 years	Operating cycle plus 1 year. (Rounded up to the nearest whole number, e.g.: 2.4 year operating cycle + 1 year = 4-year time horizon)

managerial actions and decisions taken toward the end of the budget year—hence the need to add one year to the operating cycle to determine the budget time horizon. Because it is difficult to work with periods less than a year, the time horizon is always specified in whole numbers. This practice of using whole numbers of years also fits in with an annual updating of the master budget.

The key consideration in determining the time horizon is that it should be long enough to encompass the consequences of the operating decisions and actions of managers. This is the reason why the operating cycle has such a major influence on the recommended time horizon. In addition to the operating cycle, it may be useful to identify key decisions made by operating managers and examine the normal time period over which the results of these decisions how up. For instance, in an organization that relies primarily on advertising to generate sales, the period over which advertisements are expected measurably to influence sales should be encompassed by the budget horizon. Examples of such organizations would be those whose products are discretionary or luxury purchases such as toys and cosmetics.

Some organizations might emphasize new product development as an operational rather than strategic responsibility. In the breakfast food industry, particularly the segment focusing on children, new products and packaging constantly have to be developed and phased out. In such cases, the determination of the operating cycle should take new product development times into account. In short, the master budget time horizon should encompass the period over which operating actions and decisions will have a measurable impact on the organization's performance.

The argument is often made that the degree of uncertainty affecting the organization should also influence the time horizon of budgets. The more uncertainty there is, it is argued, the shorter the time horizon should be. This is a tenuous argument at best. Regardless of the uncertainties, managers have to make decisions and take actions. The best estimate of the impact of these decisions and actions has to be made based on the current understanding of what is most likely to happen. If assumptions about the future prove to be wrong, contingency plans can respond to these developments. Thus the operating cycle of the organization, the impact period of key decisions, should determine the time horizon of the master budget, not the level of uncertainty about the future.

Applying these recommendations to AIM, it appears that the two product lines, residential and industrial, have different operating cycles. In the residential product line, manufacturing and selling are parallel processes. Thus the operating cycle for residential products probably equals the normal manufacturing time for the standard residential meters. In the industrial product line, order generation and manufacture are sequential processes because the meters are largely made to order. The operating cycle is therefore the sum of the time it normally takes to generate an order and to manufacture the product.

Advertising is maintained at a constant level, and hence the impact of advertising decisions is likely to be constant and can be ignored. New product development is not a significant activity and hence has little bearing on the time horizon.

It appears that the sum of the order-generating plus manufacturing time of the industrial product line should be the operating cycle that determines the time horizon of AIM's profit budget. The operating cycle of the residential product line is less, and if the time horizon was determined on the basis of the residential product line, it would be too short for the industrial product line. In cases such as AIM, where more than one operating cycle exists, the longest should be chosen to determine the budget horizon.

The operating cycle of AIM's industrial product line normally lies between six months and one year. From table 12–1 we determine that the time horizon of AIM's master budget should be two years.

Formulating the Operational Plan

The heart of the master budget is an operational plan focusing on actions to be taken. The skeleton of the operational plan is formed of the issues identified as part of the strategic planning exercise. (In the years between comprehensive strategic planning exercises, the strategic issue management system described in chapter 16 would ensure timely operational responses to emerging issues.) The operational plan should identify the actions or programs to be implemented in response to the key issues identified through the strategic planning (chapter 6) or strategic issue management (chapter 16) exercises. It is necessary to develop and articulate the following:

1. Specific actions to be taken.
2. Deadline by which action is to be taken.
3. Executive (identified by name and title) responsible for carrying out the action.
4. Executive responsible for monitoring the timeliness and effectiveness of the action.
5. Financial and physical consequences of the actions.
6. Contingency plans.

Action Plans

The action plans or programs that flow from the strategic issues are elements of the operational plan that are recorded as part of the budgets of the managers who have responsibility for executing these actions or programs. In AIM, actions relating to manufacturing efficiency should be included in the budget format of the foreman of the machine shop, to the extent that he or she is responsible for achieving progress to related quantitative goals. The budget document for the general manager would similarly incorporate those actions he or she has the responsibility to execute or monitor.

The importance of the articulation of these action plans as a key component of the budgeting system cannot be overemphasized. First, they are the primary linkage between the strategic planning and the management control activities of the organization. They reflect the outcome of the analysis built into the design of the budget formats. Also by responding to strategic issues, they translate into reality the organizational aspirations arising out of the matching of the firm's capabilities and the potential in the environment. Implementing the operational plan is therefore an integral step in implementing the organization's strategic plan.

Second, the action plan delineates what needs to be done differently from the way operations are carried out currently. This contributes to the communication between departments and hierarchical levels that is needed to accomplish the integration that is a basic purpose of the budgeting system. The various departments and responsibility centers can explicitly identify the changes in the support of or relationships with other departments or responsibility centers that should take place during the budget period. A budgeting system with a primarily financial orientation cannot be as effective in this regard.

Third, during a comparison of actual to budgeted performance in the review and follow-up process, the operational plan greatly facilitates the identification of needed remedial action. The explicit assignment of responsibility for implementation and for monitoring the implementation contributes greatly to motivation. In addition, it simplifies the exercise of control because the timing and consequences of actions are specified so that it can be more easily determined whether the planned action was appropriate.

Quantitative Goals

The quantitative goals define the results expected from effective implementation of the master budget and operational plan. These goals should also be part of the budget formats for all managers who have any responsibility for executing or monitoring the operational plan.

The other quantitative goals for the organization as a whole flow naturally from the performance report designed for the general manager. The key indicators of performance relating to the managers reporting to him or her would be included in the performance report and would therefore have appropriate expectations set.

In addition to these quantitative factors, it is necessary to ensure that a projected cash flow statement for the budget period is developed. The cash flow statement would normally be part of the performance report and budget format of the executive in charge of the finance function—in AIM, the chief accountant. It is desirable, however, given the great importance of cash management, that the cash flow statement also be included in the performance report and budget format of the chief executive. In AIM the general manager should receive monthly or weekly statements of the cash position and also have the projected cash flow statement as part of his or her budget documentation.

In most cases, it is necessary to generate complete pro forma financial statements (income statement and balance sheet), which can be used in the course of negotiations with external or nonmanagement bodies such as banks and unions. It would be inappropriate to use the general manager's performance report and related budget formats in such discussions for obvious reasons. If these external requirements were not present, the statement of quantitative goals for the general manager (that is, the firm as a whole) would be in formats designed exactly as discussed in chapter 10.

With regard to quantitative goals, the need for nonfinancial or physical goals in addition to financial goals must be emphasized. The ultimate, bottom-line financial measure or goal is profit. Although it is understandably the most importance measure of performance, it suffers from a variety of shortcomings. First, it is possible for a firm to have objectives other than just profits—perhaps maintaining employment levels, playing a major role in community affairs, or being the acknowledged technological innovator in the industry. These objectives are best measured in nonfinancial terms and occupy a legitimate place in performance reports and budget formats.

Second, profit is essentially a short-term measure. It is possible to increase this year's profits by taking actions such as reducing corporate advertising, cutting down on management development, and minimizing R&D expenses. However, such actions essentially exchange future profits for more profits in the present. To emphasize and understand the long-term implications of profit-maximizing decisions, nonfinancial measures such as market share and rate of new product development are essential.

Third, profits are affected by a variety of factors that may or may not be subject to the control of the firm's management. Thus it is desirable to employ other measures to help assess how much of the change in profits was due to managerial efforts and how much to chance. Indicators such as market share and work-load measures are of value in this regard.

Fourth, profits are subject to manipulation within the bounds of generally accepted accounting principles. Nonfinancial measures can shed light on performance, unaffected by accounting phenomena such as the effect of inventory fluctuations in a full-cost system and the effect of changes in accounting practices.

The need for the direction afforded by strategic planning is obvious when considering these shortcomings of the profit measure.

Contingency Plans

There are two distinctly different types of contingency plans, each effective in particular circumstances: the thermostat (or trigger variable) approach and the scenario approach. The differences between these two approaches are indicated in figure 12–1.

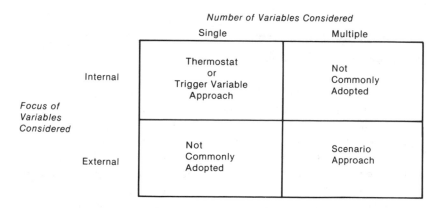

Figure 12–1. Types of Contingency Plans

The simpler type of contingency plan focuses on a single variable that is largely internal in character, such as sales or orders booked. The contingency plan in effect broadly outlines the actions to be taken when various situations arise—for example, sales or orders booked falling 10 percent below budgeted levels for two months in a row or by 20 percent for one month, and so on. A classic contingency plan of this type is the flexible budget employed in the manufacturing context (described in chapter 10). These simple thermostat-type contingency plans have been widely employed by companies such as ITT. Although they possess the advantages of simplicity, ease of development, and precise identification of responses, they are best suited to organizations operating in relatively less complex and less uncertain environments. Coca-Cola Company and McDonald's could justifiably and effectively employ the thermostat type of contingency plan because of their simple, limited product lines and the relatively few external variables of importance in the short run. For instance, Coca-Cola Company's sales of soft drinks within a budgeting period would probably be more affected by weather conditions than any other external factor.

More complex organizations operating in more complex environments should use the scenario approach (though the thermostat approach could still be used for resonsibility centers within these organizations), which focuses on several external variables that describe the relevant environment for the firm. For instance, in AIM the following variables would be of importance:

Housing starts by region.

New investment in process plants by region.

Market share of firms in meter industry that will go bankrupt.

Prime lending rate.

Inflation rate.

Expected price changes for major raw materials.

Market share captured by electronic meters.

For each of the selected variables, the most likely value or state during the budget period is decided. This will be the scenario on which the detailed operational plan is developed.

For each of the selected variables, the most unfavorable value or state and the most favorable value or state that can reasonably (5 to 10 percent probability) be expected during the budget period are identified. These two values or states give rise to two additional scenarios, the most pessimistic and the most optimistic. For each scenario, outlines of operational plans should be developed. These broad operational plans constitute the contingency plans for the organization.

This approach to contingency planning has been effectively employed in the Asian operations of Citibank. It has both advantages and disadvantages. Its primary advantage is that it focuses management attention on variables that, though largely out of its control, will have a significant impact on the organization. In comparison, the thermostat approach might contribute to managerial insensitivity to important external developments. It forces management to think through in advance the complex implications of variations in these factors.

The complexity of the exercise is a disadvantage. A more troublesome disadvantage is that the actual situation that develops will probably not coincide with any of the three (most pessimistic, most likely, and most optimistic) scenarios. Also, certain variables may move toward the pessimistic end and others toward the optimistic end. Management therefore cannot blindly apply the contingency plans developed for the pessimistic or optimistic scenarios. Judgment will be required to determine the appropriate response to actual developments.

In my experience, the advantages of the scenario approach to contingency planning appear to outweigh significantly the disadvantages. The more effective identification of the need to modify the master budget and operational plan is of great value. In addition, if adequate attention and thought are paid to the development of the contingency plans for the pessimistic and optimistic scenarios, management will possess a valuable appreciation of the range of alternative responses that should be considered. As a consequence, the speed and effectiveness with which responses to unanticipated developments are implemented is greatly improved. In organizations where the strategic issue management system discussed in chapter 16 is not perceived to be effective, the scenario approach takes on even greater importance as a means of responding to environmental developments.

Managing the Budgeting Process

To complete the design of the system, it is necessary to define the responsibilities of individual managers in developing the master budget. The timing and duration of the activities involved also have to be specified. The most fundamental consideration influencing these decisions is the form of the managerial hierarchy. In AIM, for instance, not only is there a general manager, but there are executives one level below (chief accountant, personnel manager, manufacturing manager, and marketing manager) and two levels below (product managers, foremen). Each executive has a budget and responsibility center to manage. The organization's master budget has to recognize and integrate these responsibility center budgets. A basic issue that then arises is how these responsibility center budgets and the master budget should affect one another.

The relationship between the master budget and the responsibility center budgets is complex. Should top management's goals and aspirations be the prime determinant of the content of these budgets? If the answer is yes, a top-down (master budget ⟶ responsibility center budgets), authoritarian type of managerial involvement must be defined. Should the departmental or functional manager's perceptions of what is feasible determine the master budget? If the answer to the this question is yes, a bottom-up (responsibility center budgets ⟶ master budget), highly participative type of managerial involvement must be encouraged.

Neither a top-down or bottom-up process is appropriate for most organizations. The exceptional circumstances where the process should be strongly biased toward the authoritarian or participative extremes will be identified later. In most organizations, both top management and operating management have contributions to make and insights to offer. Top management may be more familiar with or cognizant of economic, regulatory, political, and other environmental factors. The CEO is ordinarily more aware of and sensitive to owners' or stockholders' preferences with regard to growth and risk. The expectations and priorities of the communities in which plants and offices are located will probably be communicated by community officials to the CEO. The deliberations and orientation of the board of directors are known to the CEO. Most CEOs attain their position through demonstrated managerial competence and relevant experience and will have important contributions to make to the organization's profit plans. Finally, the CEO is presumably the executive most familiar with the directions suggested by the organization's strategic plans and certainly has the final responsibility for achieving strategic aspirations.

Operating management is normally most familiar with the capabilities and limitations of their departments and the characteristics of the territories for which they are responsible. Their commitment to the achievement of the quantitative goals specified in the master budget will be affected by their perceptions of how well the budget has taken into account the factors they consider important.

The process that should be adopted in most organizations should therefore represent a balance between the top-down and bottom-up extremes. Such a balance can be accomplished by designing a series of formal communications between top management and lower-level managers. An iterative process where assumptions, plans, and goals are communicated back and forth and progressively refined can exploit the insights and understanding of both top management and operating management. The process can also be designed to be biased, to the degree thought to be desirable, toward either the authoritarian or participative extremes.

Illustrative iterative processes are diagrammed in figure 12–2, which shows a variety of options available to orient the process toward the desired authoritarian or participative extreme. In simple businesses operating in

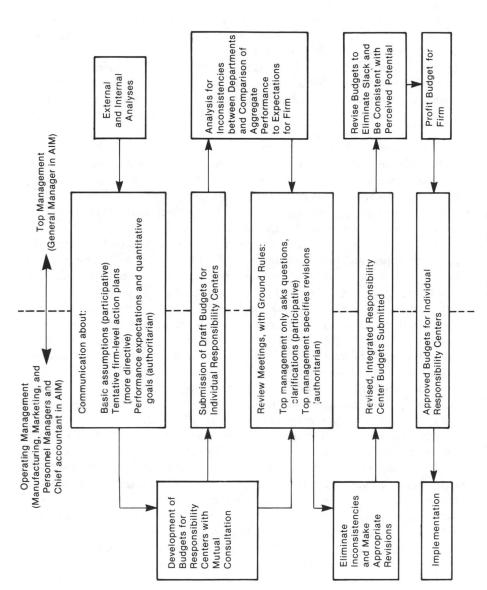

Figure 12–2. Top-Down and Bottom-Up Processes

stable environments, where top management has considerable experience in the industry, and where operating management have strongly functional rather than general management expertise, a greater top-down or authoritarian bias is appropriate. In complex businesses with highly uncertain environments, a more participative bias is usually desirable.

In some companies such as ITT where the management culture is oriented toward the authoritarian mode, the process tends to be more top-down. In my opinion, organizational effectiveness requires that the culture should reflect the type of operations and environment rather than the personal values of top management.

An authoritarian approach may be effectively employed for limited periods of time in organizations where operating management has displayed a tendency toward complacency or lackluster performance. By specifying goals that demand a high degree of effort and competence on the part of operating management, top management can shock lower levels of management into more acceptable modes of operation.

The first communication recommended in figure 12–2 is from top management to operating management. If a participative approach is desired, all that needs to be communicated are the basic assumptions that constitute the most likely environmental scenario. If more direction is thought necessary, an outline of top management's thinking about the operational plan for the firm can be communicated in addition to the assumptions. If even greater direction is to be provided, the levels of performance that will be considered acceptable could be specified, in addition to the basic assumptions and the outline of the operational plan.

Basic assumptions should always be communicated to provide consistent responsibility center budgets. If the performance expectations are specified, it is desirable to outline the tentative operational plan so as to indicate to operating management that these performance expectations have some basis and are not entirely arbitrary.

The review meeting suggested following the submission of the tentative responsibility center budgets can also be designed to promote the desired orientation of the process. At such meetings, Motorola has successfully employed the ground rule that top management will not exercise its authority to demand revisions in the budgets being considered but will only ask questions and seek clarifications. The behavioral consequences of this ground rule are significant. First, a more participative climate results. Second, operating managers do not lose face by having to recognize explicitly and publicly their budgets' shortcomings. They have the option to indicate that further study or consideration will be given to the issues raised by top management. Competent operating managers will employ the meetings as an opportunity to identify top management's preferences and orientation. Third, and this is an interesting point, top management has to do its homework before the meeting in order to identify flaws, inadequacies, or inconsistencies in the budgets. They do not have the option to mask poor preparation or understanding by exercising their authority in an arbitrary fashion.

The meeting can be made more authoritarian very easily. Top management that is sensitive to the behavioral nuances can tailor the interactions at these meetings to promote the desired climate in the organization.

At these meetings, all managers reporting to the top management should be present. These meetings are a valuable opportunity to exchange information and ideas and to promote the maximum integration and consistency of the department and functional budgets. In some organizations, the review meetings are limited to individual operating managers and top management. Although this practice reduces the pressures experienced by operating management, the communication and integration purposes of budgeting are poorly served.

As a leading behavioral scientist who had experienced administrative responsibility recently phrased it, "The boss must boss!" The revised budgets submitted by operating management must be modified by top management to eliminate inconsistencies and fully exploit the strategic potential that top management believes exists. The need for such modifications should, however, be minimal given carefully designed interactions between top management and operating management.

Time Dimension

Three important time-related decisions have to be made when designing the budgeting system: the time horizon that the budget should cover, the span or duration of the process of developing the budget, and the frequency with which the budget development exercise is to be repeated.

Three considerations should be taken into account when determining the appropriate duration of the budget development process. Two of these considerations suggest as short a duration as possible. First, when the budget development process takes a long time, momentum and executive commitment are often lost. The psychological implications are made even more adverse by the resulting perception that too much time is being taken up by the process, to the detriment of other managerial responsibilities. Second, the longer the duration of the process, the greater is the probability that the basic assumptions and scenarios will be proved inappropriate or obsolete. An organization that devotes, say, six months to the process probably develops its basic assumptions in July (assuming that the fiscal and calendar years coincide) for the final budget that may be completed in early December. Instead, if the organization had devoted two months to the process, it would develop its assumptions in October, with a great deal more reliability and accuracy.

The constraint on minimizing the duration of the process is the need to provide a reasonable amount of time for the required analysis. Judgments will have to be made about the appropriate minimum time, but the designer's bias should be strongly toward as short a duration as possible. If no complaints are heard from operating managers about inadequate time to develop the budget, the duration is almost certainly too long.

The third and final time-related design decision is the frequency with which the budgeting exercise must be carried out. Standards need to be examined annually and revised if technological or competitive developments have made them obsolete. The operational plan, unlike the strategic plan, does not necessarily suffer from annual repetition. An annual exercise enables the organization to respond to the need for updating plans that are becoming irrelevant because of unexpected developments. The master budget and operational plan are often the basis for incentive compensation schemes, and therefore plans that do not reflect reality are demoralizing rather than motivating. Given the practice of annual performance appraisals, annual operational planning and budgeting exercises are consistent. Also the budget reflects a commitment to performance unlike the strategic plan, which reflects the aspirations of the organization. If commitment to stated results is expected of the organization's executives, the budgets and operational plans must clearly reflect reality. Annual exercises can therefore be justified.

Performance Review

It is widely presumed, particularly in academic circles, that the top-down or bottom-up orientation of the process of formulating the budget and operational plan is the most important behavioral consideration when designing the budgeting system. A research project (Bhattacharyya and Camillus 1977) that looked at the systems in about ninety companies indicated that an equally, if not more, important behavioral consideration is the review and follow-up exercise. The comparison and analysis of actual performance in relation to the budget and the initiation and monitoring of remedial action appeared to be the most important determinants of the perceived effectiveness of the management control system. On the basis of in-depth interviews with executives in companies that considered their systems to be effective, the study identified the key guidelines for ensuring an effective review and follow-up process.

The importance of a well-designed and executed performance review cannot be exaggerated. Systems that have been extremely well designed in other respects founder because of poorly executed performance reviews. On the other hand, systems of mediocre design in other respects can perform quite satisfactorily if the performance review is well executed.

The quality of the performance analysis and the manner in which the review is carried out can provide strong signals about management's commitment to using the management control system effectively. The guidelines discussed take into account vital behavioral implications of the way in which the review is carried out. In particular, the resulting attitudes of lower-level managers and their approach to subsequent budget formulation processes have to be borne in mind. The master budget and operational plan is both a planning and a control tool, and top management's approach to exercising control can greatly influence the creativity and attitudes to openness and risk taking on the part of lower-level managers in later operational planning exercises.

Frequency of Review

The frequency with which performance should be reviewed jointly by the manager of a responsibility center and his or her superior is largely determined by the nature of operations in the responsibility center. The characteristics of the responsibility center that determine the frequency with which formal performance reports should be made are the characteristics that largely determine the frequency with which formal joint reviews should be scheduled.

Although weekly reports may be generated at lower levels in the organization, most of the important responsibility centers will have reports generated on a monthly basis. Consequently joint reviews cannot ordinarily be scheduled more often than at monthly intervals. In situations where the environment is stable, departmental or functional managers are competent, the product line has been in existence for years, and no significant changes in these conditions are expected, it would be reasonable to schedule meetings between the CEO and department heads as infrequently as once every quarter.

An important consideration is the possibility of encouraging adaptive control. The budgets that have been developed attempt to be effective in identifying the profit potential available. As time progresses, however, the possibility of a better understanding of the potential might emerge. In such situations, it may be desirable to encourage managers to adapt or modify their originally planned actions and decisions to exploit the improved understanding. Thus, when adaptive control is implemented, performance will be assessed not only in relation to the budgets but also in relation to the best performance that could have been accomplished, given the improved understanding. Adaptive control is a difficult process to implement successfully in the majority of situations. It demands a high degree of trust and mutual respect between superiors and subordinates at all levels. It also requires highly effective communications between departmental or functional managers so that the needed integration of their respective actions can be maintained. These managers must be committed to the organization's goals rather than to the performance goals of their individual department.

Adaptive control is not suited to every organization. In firms where the conditions discussed exist, adaptive control could be encouraged during the formal review and follow-up exercise by comparing performance to what the maximum performance could have been, in addition to comparing performance to budgeted expectations. When adaptive control has been found to function effectively in the organization, the frequency of formal reviews can be greatly reduced.

Role of the Superior

The superior executive participating in each formal joint review of performance can greatly influence the exercise through the attitude he or she brings to the exercise. In fact, the climate that exists during these reviews substantially determines the managerial climate of the organization as a whole.

The superior can make the review process an exercise in attaching or apportioning blame for shortcomings in performance or a collaborative effort where superior and subordinate apply their insights and abilities jointly to the task of improving future performance.

The superior and subordinate have distinctive and valuable contributions to make. The superior has a broader organizational perspective of the reasons for and implications of the performance of the subordinate's responsibility center. The subordinate is close to where the action is and can provide a detailed and first-hand understanding that may not be reflected in the performance reports. It is up to the superior to exploit these competences in the effort to analyze and remedy deviations from budgeted performance.

In terms of deciding on remedial action, the superior must determine when the subordinate's suggestions and preferences should be accepted and when they should be modified. In at least three exceptional circumstances, however, the superior has the obligation to overrule the subordinate. First, if the subordinate's plans are clearly inappropriate, based on erroneous assumptions, or do not take into account information available to the superior, the superior should exercise his or her authority if the subordinate does not appear to be open to reason or persuasion. If the need to exercise authority for these reasons keeps recurring, the subordinate's competence may well be in question.

Second, if a continuing trend over two or three formal reviews indicates that the subordinate's remedial actions and plans are consistently ineffective, the superior should assume a more direct and substantive responsibility for identifying and implementing remedial action. The importance of keeping track of trends is obvious in this context.

Third, if there are remedial actions that fall within the superior's capability but that lie outside the formal authority of the subordinate, it would be reasonable and appropriate for the superior to become directly involved at an early stage. An example of such actions would be the transferring of resources such as personnel from other responsbility centers to the responsibility center that is experiencing difficulty.

Except for these circumstances, the superior should allow the subordinate a free hand in selecting and implementing remedial actions. For the superior to get more directly involved in circumstances other than those discussed would probably lessen the subordinate's self-confidence and commitment to seeing the remedial action succeed and would waste a resource that the firm is paying for.

ITT has been observed to follow a pattern of responses to deviations that largely follows these recommendations. There is a graduated assumption of responsibility by the superior executive. The practice adopted is that poor performance by the subordinate over one or two review periods is left largely to the subordinate to resolve. The possibility exists that this poor performance may be the result of random occurrences and will disappear. Also, the subordinate must be given the opportunity to correct the situation, and it is presumed that most have the competence to do so on their own. It would be overly demanding on the superior and would not be utilizing the subordinate's capabilities if all deviations were treated as the superior's direct responsibility to rectify. If the deviations continue for three or more review periods, the superior is expected to give explicit directions to the subordinate as to the appropriate remedial actions. At this time the superior is expected to identify remedial actions that are within the superior's powers to implement but that are beyond the bounds of the subordinate's formal authority. Thus other responsibility centers that report to the superior and that can aid the responsibility center in difficulty may be directed to offer specific additional support. Finally, if the problem continues, it becomes the superior's responsibility to correct the situation. If the problem is significant enough, higher levels of the organization progressively get involved.

The superior executive must bear one more point in mind. It is highly desirable that the review process emphasize the management control problem of identifying reasons for deviation of performance from the budget and instituting required remedial action. The personnel problem of evaluating the subordinate's shortcomings and determining appropriate future development should be kept as much in the background as possible. If it were possible to divorce the review process from the personnel evaluation and development issue, that would be recommended. It is not feasible, however, to ignore entirely the personnel evaluation considerations when conducting the review and follow-up exercise. Ultimately the superior's perceptions about the subordinate's capabilities and characteristics will enter into the annual personnel appraisal exercise leading to decisions about training, development, and career paths. It is desirable, nevertheless, to keep the personnel evaluation considerations to a minimum during the review and follow-up process so that as open and collaborative a relationship as possible between the superior and subordinate is encouraged.

Role of the Subordinate

The subordinate's role and behavior is largely dictated by the approach adopted by the superior. If the superior adopts a fault-finding stance, the subordinate is likely to be wary, defensive, and not entirely candid. If the superior emphasizes collaborative problem solving, the subordinate will be encouraged to be open, frank, and creative in identifying remedial actions.

One of the most important judgments that the subordinate should make is whether deviations from budgets are caused by erroneous assumptions, improper goals, ineffective action plans, or poor implementation. This determination is important because the appropriate managerial response is greatly affected.

If erroneous assumptions are the problem, it may be necessary to review the entire budget, including goals and operational plans. If the goals are improper or impractical, both goals and action plans may have to be revised. If the operational plans are ineffective, alternative means of accomplishing the stated goals must be sought. If poor implementation is the key, the manager has to look to his or her own behavior and efforts as the key to improving the situation.

The adaptive control approach must be viewed as a recognition of their competence and as a challenge by the subordinates who are expected to achieve better than budgeted performance if the opportunity arises. The uncertainty under which they operate in an adaptive situation is obviously greater than in a solely budget-oriented control situation. If the subordinates do not perceive the adaptive control practices at review time as reflecting their superior's confidence in their capabilities, the adaptive control process will not work. It would be best, then, to use the budget as the primary or sole benchmark for evaluating performance.

Coping with Uncertainty

The recommended management control system is designed to recognize and reduce the uncertainties that can cause actual performance to deviate from budgeted performance. Even in the best-designed system, uncertainties can affect managerial performance. The most competent and committed managers will inevitably encounter situations where despite their best efforts, the performance of their responsibility centers will fall short of budgeted expectations. The review exercise must take cognizance of this possibility.

The superior executive can adopt several responses. First, the subordinate can be told that the budgeted expectations have to be met regardless of the problems encountered. Second, the superior can accept and operate on revised expectations for the remaining period until the budget is scheduled to be formally updated but still base rewards and penalties on the original budget expectations. Third, the superior can agree to revise budget expectations and base rewards and penalties on the revised figures. Each of these responses is appropriate in specific situations.

If the assumptions on which the budget was developed continue to be perceived as valid and if there is the possibility of the subordinate's being able to make up the shortfall in the remaining time before a formally updated budget goes into operation, the superior should not revise the budget. In other words, if the causes of the deviations are not erroneous assumptions or improper or infeasible goals, the budget should not be revised. In fact, the bias should be strongly toward not revising the budget if the assumptions continue to be correct.

If the shortcomings are due to poor implementation of the action plan, the year-end goals should not be revised. The subordinate responsible for the poor performance can in fact be arbitrarily assigned higher targets for the remaining period so that the originally set goals for the budget period can be achieved.

If the assumptions on which the budget was based are proved to be wrong, revising the goals and action plans may be appropriate. It would be desirable, however, to retain the financial goals if possible by modifying the action plan to respond to the changed set of assumptions. Under such circumstances, it may even be best to link incentives to the revised targets.

In the final analysis, the superior must make an assessment of the impact on subordinates' behavior if the budgets are revised. If revising the budget will appear fair and reasonable and motivate subordinates to greater efforts, the budget should be revised. If not revising the budgets is likely to pressure the subordinates into greater efforts, it may be desirable to retain the original budgets even if they are perceived as unfair.

Key Guidelines

There are a few demonstratedly effective guidelines that every superior should keep in mind to ensure an effective review and follow-up exercise.

First, the subordinates should be evaluated with reference to the potential available. If the adaptive control approach is likely to work in the firm, it should be adopted; otherwise performance should be evaluated only with reference to the budget. The common practice of comparing one manager's performance to another's is highly undesirable. The differences between the two situations can be exaggerated by defensive subordinates who then concentrate on explaining why their performance was different and neglect the primary task of rectifying poor performance. Comparing one manager's performance to another's is desirable at the planning stage, when the budget is being developed, so that improved practices can be adopted. Comparisons when performance is being evaluated are highly undesirable.

Second, the superior should always take into consideration the quality and magnitude of the efforts made by the subordinate because no budgeting system can identify potential with certainty. When actual performance falls short of the budget, it could be despite the best efforts of competent managers. In that case, the subordinates could use the reassurance that their superiors recognize that they have done an excellent job despite the unfavorable variances on their performance reports.

Third, importance must be given to tracking trends. The reasons for deviations are more reliably ascertained by analyzing trends than by considering performance for just one reporting period. Also the response by the superior should be influenced by the duration over which the problem has been experienced. A random single-period problem is perhaps best ignored; a continuing multiperiod problem calls for progressively greater involvement of the superior in correcting the situation.

Fourth, superiors must stress the collaborative character of the review process — that it is a joint effort by superior and subordinate to analyze and remedy unsatisfactory performance. If the review process becomes an exercise in apportioning blame, the basic purpose of correcting the situation is not served as effectively.

Fifth, the remedial actions that are decided upon in the review process must be recorded and monitored in subsequent reviews. The format used for operational plans could be used to document and monitor the effectiveness of the planned remedial actions.

Certain features of the recommended budgeting system have been designed to support and improve the review and follow-up process. The operational plans that are the basis of the budget are of immense value in determining the probable cause of shortfalls in performance. If the planned actions have not been taken in time or have not been implemented in the manner specified, probably inadequate managerial effort is the reason for poor performance. If the actions have been implemented and in a timely fashion and the results are still poor, the validity of the goals and the appropriateness of the original operational plan deserve scrutiny. The importance of comprehensive financial and nonfinancial goals in addition to a detailed operational plan should now be evident in the context of the review and follow-up process.

The recommended contingency plans are also of obvious importance. The scenario approach in particular is a powerful technique for monitoring the appropriateness of key assumptions and for reducing the lead time for identifying needed changes in the operational plan to respond to the changed assumptions.

Finally, the explicit identification of the key assumptions by top management during the process of formulating the budget is vital to the review process. Without consistency and agreement between superior and subordinate as to the assumptions on which the budget and operational plan are based, attempts at arriving at a common understanding of the reasons for deviations are likely to be exercises in futility. Also the appropriate managerial response to deviations is contingent on whether the original assumptions continue to be valid. If the original assumptions have not been stated, identifying the appropriate remedial action becomes immensely difficult.

Reference

Bhattacharyya, S.K., and Camillus, J.C. *Management Control Systems: A Framework for Resolution of Problems of Implementation.* New Delhi: Institute of Chartered Accountants of India, 1977.

Part IV
Planning and Control in Complex Organizations

13
Planning and Control in Divisionalized Organizations

In the preceding chapters, we considered the strategic planning and management control systems appropriate to functional organizations. In this chapter, we shall consider the additions to these systems that are necessary in order to respond to the divisionalized organization.

Divisionalized organizations can be visualized as consisting of two or more functional organizations all reporting to a common corporate headquarters (refer to figure 3–1). This conceptualization permits us to simplify the design of planning and control systems and to recognize the peculiarities of this type of organization. Within each division, planning and control systems substantially similar to those described in the preceding chapters would be appropriate; however, each of these divisions should function synergistically in the corporate context. In order to facilitate such synergistic interaction, additional strategic planning and management control activities are necessary.

Four significant additions to the planning and control systems appropriate for functional organizations have to be considered in the context of divisionalized organizations:

1. Cross-divisional linkages.
2. Corporate-divisional linkages.
3. Transfer pricing between divisions.
4. Divisional measures of performance.

Cross-Divisional Linkages

These linkages are of importance because most divisionalized organizations possess a corporate-wide core competence on which the strategies of all the divisions are based. Companies such as Motorola and Texas Instruments during the 1970s were typical of such organizations. In both corporations, electronics-related technology constituted the core competence on which all their divisional strategies were based. When distinctly different product-market strategies and core competences characterize the various divisions in a corporation, the organization has essentially taken on a conglomerate character. In the 1980s, Texas Instruments failed to recognize this development in the context of the consumer-oriented products it offered, in particular personal and home computers. Thus it did not respond formally to its emerging conglomerate character, and serious performance problems resulted.

Because the various divisions in a divisionalized organization employ similar competences, channels of communication and transfer of competences across the divisions should be implemented. The simplest and yet one of the most powerful ways in which cross-divisional communication and knowledge transfer can take place is the creation of task forces with responsibility for individual strategic programs. These task forces would have to be comprised of managers drawn from all the divisions that can contribute to the effective implementation of the program or benefit directly or indirectly from its implementation. They can take on a permanent character, resulting in a matrix structure such as that adopted by Texas Instruments. In such matrix structures, individual managers are assigned strategic responsibility for major programs that cross divisional lines and operating responsibility within a particular division.

Another approach, fairly similar in character, is to depute managers from the various divisions to the corporate planning or development department for a period of a few months to a year. Managers so assigned in essence become sentient communication channels between the individual divisions and the corporate headquarters. They bring to the corporate level an understanding of divisional concerns and issues that might have organization-wide relevance and in turn are sensitized to developments in other divisions and to emerging corporate-level thinking, which they take with them back to their individual divisions. Such practices have been employed with varying degrees of success by a variety of organizations. One such organization that has experienced considerable success with this practice is Time, Inc.

A simple procedure to ensure some degree of cross-divisional communication is to conduct preliminary sessions where the general managers from each division present on an annual or semiannual basis their plan and experiences to colleagues in other divisions. Although these meetings can be hectic and stressful, the benefits in communication among divisions are important.

The capital budgeting process is a powerful mechanism for alerting corporate management to projects that can have benefits to more than one division. Recognizing this possibility, some organizations (for example, Federal Express) employ financial analysts who communicate corporate priorities and perceptions to managers within each division and take back to the corporate level from individual divisions ideas and possibilities that might be of interest and value to other divisions.

Finally, the analysis necessary for effective strategic planning within individual divisions and at a corporate level might be conducted by study groups drawn from more than one division. If the study groups include appropriate corporate-level managers, the level and quality of communication within the organization will be greatly augmented.

Corporate-Divisional Linkages

Some of the mechanisms for promoting cross-divisional linkages can also be effectively employed to promote communication between the corporate and divisional levels. In addition, other possibilities exist.

An interesting approach, which is employed by some organizations, including subsidiaries of Unilever, is the specification of boundary roles. Such boundary roles essentially involve individual managers functioning at both the divisional and corporate level. For instance, the corporate executive committee could include key divisional general managers. And corporate-level boards of directors could include key general managers. These managers function as communication channels between the corporate and divisional levels. When functioning in their corporate roles, they provide detailed perspectives and understanding that can enrich corporate decision making. When functioning in their divisional roles, the quality of their decisions is clearly affected by the corporate perspectives they inevitably absorb.

A key decision that corporate-level management must make in this context is the extent to which they wish to influence or direct divisional decisions and actions. Corporate-level guidance of divisional strategic planning activities can be limited to the specification of broad assumptions about the economy or social and demographic developments that can affect all divisions. At the other extreme, preferred strategic postures for each division and even performance expectations in the long run can be specified by a corporate management that wishes to play a major and direct role in influencing the divisional activities. The more complex the organization is and the more competent the divisional manager is, the less is the need and appropriateness of corporate involvement in divisional planning and control activities.

Transfer Pricing

Analogous to but quite different from transfer pricing between production and marketing departments in functional organizations is the need for transfer pricing between the profit centers or divisions in a divisional organization. Transfer pricing between divisions (profit centers) is a complex activity.

Determining the price one division must pay to another for goods or services provided has economic, behavioral, and structural implications.

The economic imperatives are fairly obvious. The economic performance of the corporation would be adversely affected if a division purchased goods or services from outside the corporation that could have been provided by another division for an out-of-pocket cost less than the price paid to the outside source. Corporate economic performance would also be adversely affected if one division sold to another goods or services that could have been marketed outside the corporation for a greater profit than the goods or services provided by the purchasing division to outside customers.

Corporate economic performance is maximized when the transfer price between divisions is the market price of the goods or services provided. If a true market price is available from external sources, transfer pricing is a relatively simple problem.

If, however, objective and valid market prices cannot be readily obtained, the behavioral considerations pertinent to the transfer pricing issue become of great importance. Openness and trust between the managers of the two divisions concerned is of the essence. The incremental cost of manufacturing the goods or providing the services should be made available by the selling division to the purchasing division. The purchasing division in turn should make available to the selling division the additional cost, anticipated volume, and expected price for the final product or service that would be provided to customers outside the organization. A mutually acceptable sharing of the corporate profits generated by such a partnership usually results when openness in communication exists. It is often desirable to set transfer prices during the course of annual operational planning exercises. When distrust or lack of understanding of the economics of this situation is encountered, corporate-level staff with industrial engineering, cost accounting, and economics expertise can often facilitate the process of arriving at a mutually satisfactory transfer price.

In the rare instances where conflicts between the selling and purchasing divisions are severe and frequent, corporate management must reexamine its structural options. If the charge for goods and services between the two warring divisions is not of significance, an easy solution available to corporate management is to encourage the buying division to develop alternative sources. If the magnitude of the transactions between the two divisions is significant, top management should examine whether the two divisions should be maintained as separate profit centers or whether they can be integrated into a single profit center, with the buying division essentially functioning as the marketing department and the selling division as the production department. The transfer pricing problem then simplifies to the situation described in the context of functional organizations.

The involvement of corporate management in the transfer pricing relationship between divisions should be minimum. If involvement is significant and protracted, the climate within the organization may need to be critically examined. There is, however, the possibility of a situation where corporate management can usefully assume responsibility for setting transfer prices between two profit centers. A classic example is the situation in banks where some branches have more deposits than advances, and other branches are in the opposite situation. In most banks, therefore, the interest rate or transfer price for funds from deposit-heavy branches to advance-heavy branches needs to be specified. Because the overall liquidity of the bank is of critical importance, corporate management may find that managing the transfer price for funds between the branches is of great value. By lowering or raising the interest rate for advances from one branch to another, top management can influence the emphasis that managers from each branch give to seeking more deposits or endeavoring to loan more money.

Transfer pricing has long been seen by academics as an enormously complex issue. From a practical standpoint, however, awareness of the economic, behavioral, and structural implications should enable divisionalized organizations to arrive at a pragmatic response to transfer pricing.

Divisional Measures of Performance

The measures of performance that have been identified in the context of functional organizations are readily applicable to divisions within a corporation and to the corporation as a whole. There exists, however, the possibility that the use of return on investment (ROI) as a major measure of divisional performance could lead to undesirable behavior by the general managers of divisions.

ROI measures the relationship between outputs (profits) and inputs (investment) to determine efficiency. Efficiency measures can be manipulated in ways that do not promote the long-term well-being of the organization. A divisional manager can compensate for a drop in profits by reducing the investment for which he or she is held responsible. Reduction could be accomplished in ways that might have undesirable long-term effects. For instance, inventory levels might be reduced so low that customer satisfaction with delivery times drops considerably. Equipment that may not have immediate use but that could be of great value in a year or two could be disposed of to provide a short-term decrease in the investment figure.

Another interesting problem with the ROI measure is that it can lead to investment decisions on the part of divisional managers that are not consistent with the organization's best interests. For instance, a manager of a division earning a 15 percent ROI would be inclined to reject a project offering a return of 12 percent, though the cost of capital for the organization is 10 percent. Thus a project that may be highly desirable from the perspective of corporate management would be tossed aside by a divisional manager whose ROI would suffer despite the desirability of the project from the corporate point of view. Another possible error engendered by the use of the ROI criterion could arise in the context of a division earning a ROI of 6 percent. This division would be inclined to invest in projects offering a return of 8 percent despite the fact that the corporate cost of capital was in the region of 10 percent.

These shortcomings of the ROI measure are of importance, particularly because recent surveys have shown that the vast majority of corporations employ ROI as a primary measure of divisional performance. The problems with the ROI measure stem from two factors. First, ROI measures efficiency and not effectiveness. Second, investment decisions delegated to the divisional level might be based on divisional ROI rather than the economically appropriate criterion of corporate cost of capital. A performance measure that responds to these problems was developed by General Electric in the mid-1950s. It has been given various labels. Academics tend to call it residual income, and some practitioners—for example, managers at Westinghouse Corporation—call it income after capital charge.

The income after capital charge measure is best described by means of the illustration shown in figure 13–1. A measure that occupies an intermediate position between ROI and income after capital charge is the return after capital charge, also calculated in figure 13–1.

The return after capital charge is superior to the ROI measure in that it takes into account the corporate cost of capital rather than the particular division's rate of return on investment. Thus congruence between divisional decisions and corporate interests is promoted. Income after capital charge goes a step further in that it is an effectiveness measure that assesses the dollars of profit contributed by the division to the corporate coffers after recognizing the cost of funds made available to the division for its operations.

Calculating the income after capital charge requires that two factors be defined in each organization: corporate cost of capital and the investment base in each division. The corporate cost of capital should be based on the anticipated future capital structure of the corporation.

A more sophisticated approach to defining the cost of equity capital in an organization, taking into account its risk characteristics, is described in the following chapter in the context of conglomerate organizations. This approach can also be applied to divisional organizations.

The second factor—the level of investment—is not readily arrived at on the basis of objective economic criteria. The investment base chosen should reflect the elements on the balance sheet that corporate management view as significant and as meriting the particular attention of divisional managers. One possibility is to apply the capital charge to the total assets of the division.

Assumptions

1. *Sales* = $ 50 million
2. Income after tax (IAT) = $ 3.75 million
3. Total assets = $ 27 million
4. Current liabilities = $ 2 million
5. Cost of capital = 13%
6. Investment = Total assets − current liabilities
   = $ 25 million

$$\text{Profit margin} = \frac{\text{IAT}}{\text{Sales}} = \frac{\$\,3.75\text{ m}}{\$\,50\text{ m}} = 7\tfrac{1}{2}\%$$

$$\text{Investment turnover} = \frac{\text{Sales}}{\text{Investment}} = \frac{\$\,50\text{ m}}{\$\,25\text{ m}} = 2$$

$$\text{Return on investment} = \frac{\text{IAT}}{\text{Investment}}$$

or Profit Margin × Investment Turnover

$$= \frac{\$\,3.75\text{ m}}{\$\,25\text{ m}} \text{ or } 7\tfrac{1}{2}\% \times 2$$

$$= 15\%$$

Return after capital charge   =   ROI   Cost of Capital
(RACC)   =   15% − 13%
   =   2%

Income after capital charge   =   IAT − (Investment × Cost of Capital)
(IACC)

or (RACC × Investment)

= $ 3.75 m − ($25 m × 13%)

or (2% × $25 m)

= $ 0.5 m

Figure 13–1. Divisional Measures of Performance

Another popular option is to define the investment base as the sum of the net fixed assets and the net working capital. In this latter option, the divisional manager is intrinsically encouraged to focus on the management of the level of working capital employed by the division. The investment base chosen should be the sum of either the net assets or the gross assets and the net working capital.

The flexibility in the choice of the investment base stems from the fact that the budgeted income after capital charge can be derived from whatever base is chosen in a particular organization. In this context, it must be recognized that meeting or exceeding the budgeted income after capital charge indicates satisfactory or good performance on the part of the divisional managers. The magnitude of the budgeted figure should reflect the profit potential of the particular division. In the extreme instance, in the short term, a negative income after capital charge can be viewed as good performance if the budgeted figure had anticipated an even greater loss.

The shortcomings of the ROI measure must be borne in mind. The current importance given it by most companies suggests that they are inclined to turn a blind eye to its problems. Although the income after capital charge may be slightly more complex and not as well understood, it is a vastly superior measure of profitability for divisions within an organization. Decision making within the divisions with regard to new investment and evaluation of a division's economic performance are greatly improved by the use of the income after capital charge measure.

14
Planning and Control in Conglomerate Organizations

Conglomerate organizations can be visualized as consisting of two or more divisionalized organizations, all reporting to a common corporate headquarters. Relating the form of the conglomerate organization to the simpler divisionalized type, it is possible to consider only the differences and additions resulting from the need to manage two or more divisionalized organizations.

Meshing two or more divisionalized organizations is much more difficult in some ways than the task of integrating two or more functional organizations within a divisionalized corporate context. The search for synergy in conglomerate organizations can be extremely difficult. The components of divisionalized organizations tend to have core skills or distinctive competences that tie together the functionally organized subunits in these corporations. Conglomerate organizations, on the other hand, are rarely characterized by such common competences. Synergy in conglomerate organizations is normally sought through the mechanism of financial performance of the components of the corporation. Another possible source of synergy is the use of centrally developed management capabilities, both personnel and systems.

Conglomerates do not commit themselves to a particular industry, market, or technology, although functionally organized profit centers within the conglomerate organization tend to emphasize particular markets or technologies. At corporate headquarters, strategic planning emphasizes the acquisition or divestment of groups of such functional components, based on expectations regarding financial performance.

This perspective on conglomerate organizations helps us to identify distinctive requirements of strategic planning and management control in these most complex organizations:

1. Managing business portfolios.
2. Maximizing the value of the corporation.
3. Measuring subunit performance.
4. Organizing for planning and control.

Managing Business Portfolios

Strategic planning in the context of conglomerates has long been viewed as the task of selecting and managing the groups of businesses in which the corporation wishes to function. The most popular approaches in the 1970s involved the use of a variety of portfolio matrices, which essentially consisted of two dimensions—the attractiveness of the industry and the competitive strength of the corporation in that industry—measured with a variety of parameters. A generic matrix of this type is diagrammed in figure 14–1.

One of the most popular measures of industry attractiveness was the projected growth rate of the industry. Another popular practice was to relate industry attractiveness to the stage of its life cycle. Industries in early growth stages were seen as highly attractive, whereas mature, declining industries were seen as ones from which the corporation should exit.

Perhaps the most widely used measure of competitive strength was the organization's share of the market in the particular industry. Organizations with a higher share of the market are presumably further down the experience curve than other corporations and are thus well placed to experience the benefits of the economies of scale, improved practices, lower costs, and better understanding of the products and technology that accompany greater volume. Other approaches to competitive capability tended to focus on an aggregation of several measures. Here the organization's strengths in relation to those of its competitors along several dimensions would be assessed and a summary measure developed either on a subjective basis or by summing up the scores assigned to the corporation along each of the dimensions thought to be important.

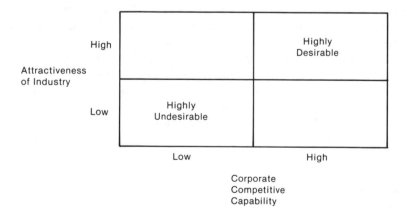

Figure 14–1. Generic Portfolio Matrix

Portfolio matrices came under severe criticism in the early 1980s because of their presumably cookbook character. For instance, research indicated that low market share did not necessarily mean that the company could not be profitable. Thus one of the key measures of competitive capability came to be viewed as highly unreliable. These portfolio matrices are, however, of significant value when viewed as tools of analysis rather than as determinants of corporate strategy. Assessing one's strengths in relation to competition and evaluating the attractiveness of various industries are highly useful activities in the context of analyses leading to the development of suitable strategic plans. Thus to discard these matrices as superficial and a passing fad is perhaps as unthinking as the original widespread acceptance of such matrices.

Recognizing the utility of portfolio matrices as tools of analysis and as a means of developing a better understanding of the business in which a conglomerate operates, there still remains the significant problem of how to decide on which business to enter or emphasize and which business to deemphasize or divest. In response to this need, much attention recently has been paid to value-based approaches to strategic planning.

Maximizing the Value of the Organization

The theoretical underpinnings of value-based approaches to strategic planning derive much of their credibility from the empirically observed relationship between the stock market's perceptions of the value of the organization in relation to its profitability. Studies have suggested the relationship of the nature diagrammed in figure 14–2. As the figure suggests, the ratio of market price per share to book value per share is related directly to the spread between the return on equity and the cost of equity. Before identifying some of the flaws and questionable assumptions in this presumed relationship, we shall first explore the possible applications.

If top management of the conglomerate accepts as its primary responsibility the task of increasing the value of the holdings of the stockholders, then clearly the focus of the corporate effort has to be on increasing the businesses in which the spread between return on equity and cost of equity is the greatest. This approach is more sophisticated than merely looking at the profitability, in terms such as ROI, of individual business possibilities. Unlike the simple profitability of the business, this approach takes into account the premiums that investors expect in the context of higher risk. In order to calculate the spread, it is necessary to arrive at a reasonable estimate of the cost of equity in individual businesses.

There are several components of the cost of equity in individual

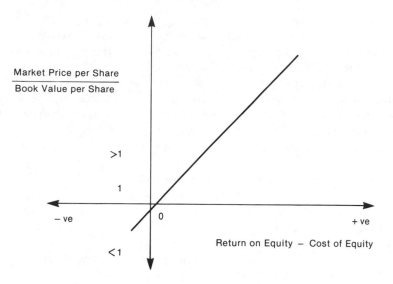

Figure 14–2. Market Value and Profitability

business. While in practical terms the cost of equity may be calculated quite differently, conceptually four components comprise the cost of equity:

1. The rate of return that investors expect on risk-free investments.
2. The premium that investors expect as a response to the riskiness of the stock market as a whole.
3. The premium or discount that investors would grant the particular business in recognition of its individual risk characteristics in relation to the stock market as a whole (that is, riskier or less risky than the stock market).
4. The premium that investors would expect in the light of the riskiness resulting from the proportion of debt in the capital structure of the business.

For example, assume the following values for each of the four components of the cost of equity:

Risk-free rate, 8 percent.

Stock market premium, 5 percent.

Business risk premium, 1 percent.

Leverage premium, 1 percent.

Hence, cost of equity is: 8 percent + 5 percent + 1 percent + 1 percent = 15 percent.

The practical determination of the cost of equity in a business is much simpler than the concept. The risk-free rate is readily available in that it is the current rate on long-term government bonds. The stock market premium and the business premium or discount for many businesses are calculated by investment services such as Value Line, which determine what are called betas for various businesses. The betas are the factor by which the market risk premium should be multiplied in order to arrive at the cost of equity for a business with particular characteristics. Betas are arrived at by measuring the volatility of the price of stock in the business over a period of usually five years and relating this volatility statistically to the volatility of an average stock on the market.

If betas of businesses similar to the one being considered by the conglomerate are not available, two options exist. First, it is possible to calculate the beta by taking into account a variety of factors, including volatility of its earnings. Second, a satisfactory approximation can usually be arrived at by interpolating between the betas of businesses that are viewed as riskier and less risky than the one being considered. Of these two options, the second is vastly preferable because, in addition to the complexity of calculating a beta for the business, such calculated betas do not take into account the risk factor stemming from the extent of leverage in the business. Further calculations are necessary in order to arrive at a leveraged beta. Published betas, on the other hand, also include the impact of leverage, typical of the particular business.

The values of betas usually range between .5 and 1.6. If a business being considered has a beta of 1.2, if the risk-free rate of return is 8 percent, and if the market risk premium is 5 percent, the cost of equity for the business would be calculated as follows:

$$\text{Cost of equity} = \text{risk-free rate of return} + (\text{beta} \times \text{market risk premium})$$

$$= 8\% + (1.2 \times 5\%) = 8\% + 6\% = 14\%.$$

The attractiveness of a business can therefore be readily ascertained by comparing its actual or projected return on equity with the cost of equity calculated as described. For existing subunits of the organization, this calculation normally involves an estimation of the equity investment in the subunit, which can be arrived at by determining the total investment in the business and subtracting the amount of debt the business can reasonably be expected to bear. Several treatises have been written on the appropriate amount of debt for a business. A popular rule of thumb, however, is to arrive at an estimate of the appropriate level of debt by looking at the earnings before interest and taxes. If projected interest payments are covered ten times by projected earnings before interest and taxes, the business would qualify for a very high rating in terms of safety.

Although value-based approaches to strategic planning have been receiving much attention and acceptance, they are by no means the final answer. Relationships such as the one diagrammed in figure 14–2 can be justifiably criticized as meaningless if one recognizes the number of assumptions and judgments that go into determining the book value per share. Furthermore, projected return on equity is very much dependent on the quality of the strategic thinking that is the basis for the expected profitability. If the world were certain and strategic plans entirely reliable, then clearly businesses with a greater spread between return on equity and cost of equity could rightly claim top management's positive attention. However, the world is not certain and strategic plans all too often go astray, and it must be recognized that value-based approaches can provide only a lens through which to view the strategies and businesses that management has identified.

Just as in the case of business portfolio matrices, variations on the basic theme are currently being generated. One school of thought promotes the not-unattractive notion that businesses that top management should target for increased investment are those where value ascribed to the business by the stock market exceeds the replacement value of the assets in the business. While attractive in concept, determining current values of business assets is a complex and subjective activity. However, such estimates have to be made in response to the requirements of the Financial Accounting Standards Board. At least, it provides one more perspective that could either corroborate or raise questions about analyses that adopt the approach described previously.

The particular merit of value-based approaches to strategic planning in conglomerates is that they address the key decisions that need to be made by corporate management: which business should resources be allocated to and which business should be harvested or divested. Also, calculating the cost of equity provides a powerful linkage with the control activity in conglomerates. It is rare that a key measure employed in strategic planning is also readily applicable to the exercise of control. The cost of equity is perhaps the most relevant benchmark against which the subunits' performance can be evaluated.

Measuring Subunit Performance

The task of measuring the performance of subunits in conglomerate organizations has to recognize the unique need to assess the performance of groups of related divisions. In this context, the income after capital charge measure is appropriate because it calculates the effectiveness and efficiency with which the managers of groups handle the divisions for which they are responsible. In these organizations, it would be some what presumptuous for top management to control the processes that take place in each of the groups reporting to them. In conglomerate organizations, top management is confined to output-oriented control rather than process-oriented control because of the inevitable lack of familiarity with what goes on in a variety of disparate businesses. Thus having assessed the relative attractiveness of various businesses, top management essentially has to recognize that its control possibilities are limited to determining the amount of resources to be made available to each group and evaluating the profit performance of each group.

The value-based approach focuses on resource allocation decisions. The cost of equity for each business can be used as a benchmark against which to evaluate performance. By calculating the return on equity of a group and thus arriving at the spread between the return on equity and cost of equity, top management can take into account the influence of risk characteristics of the business on expected return.

The return on equity for each group can be calculated by taking the total investment in the group and arriving at the equity component of this figure by estimating the amount of debt each group can suitably bear. It must be borne in mind that groups within a large and successful conglomerate are likely to receive the benefit of belonging to such a corporation. Just as an individual would be treated differently by a bank if he or she belonged to a particularly prosperous or penurious family, the amount and cost of debt available to a group in a conglomerate might be more or less favorable than if it was an independent, free-standing enterprise. In calculations of the amount and cost of debt for each group, as part of the exercise of determining the return on equity, this factor must be borne in mind. The amount of debt that a group within a conglomerate can support as an independent unit can be easily estimated by assessing the coverage of interest payments by the earnings before interest and taxes. A caveat in this analysis is that the volatility of the earnings of the group can affect the amount it can borrow. When estimating the number of times interest payments are covered by earnings before interest and taxes, it may be more appropriate to employ the lower range of estimated earnings rather than an average figure.

In addition to looking at the spread between return on equity and cost of equity as a basis for measuring the performance of a group of divisions within a conglomerate, it may be useful to assess the performance of groups by calculating the ratio of return on equity to cost of equity. Thus divisions with a very high cost of equity, say 18 percent, and a spread of 6 percent will not be given unmerited recognition in relation to another group with a cost of equity of, say, 12 percent and a spread of 4 percent. In the case of the first group the ratio of return on equity to cost of equity would be 1.33 ([18 + 6] ÷ 18). In the second group, though the spread is less, the ratio of return on equity to cost of equity would also be 1.33 ([12 + 4] ÷ 12).

Organizing for Planning and Control

The most important difference between divisionalized organizations and conglomerate organizations is that in the latter, the corporation probably will engage in new businesses about which top management might have a very limited understanding regarding the technical and market characteristics. Synergy, if at all existent, in such conglomerate organizations stems from financial considerations and possibly from improved management resulting from the application of more effective systems to previously less effectively managed businesses. Planning and control at the top management level in conglomerate organizations therefore involve activities that are not necessarily a desirable part of the responsibilities of managers within existing groups or divisions in the conglomerate. A strong corporate planning unit is therefore usually needed in conglomerate organizations.

In addition to identifying potential new businesses, an activity that may not perhaps be done most effectively below the corporate level, this planning group would have to conduct the key exercise of strategic control: identifying the groups to be given added resources and groups to be phased out or divested.

The close relationship between planning and control is perhaps most evident at the strategic level in conglomerates. Strategic planning and control are essentially similar in nature. Both require the identification of the most attractive investment opportunities from the corporate perspective.

In organizing the planning and control function at the corporate level, top management must recognize that executives responsible for these areas will tend to play active managerial roles. Top management decisions will be substantially based on the alternatives and advice provided by these planning and control executives. Paradoxically although the complexity of strategic planning and control in conglomerates requires substantial technical expertise, the nature of the planning and control responsibility requires managerial skills in equal, if not greater, measure. Clearly the planning and control function must be given enough prestige to attract technically competent line managers to the function. In fact a persuasive argument can be made that elevation to top management in conglomerates should be preceded by an assignment to the corporate planning and control function.

The control function becomes even more important when the conglomerate relies on increased managerial productivity and business profitability in newly acquired business as a result of introducing more effective management systems. A substantial part of most management systems is comprised of the reporting and control function—hence the importance of the corporate control function as the main source of competence and consulting services in relation to these management systems.

Part V
Administrative Systems to Support Planning and Control

15
The Capital Budgeting System

The capital budgeting system in organizations is perhaps the most important link between strategic planning and management control. This system translates strategic plans into resource allocation decisions that propel the organization in the desired direction.

The design of systems for planning and controlling capital expenditures has evolved significantly over the years. The original portfolio of projects approach visualized in the 1950s has been determined to be wishful academic thinking rather than pragmatic reality. Although the surprisingly complex nature of the process of making capital expenditure decisions is now widely recognized, the design of formal systems to manage this process and thus effectively link strategic planning and management control has yet to utilize fully the insights that have been developed.

Recent research has generated a pragmatic understanding of the processes involved in making capital budgeting decisions. This understanding, however, has not yet affected the accepted guidelines for designing capital budgeting systems. One of the reasons for this lag between changes in systems design and the improved understanding of the nature of the capital budgeting process is that it is not possible to make universally true generalizations about suitable system design. System designers have not recognized the value of tailoring capital budgeting systems to different organizational types in order to allow the development of guidelines that are responsive to differences between organizations and at the same time permit the articulation of principles and approaches that apply to organizations belonging to a particular category.

The framework suggested in this chapter is based on the type of organization and incorporates the most recent understanding of the nature of the capital budgeting process. The framework is also intended to be responsive to the issue of building bridges between strategic planning and management control and, further, is intended to facilitate the linkage between planning and control systems with other supportive management systems in organizations.

Defining the Process

The traditional perception of the capital budgeting process is that a basket of investment proposals is submitted at specified intervals to evaluation committees set up by top management. These committees are expected to study the technical, marketing, and financial feasibility of the proposals and rank them in order of attractiveness. Top management then selects for implementation the portfolio perceived by them as most desirable and that can be supported by available and planned resources. Studies have shown, however, that this perception of the process is deficient, erroneous, and misleading. In reality, the capital expenditure decision process is vastly different in several ways:

1. It is incremental and not holistic in character.
2. Proposals get crystallized at low levels in the organization and do not readily permit the subsequent consideration and incorporation of wider or different perspectives or alternatives.
3. Proposals submitted for top management evaluation are those that lower levels of management expect will (not may!) be approved.
4. Political and personality considerations play a large role.
5. Strategic, noneconomic, or nonquantifiable criteria are often employed by top management.
6. Top management attitudes to risk and perceptions of new strategic directions are often not shared by or communicated to lower levels of management.

In what is perhaps the best known of these studies (Bower 1970), it was found that in divisionalized organizations, capital investment proposals were first defined and justified within the functional departments in each division. Second, the management of each division assessed whether the proposals could be sold to top management. The proposals that were thought likely to obtain funding were then submitted to top management and were provided with all the political backing that divisional management could generate. In the third stage, top management determined how well the proposals fitted in with their explicit strategic thinking regarding the corporation's future direction. The perceived likelihood of individual proposals' meeting their performance expectations was often arrived at in the light of the concerned divisional manager's track record rather than on the merits of the proposal. Case studies have also shown that failure to obtain top management approval tended to be viewed by divisional management as a personal slight, resulting possibly in a lower position in the informal pecking order among divisional managers.

Based on this revised understanding of the process in divisionalized organizations, modifications to the traditional, simple, three-stage (definition-evaluation-approval) model of the process have been proposed. Based on case studies, it is possible to identify the following modified and comprehensive process, applicable to the most complex organizations, which includes eight stages rather than the simple three stages in the initial model of the capital budgeting process:

1. Communication.
2. Triggering.
3. Screening.
4. Definition.
5. Evaluation.
6. Transmission.
7. Decision.
8. Monitoring.

Communication is the provision of top management's strategic thinking to lower levels of management. In particular, such communication would point out not only strategic direction but the assumptions on which the preferred strategies have been based. At the very least, top management must communicate the basic assumptions on which strategic plans are built in order to ensure that inconsistent assumptions at lower levels do not lead to meaningless proposals. To the extent that lower levels of management participate in corporate strategic planning, the problems surrounding the communication stage of the capital budgeting process are proportionately reduced.

Triggering is the process by which possible capital projects are brought to the awareness of management. It could emanate from the strategic plan, environmental developments, or internal problems. The communications stage is of great importance in directing managerial attention to relevant issues. Without an understanding of corporate objectives, subunits may not be able to identify the capital projects that need to be implemented in order to move the organization effectively and efficiently toward strategic objectives. In the case of internal or external issues requiring a response, an understanding of corporate strategy can prove invaluable in directing managerial attention to the most significant concerns.

Screening is designed to select from among a host of possible alternatives those that merit particular attention. The triggering stage might result in the identification of an impossibly large number of potential projects. Even before a preliminary analysis of all these projects is undertaken, resource limitations would mandate that the range of possible projects be screened in order to identify those few that merit further attention.

Definition of individual projects is a difficult stage in the process. Although the intent of a project being developed might be well understood, translating this understanding into a definition of what should be done by whom and at what cost in order to obtain desired results is a demanding task.

The importance of the screening process is most evident when considering the effort required to define the parameters of a project in such a fashion as to allow an assessment of its contribution to the organization's goals.

Evaluation of projects has tended to be a highly financial exercise. Discounted cash flow calculations, rooted in rational economic theory, have been the basis for the evaluation of capital projects. The inevitable uncertainties and the difficulties of incorporating strategic and qualitative considerations in such rational analyses suggest a strong need to broaden the traditional approach to this evaluation.

Transmission of the project details to top management constitutes the next step in the capital budgeting process. Although this step may appear obvious and trivial, several possible modes of transmission are possible. Oral presentations by champions of a particular project are very different from the situation in which top management bases its decision on written descriptions of a project. The former approach, though extremely time-consuming, allows top management to explore the thinking of managers who are closer to the front lines. The possibility of a small change in the project, making it more attractive to top management, exists when those who have developed it are able to interact with senior management. Of course, refusal to sanction a project could be particularly painful to its proponents if they have had the opportunity of face-to-face discussions with top management.

Decisions regarding which projects to approve are the responsibility of top management. Those with strategic responsibility have the obligation to make these critical decisions, which steer the organization in the desired strategic direction. Delegating the decision-making authority in the context of capital budgeting can be done only when top management is confident of the understanding and sensitivity of lower levels of management regarding the strategic orientation of the organization.

Monitoring and control of the implementation and effectiveness of the approved capital projects is an activity of great importance. The nature of control of projects is quite different from the task of controlling ongoing operations of a business. In the case of capital projects, the most basic decision that must be made while the effectiveness of the project is being evaluated is whether to continue with it or to drop it. Updated estimates of time and cost to complete projects are of vital importance in exercising control over the capital budgeting process.

Impact of Organizational Types on the Nature of the Process

All of the stages in the process are not equally important in all types of organizations. In simple organizations, with only a few hierarchical levels, some of the stages of the process become less important or even irrelevant. Communication and transmission are of much greater importance in complex organizations than in simpler organizations. Communication in functional organizations can take place as a natural outcome of the many interactions that functional managers tend to have with the organizations' CEOs. Also, the likelihood of department-level managers' participating in the strategic planning processes in functional organizations is much greater than in more complex organizations. Thus the appreciation of the strategic direction of the organization that exists at lower levels is likely to be greater in these simpler types of organizations.

Because of the likelihood of frequent interactions between concerned levels of managers, the formal process of transmitting proposals to the upper levels becomes less influential in determining the outcome in these simpler organizations.

In complex organizations, on the other hand, it becomes imperative to ensure that these important stages in the process are effectively executed. Consequently the need for formalization of these stages is greatly increased in these organizations.

In addition to the need for greater formality and comprehensiveness of the capital budgeting process in complex organizations, the nature of the activity and the options that exist tend to vary depending upon the type of organization. In conglomerate organizations, managers at the group level just below the corporate level may need to know only the most important assumptions being made by top management and a rough estimate of the magnitude of resources likely to be made available. In functional organizations, on the other hand, departmental-level managers, just below the corporate level, may need and obtain much greater guidance regarding the nature of projects that top management views as desirable. In short, the possibility of exercising control over the process of management in simpler organizations affects the design of the process. In contrast, the focus on output controls that is inevitable in more complex organizations will influence the nature of the stages in their capital budgeting processes.

The matrix in figure 15–1 shows the importance of the various stages in the capital budgeting process in the context of various organizational types.

Relevant Techniques

Communication among corporate-level, group-level, and divisional-level management can be designed to take place through involving them simultaneously in management processes or through the medium of formal statements. One significant possibility is the active involvement of both corporate and divisional or group and divisional managers in the process of developing

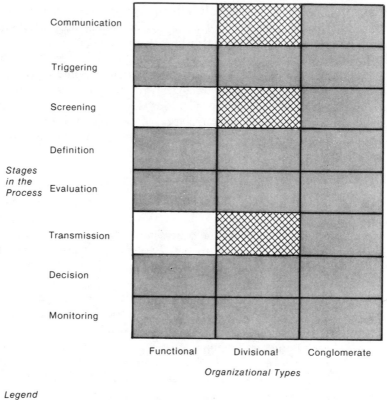

Figure 15–1. Relating the Capital Budgeting Process to Organizational Types

each division's strategic plans, which should serve to direct divisional management's attention toward the divisional strengths and weaknesses and environmental opportunities and threat that senior managers perceive to be of importance from a corporate perspective.

Additionally, formal communication can focus on corporate- or group-level assumptions regarding the environment, the divisional business areas or charters, the divisional or group strategies, the probable level of resources that will be made available, and the expected performance of the groups or divisions. Such formal communications are particularly necessary in conglomerates because in these organizations, top management is limited to controlling the output of the investment centers or groups and lacks in-depth knowledge regarding the operational and managerial processes of all the groups. Active involvement of corporate-level management in divisional strategic planning processes is therefore of doubtful value and feasibility in conglomerate organizations. The desirable content of such formal communication will become evident on considering the mechanisms employed in subsequent stages of the process.

Another device is to have annual plenary meetings of managers from all parts of the organization and from several levels to present and discuss their plans for the future. Such meetings often result in elimination of duplication of effort and identification of shared interests and efforts of managers who would otherwise have not met.

Triggering of the identification of capital expenditure possibilities can be influenced by a variety of mechanisms. First, a formal information system focusing on process efficiency, capacity utilization and backlogs, rejections, rework, and customer complaints would cover the traditional problem areas that require responses in terms of capital expenditure.

Second, channels other than the usual hierarchy for submitting ideas could be set up. Illustrative of such idea systems is the one that Texas Instruments has as part of its formal management system to provide funding for ideas separately from the formal capital budgeting system. Ideas are evaluated directly by carefully constituted committees with no commitment to the status quo but with control of funds for supporting further work on promising, out-of-the-ordinary proposals.

Third, analysis of strengths, opportunities, faults, and threats, or SOFT analysis, constitutes a formal and significant source of ideas in large, complex organizations. Involvement of corporate-level managers in divisional SOFT analyses could simultaneously provide a corporate perspective and a screening mechanism. Opportunities that divisional managers might rule out as too speculative or requiring inordinate resource commitments might find favor from a corporate perspective. Threats that might be perceived as inevitably realities might lead to corporate emphasis on other divisions.

Fourth, triggering can be forced by the corporate imposition of what one organization terms shocking objectives. In conglomerates, where corporate-level managers probably possess only limited knowledge of the diverse business in which their divisions are engaged, corporate management's participation in SOFT analysis at the divisional level becomes of doubtful value. In such situations the responsibility of corporate managers is to create a climate where ideas are both nurtured and demanded. Complacency is all too often a concomitant of success, and successful groups or divisions may require the goad provided by highly demanding objectives set by corporate managers.

Fifth, the portfolio planning models that have attracted much attention in the past decade offer valuable tools that have particular relevance to divisionalized and conglomerate companies. The BCG Growth/Share Matrix, Royal Dutch Shell's Directional Policy Matrix, and derivatives of GE's seminal work such as McKinsey's Strength/Attractiveness Matrix, and A.D. Little's life-cycle-based approach are of significant value to the conglomerate and divisionalized organizations at the triggering and screening stages. These models not only suggest areas and strategies for growth but also indicate likely candidates for divestment and harvesting.

The screening stage is largely informal in most organizations. In fact, the problem identified by studies is one of rejection at lower organizational levels of ideas or projects that would have been favorably viewed by higher-level management. The systems design response needed, therefore, is not only to provide filters for ideas generated by triggering techniques but to involve higher-level managers in the idea generation stage of the process and to communicate top management's criteria to lower-level managers. Both objectives are supported by involvement in the SOFT analysis and by the use of the portfolio planning models.

The definition, evaluation, transmission, decision, and monitoring stages are adequately served by conventional capital budgeting systems.

At the definition stage, the use of standard formats ensures that all bases are touched and facilitates evaluation. Such formats should recognize project classes such as necessities, replacement and renovation, cost reduction, expansion, and new products or markets. This classification correlates well with the degree of risk.

At the evaluation stage, classification of projects makes it easier to employ risk-adjusted, discounted cash flow techniques. At the appropriate levels (division, group, corporate), committees, carefully constituted to minimize undesirable biases, are needed to scrutinize and evaluate each proposal from the technological, marketing, and financial perspectives.

Transmission of the proposals to higher levels is an intrinsic part of the evaluation stage. The option to make oral presentations on key proposals should be available to lower levels of management seeking approval of their proposals. Often such presentations add insights, such as the level of commitment of the managers making the proposal, that senior managers evaluating the proposals may not be able to derive from the written description of the project.

The decision stage occurs at different levels in the organization because authority is usually delegated to lower levels to sanction expenditures up to specified limits. The specification of ceilings on the total capital expenditures for each class of projects for each of the divisions also greatly assists decision making. Such ceilings are particularly useful in the context of projects classified as necessities that are mandated by regulatory requirements or motivated by nonquantifiable considerations such as labor welfare and morale. Without such ceilings, these projects could consume excessive quantities of corporate resources.

Monitoring and control of the implementation and effectiveness of the approved capital expenditures could be achieved by such conventional project management devices as time- or milestone-triggered reports on updated estimates of time and cost to complete the project. Mandatory reevaluation of projects where time or cost variances exceed prespecified percentages are useful. Commitment of resources provided for a particular project to some other project should not be allowed. Formal postaudits of completed projects, the results of which can be measured separately from ongoing operations, should be the normal practice. Anticipated savings or revenues from projects that do not result in separately measurable consequences should be incorporated in divisional operating budgets.

To summarize, the key features of a conventional or standard system of capital budgeting that would support the definition, evaluation, transmission, decision, and monitoring stages are listed below:

Definition
   Specification of standard formats for capital appropriation requests.
   Classification of projects into categories such as
      necessities
      replacement and renovation
      cost reduction
      expansion
      new projects or markets.

Evaluation
   Utilization of discounted cash flow techniques.
   Determination of risk-related discount or hurdle rates.
   Constitution of committees at profit-center levels to evaluate technological, marketing, and financial aspects of proposals.

Decision
   Delegation of authority to lower levels in the managerial hierarchy to sanction expenditures up to specified limits.
   Specification of ceilings on total capital expenditures for each category of project for each organizational subunit.

Monitoring
   Provision of time- and/or milestone-triggered reports, updated estimates of time and cost to complete projects.
   Specification of mandatory reevaluation of projects when actual or estimated variances exceed a specified percentage.

Elimination of automatic acceptance of alternative uses for capital appropriations granted to organizational subunits for a specified project.

Institution of formal postaudits focusing on actual results compared to those anticipated in the proposals.

Inclusion of benefits specified in project proposals in the operating budgets of concerned subunits.

It is now possible to specify the techniques appropriate to each stage of the capital expenditure process for each type of organization. The result is diagrammed in figure 15–2. Each column of the matrix in the figure specifies the formal capital budgeting system required for a particular type of organization. Each row of the matrix provides a listing of the techniques available to support one of the several defined stages in the capital expenditure process.

Supportive Systems

In addition to tailoring the capital budgeting system to the type of organization, other means of increasing the effectiveness of the capital expenditure decision process should be considered. A variety of structural devices have been successfully employed or are planned by organizations. The relevance of these devices, not surprisingly, is dependent on the type of organization.

A structural device relevant to functional organizations or divisions of larger organizations is the provision of what one organization terms dedicated financial analysts (DFAs). The DFAs are assigned responsibility for individual functional areas or parts of a functional area. Unlike traditional financial analysts, the DFA is expected to be involved at the triggering, screening, and definition stages of each proposal, not only at the evaluation stage. As a consequence, the quality, perspective, and relevance of proposals are expected to be greatly improved.

Another increasingly common structural device is the institution of new business planning cells at divisional levels and acquisition or divestment analysis cells at group and corporate levels. Clearly such cells greatly mitigate the problems in idea generation arising from a lack of corporate perspective or from differing attitudes to risk at various levels in large organizations.

A third structural device is the specification of dual responsibilities for individual managers. For example, in a large functional organization, the production, marketing, and finance department heads could be given seats on the board of directors. Communication of the corporate viewpoint to the functional departments would be highly effective. In addition, such executives would constitute a communication channel for bringing corporate attention to bear on operational problems with policy or strategic implications.

	Functional	Divisional	Conglomerate
Communication	*Corporate to functions* Corporate mission, strategy policies, and assumptions Plenary meetings recommended	*Corporate to divisions* Corporate mission, strategy, policies, assumptions, and resource availability Divisional charters *Divisions to functions* Divisional charters strategy, policies, and assumptions Plenary meetings desirable	*Corporate to groups* Corporate mission, objectives, strategy, policies, assumptions, and resource availability Group concept of business *Groups to division* Group concept of business, strategy, policies, assumptions, and resource availability Divisional charters *Divisions to Functions* Divisional charters, strategy, policies, and assumptions Plenary meetings needed
Triggering	MIS Idea system SOFT analysis	*Corporate level* Idea system Involvement in SOFT analysis Portfolio planning models *Divisional level* MIS Idea system SOFT analysis	*Corporate level* Portfolio planning models Shocking objectives *Group level* Idea system Involvement in SOFT analysis Portfolio planning models *Divisional level* MIS Idea system SOFT analysis
Screening	Implicit in idea system and SOFT analysis	Implicit in idea system and SOFT analysis Shortcomings responded to by involvement in SOFT analysis	Implicit In idea system and SOFT analysis Shortcomings responded to by SOFT analysis and shocking objectives
Definition	Standard system necessary	Standard system necessary	Standard system necessary
Evaluation	Standard system necessary	Standard system necessary	Standard system necessary
Transmission	Formal transmission not necessary	Standard system necessary	Standard system necessary
Decision	Standard system necessary	Standard system necessary	Standard system necessary
Monitoring	Standard system necessary	Standard system necessary	Standard system necessary
	Functional	Divisional	Conglomerate

Types of Organizations

Figure 15–2. Recommended System Design

The committees for evaluating capital expenditure proposals could usefully employ this two-hat concept. In its ultimate form, the two-hat concept results in a matrix organization typified by that employed by Texas Instruments, where individual managers function in both strategic and operating modes.

The parameters employed for evaluating managerial performance should reflect and support the capital budgeting system. Thus, cost efficiency and output volume parameters are needed in the context of functional departments. At the corporate level of all types of organizations and at the divisional level of divisionalized and conglomerate organizations, the relevant financial parameters are profits and the growth rate of profits. In addition, for each functional organization and division, nonfinancial parameters such as market share, productivity, and rate of introduction of new projects need to be specified given its strategic thrust and desired emphasis on long-term versus short-term profits.

At the group level within conglomerates, the income after capital charge, or residual income, becomes an appropriate and useful measure of groups' effectiveness and efficiency. This is so because the corporate level allocates a sum of money to each group, which then largely determines which capital expenditure projects to fund. Thus at the corporate level, control is basically limited to output measures. Here the residual income measure is vastly superior to both profits and ROI because it measures the effectiveness of operations (which profits does) and the efficiency of operations (which ROI does) and furthermore ensures that group investment decisions will be congruent with corporate interests (which neither profits nor ROI intrinsically ensures).

Applying the Dimensions of Strategic Choice

The inadequacy of traditional discounted cash flow techniques in terms of the ability to capture qualitative but important strategic consideration has been mentioned. The process of strategic planning described in the context of functional organizations was based on the notion of identifying the key dimensions of strategic choice. These dimensions can be effectively applied to the evaluation and decision stages of the capital budgeting process. They provide a strong link to the strategic planning exercise itself and introduce qualitative criteria employed in the formalization of corporate strategy.

The dimensions of strategic choice can be applied in exactly the same fashion as described in the context of strategic planning in functional organizations. In the earlier context, the dimensions of strategic choice were employed to evaluate strategic alternatives. In the current context, these dimensions could be applied to individual capital projects.

The immense potential of this approach is evident when considering some interesting decisions that have been made by corporations. A classic example is the experience of BIC corporation, whose great success in the United States stems from its consistent application of certain key criteria. BIC's operations in the early years were characterized by

1. Mass production,
2. Inexpensive products,
3. Disposable products,
4. High-quality products,
5. Early entry into markets.

Every one of these important strategic characteristics that typifies BIC's early operations in disposable ballpoint pens, cigarette lighters, and razors reinforced the others. BIC's profitability stems from its great competence in the area of mass production, where high volumes enable cost to be lowered. The inexpensive characteristics of BIC's products promoted greater sales. Inexpensiveness permitted disposability, which in turn increased the volume of products consumed. Although disposable, the products were reliable and of high quality as a consequence of BIC's manufacturing capabilities. Early entry into markets enabled BIC to increase its volume and to capture a dominant share of the market.

An understanding of these dimensions of BIC's successful early strategy should have led to a better decision than was made in the context of BIC's abortive venture into pantyhose, originally seen as attractive in that the projected rates of return on the expansion of BIC's products line looked promising. In addition, existing distribution channels could be employed for this new product. But BIC made mistakes. The pantyhose were manufactured in France, eliminating BIC's major source of profits to which the U.S. unit had traditionally had access. The product was not inexpensive in relation to its competition, and disposability was not necessarily seen as a desirable characteristic of the product. Higher-quality products were available in department stores, and the market was already saturated by large corporations.

The use of the dimensions of the strategic choice approach would have highlighted these inconsistencies in the new product. The projected ROI would have been questioned, and more realistic estimates would probably have been developed.

In addition to aiding in the evaluation and decision stages, an understanding of the dimensions of strategic choice could lead to a better definition of capital projects. Recognizing the strategic criteria explicit in the dimensions of choice, capital projects could be developed in ways to promote the desired strategic orientation more effectively.

Applying Value-Based Planning

The value-based approach to strategic planning can provide a valuable perspective on the relationship between the capital budgeting and the strategic planning processe. Adopting for the moment a financial perspective, the fundamental decisions to be made by corporate management can be diagrammed as indicated in figure 15–3. Based on stakeholder priorities and perceptions regarding opportunities and the competence to take advantage of these opportunities, the strategic planning process arrives very broadly at the determination of desired growth, stability, or contraction of operations. The identification of opportunities substantially drives the capital budgeting process. Also alternatives identified independently of strategic planning and brought to management's attention through the capital budgeting process would clearly affect the strategic planning exercise. Both capital budgeting and strategic planning influence the capital structure of the organization and are further linked through this relationship. Capital budgeting affects the capital structure in that the investment alternatives considered possess risk characteristics that affect the cost of equity. In turn, the capital structure affects the capital budgeting process in that the financial leverage substantially determines the amount of risk that is tolerable with regard to investment alternatives.

The relationship between strategic planning and the capital structure is

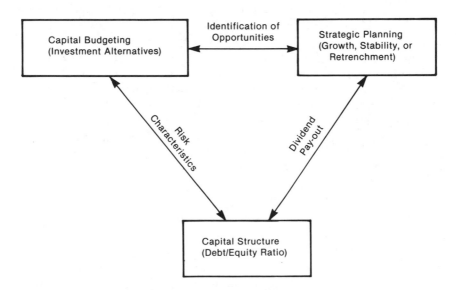

Figure 15–3. Financial Integration of Strategic Planning and Capital Budgeting

also quite close in that the attitude toward growth fostered by the strategic planning process clearly affects the need for funds and thus the capital structure. Similarly the availability of funds would constrain or stimulate the strategic planning exercises. The choice that top management makes regarding the magnitude of dividends paid to stockholders flows substantially from this relationship between strategic planning and capital structure.

The value-based approach to planning is of great importance from this financial perspective in that it effectively takes into account the impact of risk on the attractiveness of the project. While essentially applicable to conglomerate organizations, relating the cost of capital to risk characteristics of the investment is certainly of importance in simpler organizations even of the functional type. It must be recognized, however, that simpler approaches to handling risk could be effectively applied in the context of functional organizations.

Recognizing Risk Characteristics

Recognizing and responding to the risk characteristics of investment alternatives is a fundamental requirement in the capital budgeting process. Value-based approachs to planning intrinsically respond to the riskiness of a business. The riskiness of individual projects, however, requires different approaches.

The simplest approach is to classify the projects in terms of their riskiness. Classification schemes proposed in the context of the definition stage of the process reflect the relative riskiness of the alternatives. Other classification schemes are also widely used. For instance, Westinghouse Corporation managers are required to assess whether the investment projects involve:

new products or technology,

new markets, or

new facilities.

If only one of the three factors is new, the project is put into a category with the least risk. Increased riskiness is assumed for projects when two of these factors are new; extending this classification scheme, the riskiest projects are those in which all three factors are new. The rates of return that are expected of riskier projects would necessarily have to be higher than those that are less risky in character.

The discounted payback period, in which the number of years required to recoup the investment is calculated, taking into account the time value of money, is of particular relevance to extremely risky situations. When either technological or political developments might abruptly terminate a project, knowing the number of years required to recoup one's investment can be a valuable perspective on whether to go ahead. If the payback period is calculated as one or two years, some judgments will have to be made regarding the likelihood of the environment's turning sour within this period. If the payback period extends to five or seven years, such risky projects are best avoided.

A third approach to managing risk in the capital budgeting process is to seek a mix of risk characteristics in the alternatives that are developed and subsequently approved. Thus the cash flow that is generated by relatively sure projects could sustain the corporation if risky projects turn out to be disastrous in character.

The capital budgeting process is similar to the strategic planning process in that both tend to be triggered by the passage of time rather than by the occurrence of key events. This is a shortcoming that requires the addition of another element in the total management system: the strategic issue management process.

Reference

Bower, Joseph L. *Managing the Resource Allocation Process*. Boston: Harvard Business School, 1970.

16
The Strategic Issue
Management System

A fundamental premise in this book is that strategic planning is good for organizations and good strategic planning systems can be designed. But even the most effectively designed strategic planning systems have intrinsic shortcomings. One is that formal strategic planning tends to be a time-triggered activity. During the period between two formal strategic planning exercises, events will occur within and outside the organization that require a strategic response different in some fashion from the strategic posture envisioned in the most recent plan. This shortcoming is made more severe by the strong recommendation that has been made that formal strategic planning exercises be conducted less frequently than on an annual basis. The longer the duration between formal exercises, the greater is the likelihood that there will be a need for midcourse corrections. Reducing the period between two formal exercises has drawbacks, among them that overly frequent exercises tend to result in pedestrian form-filling exercises rather than sensitive and creative activities.

Purpose of the SIMS

In order to respond to this fundamental problem, organizations have widely accepted the need for a strategic issue management system (SIMS). SIMSs are designed to be flexible, sensitive, and action oriented and are intended to reduce the probability of strategic surprises or at least reduce the negative impact of unanticipated events. Identifying, analyzing, and responding to emerging developments is not an easy task; however, it is essential in order to complement and strengthen the formal strategic planning system (SPS).

Although both the SPS and the SIMS have their relative advantages and different orientations, operating both systems in parallel poses some problems. In designing the SPS and the SIMS, careful attention must be paid to the integration of the two systems. There must be congruence in terms of the actions taken on the basis of the strategic planning and the strategic issue management activities. A mutually supportive and synergistic relationship between the two systems is both possible and desirable.

SIMS makes its greatest contribution in the context of what Ansoff (1975) calls "weak signals." When unexpected developments are of crisis proportions, no system is necessary to alert management to the need for a response.

The SIMS must be designed to ensure that it is alert to faint indications of impending problems and that managerial actions resulting from it are consistent with the actions being taken on the basis of the strategic planning process. The integration of the two systems is greatly facilitated by the recommended design of the SPS. The SPS that I propose is periodic and not a continuous activity like the SIMS, but it is similar in that it is driven by identified issues. In planning systems where aspirations or visions drive the activity, linking the SPS and the SIMS is considerably more problematic.

Designing the SIMS

The SIMS consists of the following elements:

Environmental scanning.

Issue analysis.

Issue classification.

Response identification.

Response implementation.

The environmental scanning required for the SIMS is necessarily of a continuous nature. This continuous scanning between the formal strategic planning exercises complements the periodic character of formal strategic planning. In designing the environmental scanning activity, the key trade-off is the balance between investing excessive effort in identifying issues and not being broadbased enough to be sensitive to unanticipated developments. In order to promote a cost-effective scanning process, a semidirected approach is necessary. The directed component of the scanning activity focuses on the key assumptions that were the basis of the strategic plan. The occurrence and evolution of events and developments that were not anticipated during the strategic planning exercise alert the organization to the need for midcourse corrections. The undirected component of the semidirected scanning activity is somewhat more difficult to design. The key to design is to identify the appropriate sources of information rather than the events that need to be monitored. The sources for the identification of issues include appropriate literature, including technical and industry journals, as well as selected popular journals; special interest groups whose activities may affect the organization; related professional associations; people in the organization with boundary-spanning roles; and opinion polls. These sources need to be continually tapped in order to identify relevant issues.

An excellent example of the issue identification process is the trend analysis program (TAP) of the American Council of Life Insurance. Volunteers regularly reviewed close to 100 publications in the fields of science and technology, social sciences, business, economics, and politics and government for issues that could be relevant. In another example, PPG Industries, recognizing that people within the organization itself are rich sources of information, encourages managers to bring up any important issue that comes to their knowledge by filling out a standard form, labeled "New Issues Alert".

In order to ensure that biases and possible insensitivity of individual executives do not reduce the effectiveness of the process, careful measures must be taken in assigning responsibility for identifying issues. The constitution of study groups can greatly affect the quality of analysis. In order to ensure that the existing product-market-technology does not overly condition executives, individuals who do not have formal responsibility for the area or function being studied should be included in the group responsible for analyzing this element. Similar care can be taken in assigning responsibility for scanning the environment for emerging issues. In addition, responsibility for scanning particular sources can be assigned to different individuals on an annual or biennial basis. Of course, if obtaining information requires setting up a personal relationship with an organization or individual, such rotation is not a good idea.

Issue classification and analysis are the next elements in the SIMS process. Essentially the objective at this stage is to determine the merits of exploring a particular issue further. This is best done by a group with access to the entire range of issues being identified. This stage requires sensitivity and judgment. The members of the group of executives charged with the responsibility are best selected from a variety of backgrounds, hierarchical levels, and functional areas, and it would be ideal if all were open to new points of view. It is not uncommon to find this select group of executives being charged with responsibility for other elements of the SIMS process. For instance, in Sun Company, a Future Issues Committee, which was viewed as a freewheeling group operating in an unstructured fashion, had responsibility for environmental scanning, issue identification, analysis, and classification. Such a group could also be given the responsibility for subsequent stages in the SIMS process. The major argument for such a broad range of responsibilities is the presumed high quality of the individuals involved. Rotating membership in the group could minimize the inevitable conditioning and biases that emerge in any group. Also rotation through such a group could be an invaluable learning experience for an executive being groomed for senior positions in the organization.

Preliminary analysis of an issue should lead to the application of the importance-imminence matrix. The issues that are assigned to the high importance–high imminence quadrant would then be filtered through to the next stage in the SIMS process.

The strategic planning process is readily applicable to the issues identified and classified in the early stages of the SIMS process. The dimensions of strategic choice identified as part of the strategic planning process would be employed here also to prioritize the issues. The value of the process is demonstrated by its relevance and applicability to all three strategically oriented components of planning and control systems: strategic planning systems, capital budgeting systems, and strategic issue management systems.

The effective execution of the final stages in the SIMS involves two factors. First, implementation is normally best assigned as the responsibility of ad hoc task forces. Effective responses to strategic issues by definition require changes from the status quo. It is difficult for executives responsible for the status quo to accept and implement such changes. Hence there is a need for task forces that do not have such behavioral and emotional impediments to making needed changes. Second, the nature of the responses identified needs to be carefully categorized so as to facilitate integration of these responses with the thrust of the existing formal strategic plan. These responses need to be identified as one of three possible types. The first type would be responses that suggest the need to reassess the organization's objectives. The Iranian crisis, for example, could have generated the need for this type of response from organizations with major involvement in that country. It is possible that responses of this type will require an immediate (event- rather than time-triggered) formal comprehensive strategic planning exercise. It is hoped that issues that require such significant responses would be rare. If objectives have to be changed substantially, it essentially means that the strategies identified in the earlier formal strategic planning exercise have become obsolete. Unanticipated deregulation of an industry is an example of an issue that requires responses of this nature.

The second type of response is that which requires incremental changes in the organization's existing strategies. An oil price hike that results in General Motors' changing its emphasis with regard to smaller, more fuel-efficient cars is typical of an issue that leads to responses of this type.

The third type of response affects only the organization's operational plans or action programs. Such responses usually mean that individual actions may need to be accelerated or postponed; the fundamental strategic plans would remain basically unchanged. An example of such a response is the reaction of the competitors of Coleco, who speeded up the availability of their products for Christmas shopping when Coleco experienced problems with regard to its highly touted Adam computer. Identifying the nature of the response using this classification scheme greatly facilitates the integration of the SIMS and SPS because the focus of changes in the SPS is explicitly identified.

An effective SIMS that responds to the intrinsic shortcomings of the SPS has three important characteristics:

1. Continuous semidirected scanning to identify emerging issues.
2. The use of task forces for categorizing issues and implementing needed responses.
3. Classifying the responses in terms of their impact on the SPS.

Effectively integrated SIMSs and SPSs provide powerful planning and control capabilities to organizations that find themselves in a highly turbulent environment.

Reference

Ansoff, H. Igor. "Managing Strategic Surprise by Response to Weak Signals." *California Management Review* (Winter 1975).

17
Systems in the Context of Strategic Management

The Administrative System

Strategic management is widely used in place of *general management* to describe top management responsibility in an organization. In order to translate the concept of strategic management into concrete terms, it is necessary to identify the levers that top managers can manipulate in order to influence the effectiveness with which organizations function. Top management's influence on the organization's effectiveness is exerted through an administrative system that consists of four key components: the planning and control systems in the organization, organizational structure, the organization's competitive strategy, and management style. (See figure 17–1.)

Planning and Control

Planning and control are among the most clearly defined management systems or technologies and play an important role in affecting the organization's performance. Strategic planning systems identify the organization's raison d'être, its enduring objectives, and the key programs that merit managerial attention. Control systems motivate and monitor the efforts and accomplishments of managers in the context of the organization's objectives, strategies, and programs. Thus formal planning and control systems constitute a well-defined and discrete component of the total system of management technology available to top-level managers.

Organizational Structure

Discussing the planning and control system without considering organizational structure is inappropriate, if not impossible. Sociologists tend to view *control* and *structure* as synonymous. In a management control system, organizational structure serves as a key determinant of what is appropriate. The structure of organizations directly affects the processes and perspectives of

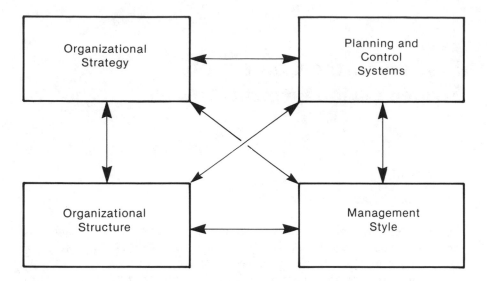

Figure 17–1. Strategic Management: The Administrative System

formal strategic planning. For instance, in multinational organizations, choosing to assign profit responsibility to managers in charge of a product line in all the countries in which the multinational operates would create a strong orientation toward a technology-driven strategy. In contrast, assigning profit responsibility to managers in charge of different regions or countries would result in strategies driven by market needs. The responsibility allocated to and reporting relationships of the planning and the control departments are another structural variable related to planning and control that affects organizational performance. Organizational structure therefore represents a set of variables or choices that top management can influence or make that are fundamentally related to the planning and control system and also clearly affect the organization's performance. In short, in order to describe top management's responsibilities, it is necessary not only to consider the design of the planning and control system but also the chosen form of organizational structure.

Competitive Strategy

Organizational structure has been closely linked to organizational strategy since Chandler's (1962) treatise. Following Chandler's proposition that structure follows strategy, there have been attempts to elaborate on or justify conceptually and empirically the theory that treats organizational performance as a variable dependent on the organization's choice of strategy and structure. What has emerged in the post-Chandler period is the recognition that strategy is clearly not only an independent variable but is also dependent on organizational structure. The multinational example in the preceding section illustrates this point. One might be tempted to argue that in complex organizations, strategy is structure, or vice-versa, just as the sociologist views structure as control. The organization's competitive strategy therefore is one additional lever that top management can employ in affecting the organization's performance. This third component is almost inextricably meshed with the planning and control system and organizational structure.

Management Style

A fourth component of the total management system now becomes evident. The control system is ordinarily visualized as encompassing the reward system, including monetary compensation. The compensation system inevitably influences the climate of competitiveness that exists in the organization. The manner in which goals are set both reflect and impinge on the style of decision making in the organization. The nature of the review of planned versus actual performance can greatly affect managerial motivation and behavior. The design of the planning and control system evidently influences and is influenced by the decision-making style or climate in the organization.

That strategy and managerial style are related is gaining increasing recognition. In fact, typologies of strategies have obvious and explicit implications in terms of climate and style (Miles and Snow 1978). The role of leadership in the formulation and implementation of strategy is universally accepted. Similarly, the interaction of style and structure is apparent in that delineations of responsibility and authority reflect and influence the decision-making style of the organization (Ouchi 1980).

This fourth component, somewhat arbitrarily labled management style, encompasses variables such as leadership, decision-making style, and organizational climate. It is also closely linked to the other three components.

Summary

This administrative system is useful and in fact necessary in terms of understanding the role of planning and control systems in the context of strategic management. By exploring the practical implications of this perspective on the administrative system, it can be demonstrated that without a simultaneous appreciation of all four components of this system, the effectiveness and influence of each of the individual components cannot be meaningfully defined.

The Administrative System in a Corporate Context

In illustrating the practical utility and nature of this administrative system, one can usefully examine the widely known, once highly regarded, and complex set of management practices that existed in Texas Instruments in the 1970s and early 1980s ("Texas Instruments" 1972; "TI Shows U.S. Business" 1980).

Viewing Texas Instruments' (TI) management practices from the perspective afforded by the proposed administrative system, some interesting conclusions may be drawn. The organizational structure TI adopted is striking in its contradiction of conventional practice and principles. In the 1970s, TI organized itself into four groups, focusing on materials, components, equipment, and services. The consequence of this mode of forming groups meant that all groups could be involved in serving a single customer, with obvious implications in terms of intergroup relationships. This mode of forming groups goes against the normal practice of attempting to form groups that are largely independent. In addition, a complex matrix organization was employed where each manager could be expected to function in two modes. In an operating mode, he or she would have profit-related responsibility within a group, and in a strategic mode he or she would have responsibility for strategic projects cutting across all groups. This two-hat responsibility extended to management committees in addition to individual managers. The dual roles that managers were expected to play were unusually complex and demanding. In short, TI's organizational structure was characterized by unusually high interdependence of subunits just below the corporate level and by a complex matrix structure that almost demanded that managers and committees possess schizophrenic qualities.

TI's planning and control systems were more complex than those found in most other organizations. Two parallel planning systems operated, with strategic and operating orientations, respectively. Management reports again incorporated two modes, with strategic expenditures being distinguished from operating expenses. The complex systems employed were clearly demanding in terms of managerial abilities and the accounting and data management infrastructure.

The incentive compensation systems were not only complex but peculiar in their implications. Incentive bonuses appeared to be more influenced by hierarchical level than performance against expectations. Managers at all levels were compared through a complicated system that progressed from lower to higher levels, with the probability being very slight that lower-level managers would make it to the final group to be rewarded. Stock options for senior managers were part of the system and did not appear to be distinctive in comparison to conventional practices. TI's planning and control systems were, in summary, extremely complex, demanding in terms of managerial abilities and the accounting and data management infrastructure, and peculiar in that tenure or level more than performance influenced rewards.

TI's managerial style was quite distinctive. Senior managers rose through the ranks rather than being brought in from other corporations. Openness and communication were encouraged through formal mechanisms such as plenary sessions in the planning process, involving as many as five hundred managers. At these sessions, managers presented their strategic and operating plans to managers from other groups in addition to their own. The managerial style did appear to mitigate some of the difficulties arising from the unusual organizational structure and planning and control systems.

The total administrative system fell into place with the incorporation of the component of organizational strategy. TI's distinctive competence was technology. The groups in TI all relied on technology as their core competence and basis for dealing with competition. Innovation as the key to growth was stressed. Barring a major acquisition in the late 1950s, growth, which had been rapid, had been internally generated. With this perspective on strategy, the peculiarities in the design of structure and systems are transformed into insightful and defensible choices that ensure a symbiotic integration and synergistic reinforcement of the four components of the administrative system.

The structure, which in essence emphasized the interdependence of the groups, made for cross-group communication and understanding, which in turn facilitated the functioning of the matrix of strategic and operating responsibilities. The cross-group strategic dimension of the structural matrix ensured the exploitation of the corporate technological capabilities that were fundamental to TI's strategy. In fact, the dual roles of individual managers and committees can be said to have reinforced each other in this strategic context instead of making for the confusion that the structure might seem to have promoted.

Given the matrix structure, the parallel systems of planning and reporting were inevitable. The system, though complex, functioned because of the long tenure of senior managers with TI. The style or climate, which promoted the loyalty and long tenure needed to operate the complex systems and provide the necessary familiarity with corporate-wide technological capabilities, was reinforced by the compensation system that rewarded tenure. The stock options mitigated cross-group rivalries, and the plenary session promoted cross-group familiarity and strengthened both strategic and operating relationships.

The essence of this administrative system is diagrammed in figure 17–2.

The importance of this comprehensive perspective is reinforced by its ability to explain TI's recent highly publicized travails. TI's venture into home computers encountered several problems after a brief period of success. These problems could have been anticipated in that success in the home com-

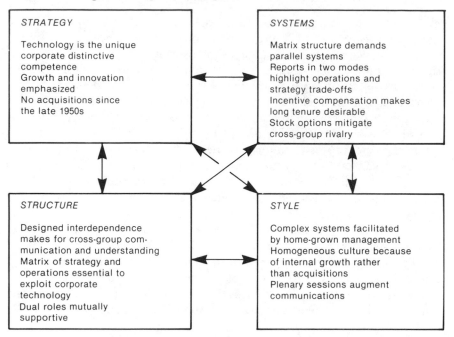

Figure 17–2. TI's Administrative System

puter market requires more than just technological competence. People buy home computers for a variety of complex and not particularly rational reasons. They are seen as tickets to success and a college career, as gateways to mastering high technology, as symbols of sophistication and affluence, and occasionally as tools for word processing or spread-sheet applications. Understanding these complex motivations and responding to them requires marketing competence that TI may or may not have possessed in adequate measure. What resulted from the emergence of the need for this additional core competence was that the complex interdependent structure became a burden rather than a benefit. The need for a new competitive strategy mandated a redesign of the other three components of TI's administrative system.

The administrative system also affords a valuable perspective on what changes in the organization are strategic in nature. A change in the design of any one of the four components of the administrative system that requires changes in any one of the other components of the system qualifies as a strategic change. Changes in any component of the system that do not require matching changes in the other components do not fall into the strategic category. From the point of view of the planning and control system, however, the most important contribution of this administrative system's perspective is an understanding of how planning and control systems can and should mesh within the total management framework of organizations.

References

Chandler, Alfred D. *Strategy and Structure: Chapters in the History of American Industrial Enterprise.* Cambridge: MIT Press, 1962.

Miles, R., and Snow, Charles. *Environmental Strategy and Organization Structure.* New York: McGraw-Hill, 1978.

Ouchi, William G. "Markets, Bureaucracies and Clans." *Administrative Science Quarterly* (March 1980): 129–141.

"Texas Instruments, Incorporated: Management Systems." Boston: Harvard Business School Case Services, #9-172-054, 1972.

"TI Shows U.S. Business How to Survive in the 1980s." *Business Week* (September 18, 1978): 72–74.

18
The Process of Implementation

A few significant questions have to be answered with regard to the issue of implementing planning and control systems. First, who should design the system? Second, should new systems be introduced overnight or over a long period? Third, how can the functioning of the planning and control system be assessed? Fourth, what considerations might guide design choices so as to increase the organization's effectiveness?

Designing the System

The most important issue in this regard is the role of the CEO, who must demonstrate commitment to the planning and control system if it is to succeed. This commitment must be expressed in the following ways:

1. Initiating or fully supporting the design and introduction of new systems or major changes in existing systems.

2. Understanding the benefits and limitations of the planning and control system so that reasonable expectations about its contributions to the organization's performance are developed.

3. Ensuring the availability of needed design resources: assignment of appropriate executives to the task of designing and introducing the system, obtaining outside technical assistance if required, and participating in key design decisions such as the top-down or bottom-up bias to be incorporated in the process of formulating the budget.

4. Providing the resources needed to administer the system when it is in place and appointing executives to carry out the various roles required to operate the system.

5. Using the system as a major mechanism for better management by participating actively in the processes and demonstrating familiarity with the behavior that is most appropriate.

The most effective approach to designing the system is for the CEO to appoint a team of executives to carry out the task. This team should include the executive(s) in the organization most responsible for promoting the idea of the new system if the idea was not originally conceived by the CEO. No more than five, or at the most six, executives for a functional organization or each division of a complex organization should be on the team.

The team members should possess the range of expertise needed to design the system effectively. The accounting, economic analysis, and MIS functions should be represented, if possible. Line managers from key departments should also be included. The team members should be able to provide an understanding of the existing management systems and existing operations of the organization. They will shoulder the responsibility of educating and convincing other managers in the organization regarding the characteristics and benefits of the system. They should therefore be highly regarded executives who are viewed by their colleagues and superiors as competent and trustworthy.

If the CEO believes that it is not possible to spare the time of the organization's executives to design the system, an outside consultant may be retained. In my experience, however, outside consultants who do not work closely with an in-house team in designing and installing the system are often not effective. Regardless of the consultant's technical expertise and experience, each organization's history and characteristics are different. Executives who have been with the organization for some time will have insights, understanding, and knowledge about sources of information that the consultant needs and would take too long to develop on his or her own. Also, the consultant's services will not ordinarily be indefinitely available to the organization, and an in-house understanding of the rationale for design choices that have been made is necessary.

This understanding will be required when modifications to the system are needed because of the inevitable changes in the characteristics of the organization and its environment. By working closely with the consultant, an in-house team can provide valuable help and develop useful knowledge about the system. Also, when introducing the system, the members of the in-house team will provide a much-needed core of committed and knowledgeable executives who will be eager to convince colleagues about the benefits of the new system.

Introducing the System

The basic questions in relation to introducing a strategic planning or management control system are whether a phased approach is necessary and, if so, how the phasing should take place. Phasing is necessary if the firm is extremely large (over $100 million in annual sales, several hundred or more employees) and complex (several different product lines, multiple manufacturing locations, many sales territories) and if formal planning and control systems that have existed before the new system are rudimentary or nonexistent.

A phased introduction can take place along two dimensions. It can be gradually implemented over a period of two or three years or introduced in selected segments of the organization before being implemented in remaining segments of the organization.

If phasing has been adopted because of the size and complexity of the organization, a segment-wise approach is recommended. This approach does not permit comprehensive strategic planning or operational planning at the corporate level until all segments are covered.

In selecting the segment of the organization where the initial implementation is to take place, top management must choose between segments that are relatively simple to handle and those that are likely to give rise to problems. If top management senses a need to demonstrate the viability and benefits of the new system, the difficult segments should be tackled first so as to create a positive and significant impact on the attitudes of the organization's executives. If the organizational climate is favorable to the introduction of more effective management systems, then the easier segments can be taken up first, thus enabling the design team to build the confidence and practical understanding necessary to tackle the difficult segments.

Coming back to the rationale for phasing the introduction of the system, if the lack of prior experience with formal management systems is the reason, then a careful step-by-step introduction of the strategic planning and management control system is necessary. The reporting system can be designed and installed first. The development of standards and performance expectations can be postponed for a few months until managers are familiar with the content of the reports. Performance in the same month or period of the previous year, if available, can be reported as a substitute for more meaningful benchmarks.

Once a historical record is built up, standard setting can be carried out. Budgets for individual responsibility centers can be developed, essentially using past performance as a guide. A year later, the comprehensive master budget and operational planning process for the organization can be introduced since managers will have developed a formal understanding of the impact on performance of resource levels, relationships with other responsibility centers, and the decisions that have been made. When the management control system has been implemented, the first thorough formal strategic planning exercise can be initiated. Workshops or discussion sessions in which the design team explains the purposes and operation of the system to other executives can be helpful in facilitating implementation.

Assessing System Effectiveness

After a planning and control system has been in operation for a year or more, it should be evaluated with a view to effecting improvements. A senior executive or team of executives can carry out this task quite adequately. If a team of executives is assigned the task of assessing the system, it should be a small group of three or four. One or two but not all of its members should have been on the team that was responsible for designing and implementing the system.

An outside consultant can be valuable when conducting the evaluation exercise. Executives who may not be entirely frank when interviewed by a colleague often tend to communicate without as much hesitation with outsiders who have less or no involvement in the politics of managing the organization. Consequently executives might perceive the outsider as an individual who can understand and appreciate their points of view without any bias. Also, the consultant can offer the assurance that comments and criticisms will not be attributed to individual executives. Such an assurance of confidentiality is not as meaningful when offered by an executive from within the organization.

Evaluation should be carried out with a view to improving the system, not with the intent of finding fault with or criticizing the efforts of those who designed and implemented it. The sources of information should include the formal documentation of the process of formulation and the output of the strategic plan or budget, as well as interviews of executives involved with the system and any other executives who wish to offer their reactions to the system. In large organizations, a questionnaire-based survey of reactions to the system may be useful.

Caution should be exercised when carrying out the evaluation. Planning systems and, in particular, control systems create pressures for improved performance. Often executives react to these pressures or to the analytical and management skills and competence demanded of them by the system rather than to the question of how the system can be improved. Such reactions should not be encouraged, and the reviewing executive(s) should be sensitive to the motivations of the executives making the comments.

The evaluation should be wide-ranging in scope. First, the appropriateness of the analytical, management, and time dimensions of the process that was employed to formulate the strategic plan or budget should be assessed. The actual process followed should be compared to what the designers had intended it to be and then to what is recommended in this book. Were the analyses comprehensive? Were the right personnel involved? Was the time allowed appropriate?

Second, the outputs of the process should be examined. Was the strategic plan or the master budget and operational plan comprehensive? Did it include all recommended elements of mission, objectives, strategy, policies, resources, and assumptions or the action plans, quantitative goals, and contingency plans? Was the matching of environmental issues with the organization's capabilities and limitations thorough? Did the strategic or action plans represent the conscious selection of the best alternatives from sets of meaningful and creative options? Were the standards employed in responsibility center budgets appropriately and effectively developed? Were the parameters or measures of performance suitable, and did they include the critical variables? Were remedial measures documented and monitored as part of the review and follow-up process? Were the goals set too high or too easily attained? Were the assumptions valid? Were needed modifications to the assumptions and related marginal changes in the strategic plan or master budget identified in the time between the comprehensive exercises? Were the capital budgeting system and the strategic issue management system complementary to the strategic planning system, and were the strategic planning and management control systems effectively linked?

Third, the spinoff or fringe benefits of the system should be evaluated. Do managers now understand better the various forces that influence their performance? Are the interrelationships and communications between responsibility centers understood and handled better than they were prior to the system? Do managers feel that the system has provided them with a learning experience, broader perspectives about the organization, and improved insights regarding their own operations? Do managers feel that they have better relationships with their colleagues, subordinates, and superiors?

The fourth area to be examined could have been covered under the outputs of the system; however, it is key to evaluating the effectiveness of any planning and control system and also different from the previous foci of evaluation in that it does not directly lead to improvements in the system design, only to an understanding of whether the present design is useful. Consequently it is considered separately from the evaluation of the outputs of the systems.

In this aspect of the evaluation, the reviewing executive(s) should attempt to identify pockets of strategic potential or plans of action that would not have been identified and developed if the planning and control system had not been implemented. Have successful new product ideas emerged? Have customer service and satisfaction improved? Has market share increased? Have new applications for existing products and new customers and customer types been identified? If the planning and controlling system does not improve the value of the organization, raise the organization's profits, and increase its prospects for profits in the future, it has not served its primary purpose.

Guidelines for Greater Effectiveness and Efficiency

Recent research has developed some guidelines that might help facilitate the design of more effective planning and control systems. Calingo (1984) has identified four characteristics common to strategic planning systems that are perceived to be effective:

1. A comprehensive analytical process as described in chapter 6.
2. A comprehensive statement of output as described in chapter 5.
3. Extensive participation by a large number of executives.
4. Less frequent repetitions of comprehensive strategic planning exercises.

The strategic planning systems recommended in this book possess all of these prerequisites for effectiveness.

Veliyath (1985) also provides some useful insights regarding how planning and control systems can be tailored to their environmental context. Veliyath found that organizational performance was strongly affected by the organization's orientation toward the future or the past. The more dynamic was the environment in which the organization found itself, the more important it became for the organization to focus on the future, anticipating discontinuities and critical events as opposed to relying on insights derived from experience. When organizations perceived their environments as hostile, it became necessary to balance the emphasis placed on anticipating future events and understanding past experiences. Hostility is largely a matter of individual perception. Organizations that view their environment as hostile have often been conditioned to do so as a consequence of unsuccessful experiences. These experiences can be useful sources of insights as to what the organization needs to do differently. In contrast, organizations that have been successful ordinarily find it much less useful to focus on the past. They have already learned how to deal with the context that they have experienced and are unfortunately prone to continue practices that have been successful in the earlier context when faced with unrelated new contexts.

A final broad guideline for designing planning and control systems can be derived from studies that have examined the implications of being technology driven or market driven in terms of the organization's strategic posture. Market-driven changes tend to be gradual in nature, as opposed to the tendency of technology-driven changes, which are more disjointed and quantum in character. As a consequence, market-driven firms tend to emphasize cost minimization strategies, have formal, centralized structures with many levels of authority, and tend to be more rigid and hierarchical in character. Technology-driven firms, in contrast, tend to rely on product differentiation strategies and skim pricing for profitability. Organizational structures reflect flexibility and more communication between hierarchical levels.

The strategic planning and management control systems developed in this book can offer to technology-driven or market-driven organizations the potential to achieve a balance and to develop new and needed competences.

The experiences of organizations over the past decade point to three lessons that can be learned (Camillus 1984). First, organizations that are masters of neither technology nor marketing are sure to encounter problems of survival. The U.S. Post Office, the old-time movie industry, many domestic airlines, and companies in the health food industry illustrate this grim reality. The emphasis in such organizations has to be on the development of competence in responding to either technological or marketing developments by an appropriate orientation in their planning and control systems.

Second, organizations that choose to be technology driven when the product or industry life cycle is market driven (or vice-versa) encounter serious problems. The cable and satellite television industry provides painful examples of this proposition. The moral of this observation is that the strategic planning exercise should identify the origins of strategic change in the organization's industry, and the management control system should provide the appropriate orientation to the market-driven or technology-driven nature of the organization's environment.

Third, organizations that are popularly perceived to be preeminent in competence and performance — IBM, Federal Express, Marks & Spencer, and Merrill Lynch — demonstrate a mastery of the management of both the technological and market sources of strategic change. The strategic planning and management control systems that we have discussed can be perhaps the most important vehicle for moving an organization toward the desired goal of being a master of both technology and marketing, ensuring not only the survival of the organization but also generating a momentum toward success.

References

Calingo, Luis Ma. R. "Tailoring Strategic Planning Systems to Corporate Strategy." Ph.D. dissertation, University of Pittsburgh, 1984.

Camillus, John C. "Technology-Driven and Market-Driven Life Cycles: Implications for Multinational Corporate Strategy." *Columbia Journal of World Business* (Summer 1984): 56–60.

Veliyath, Rajaram. "Feedback and Feedforward in Strategic Management: A Contingent Framework." Ph.D. dissertation, University of Pittsburgh, 1985.

Index

About the Author

John C. Camillus is Associate Dean and Professor of Business Administration at the Graduate School of Business of the University of Pittsburgh. He received his doctorate in business administration from Harvard Business School in 1972.

He has published several books and dozens of articles in professional journals such as *Sloan Management Review, Strategic Management Journal, Financial Executive, Planning Review, Columbia Journal of World Business, Academy of Management Review,* and *Long Range Planning.* His previous book, *Budgeting for Profit,* has appeared in multiple editions and has been translated into Spanish and Swedish.

Dr. Camillus has thrice received awards from the Foundation for Administrative Research for contributions to corporate and organizational planning and his research has been supported by several organizations including the Touche-Ross Foundation. He has consulted extensively, both in the U.S. and abroad, for a variety of manufacturing, service, and not-for-profit organizations. His research and consulting has focused on strategic planning systems, management control systems, management information systems and organizational structure.